Crime and Delinquency: Dimensions of Deviance

edited by
Marc Riedel
Terence P. Thornberry

Published in cooperation with
the American Society of Criminology

The Praeger Special Studies program—
utilizing the most modern and efficient book
production techniques and a selective
worldwide distribution network—makes
available to the academic, government, and
business communities significant, timely
research in U.S. and international economic, social, and political development.

Crime and Delinquency:
Dimensions of Deviance

PRAEGER SPECIAL STUDIES IN U.S. ECONOMIC, SOCIAL, AND POLITICAL ISSUES

Praeger Publishers New York Washington London

Library of Congress Cataloging in Publication Data

Riedel, Marc.
    Crime and delinquency: dimensions of deviance.

    (Praeger special studies in U.S. economic, social, and political issues)
       1. Crime and criminals—Addresses, essays, lectures.
I. Thornberry, Terence P., joint author.   II. Title.
HV6028.R53   364   74-19191
ISBN 0-275-05650-3

PRAEGER PUBLISHERS
111 Fourth Avenue, New York, N.Y. 10003, U.S.A.
5, Cromwell Place, London SW7 2JL, England

Published in the United States of America in 1974
by Praeger Publishers, Inc.

Printed in the United States of America

In November 1973, the American Society of Criminology held its annual meeting in New York. The meeting saw several hundred scholars, primarily concerned with crime, delinquency, deviant behavior, and corrections, gather together to present papers and exchange views.

The present volume is a selection of papers that were delivered at the New York meeting. It is one of a series of books coming out of that meeting, and is published in response to a demand that the research information, data, ideas, and proposals heard in New York be made permanently available to professionals, students, government officials and others engaged in the effort to understand the phenomenon of crime in modern society.

The editors would like to express their appreciation to Robert G. Green, Doctoral Student, School of Social Work, University of Pennsylvania, for additional editorial assistance. We are also grateful to Teresa E. Dudley for the many and yeoman secretarial services involved in the preparation of this volume.

The officers of the American Society of Criminology at the time of the New York meeting were: Dr. John C. Ball (Temple University), President; Dr. Edward Sagarin (City University of New York), President-Elect; Dr. William E. Amos (United States Board of Parole), Vice-President; Dr. Nicholas Kittrie (American University Law School), Vice-President; Dr. Sawyer Sylvester (Bates College), Secretary-Treasurer; Dr. C. Ray Jeffrey (Florida State University), Editor, Criminology: An Interdisciplinary Journal.

CONTENTS

LIST OF TABLES AND FIGURE

Crime and Delinquency: Dimensions of Deviance

CRIME AND DELINQUENCY: DIMENSIONS OF DEVIANCE

Terence P. Thornberry
and Marc Riedel

One of the dominant characteristics of contemporary criminology is that it does not have a single, overriding perspective or orientation. A variety of different orientations, each with its attendant set of assumptions and biases, have been used by criminologists in their attempts to unravel the complexities of criminal behavior.

Part of this diaspora can be attributed to the multifaceted nature of the phenomenon of crime. The empirical complexities of criminal behavior are by no means fully delimited, and as new facets come to light new explanatory modes are brought into being.

But to explain the variety of orientations that have been used in our discipline in terms of the complexity of crime alone would put us in the rather awkward position of explaining very little of the variance, indeed. Other dimensions—such as developments in related disciplines, cultural values and reigning ideologies—all play a role in explaining why certain orientations have been used at particular times and, more importantly we think, why certain orientations are currently being employed.

Indeed, the first essay in this collection—"Paradigm Conflict in Criminology"—presents a cogent discussion of such dimensions as they impinge upon the major orientations or paradigms of contemporary criminology. These orientations are, according to Professor Reasons, "kinds of people" approaches, "kinds of environment" approaches, and "power/conflict" approaches. The first, and historically the oldest, "assumes a basic difference between the criminal and non-criminal which can be discovered through scientific analysis. Methodologically, emphasis is placed upon case study and statistical verification of the differentness of criminals and the implications of such differences for 'remedying' the crime problem." In kinds of environment approaches "the circle of causality expanded with a change from focusing upon the individual to the conditions that 'produced' the criminal." The perception that crime is a product of the social system "appears in the nature of 'kinds of environment' theories emphasizing differential opportunity structures, poverty, racism, etc., as important causal factors." Finally, the most recent paradigm—power/conflict—"demystifies the traditional conception of criminal and non-criminal pervading criminology. By focusing upon the political nature of criminal definitions, their application and enforcement of the 'power/conflict' perspective asserts that crime is a product of current power differentials and conflicting world views. Crime is a definition of behavior made by officials of the state and not inherent in the act."

From the point of view of this introductory essay, the intriguing thing about Professor Reasons' paper is that it could well stand in the place of this essay. In his paper, Professor Reasons claims that contemporary criminological work tends to fall into "kinds of people," "kinds of environment" and "power/conflict" approaches, and the papers in this volume tend to do just that. Thus, one could easily use the first essay to organize and introduce those that follow.

In many ways this convergence should not be surprising since these papers were all presented at the most recent meetings of the American Society of Criminology and, as such, represent a cross-section of on-going research in the field. Also, it should not be surprising that no paper fits exactly into any of the three paradigms. since the paradigms are ideal types. Yet the convergence seems to us quite real.

Among the papers, three seem to the editors to derive from a "kinds of people" orientation. The paper by Ferracuti and Dinitz compares matched samples of Puerto Rican delinquents and nondelinquents in terms of a variety of variables that replicate and extend the criminological work originated by the Gluecks. Landau examines the relationship between pathology—defined to include both physical and mental disorders—and homocide among Israeli offenders. Finally, the paper by Zahn and Bencivengo examines the differences between drug users and non-users in relation to being victims of homicides.

Five of the papers in the volume are concerned with "kinds of environment" issues. Bailey examines the relationship between homicide and a number of socio-cultural variables, especially the Southern tradition of violence, concluding that "Southerness" is not a good predictor of homicide rates. Two papers deal with drug usage —the one written by Krohn tests the utility of a differential association model in explaining marijuana use and the paper by Wallace, Rosenthal and Young examines the interrelationships of social structure, narcotic use and the commission of other crimes. Fishman's paper examines the recent upsurge in international terrorism by focusing on

2

Palestinian terrorism since the 1967 war. Yearwood's article discusses the relationship between the use of firearms and the commission of homicide in a cross-cultural perspective.

Finally, the power/conflict paradigm is represented by six papers. Farrell and Hardin's paper on homosexuality examines the effects of formal labelling on the formation of deviant careers. Abbott and Calonico's paper deals with a very understudied criminological topic—the creation of popular images about crime—by examining the way in which the press in New Orleans portrays the crime of rape to its readers. The next four papers all deal with one of the major topics of the power/conflict model, namely, the discretionary enforcement of criminal statutes. These papers deal with discretionary decision making in the juvenile court (Rosen and Carl), in the prosecutors office (Garabedian), in judicial decisions concerning the incompetency to stand trial (Stedman and Braff), and in parole hearings (Scott and Vandiver). Together these four papers make a considerable addition to our understanding of the nature and effects of discretion in the criminal justice system.

Given the nature of the articles that appear in this volume it is clear that the three paradigms discussed by Reasons are major orientations in the current study of crime and delinquency. Whether they will continue to be so in the future or will prove to be the proverbial blind alleys of science is as yet an unanswered question, we hope that the content of the papers in this volume will contribute to that answer.

CHAPTER

2

**PARADIGM CONFLICT
IN CRIMINOLOGY**
Charles E. Reasons

It appears that an era of radical writings has descended upon
academia. This seems to be particularly the case within the social
sciences (Hampden-Turner, 1970), and increasingly so in sociology.
As Kuhn (1970) has noted, the route to "normal sciences" can be
quite trying for a young discipline attempting to establish its creed.
He presents his own year retreat with a group of social scientists:

> Particularly, I was struck by the number and extent of
> the overt disagreements between social scientists about
> the nature of legitimate scientific problems and methods.
> Both history and acquaintance made me doubt that prac-
> titioners of the natural sciences possess firmer or more
> permanent answers to such questions than their colleagues
> in social sciences. Yet, somehow, the practice of astron-
> omy, physics, chemistry, or biology, normally fails to
> evoke the controversies over fundamentals that today often
> seem endemic among, say, psychologists or sociologists.
> Attempting to discover the source of that difference led
> me to recognize the role in scientific research of what I
> have since called 'paradigms.' These I take to be uni-
> versally recognized scientific achievements that for a
> time provide model problems and solutions to a com-
> munity of practitioners. (Kuhn, 1970: viii)

Therefore, the recent emergence of radical writing could
easily be interpreted as an attempt to view the world through a new
paradigm. While discrediting "traditional," "status-quo" paradigms,
new paradigm entrepreneurs attempt to erect their own paradigm as
"the" paradigm. The importance of scientific revolutions and paradigm change is that (Warren, 1971) "data which were formerly thought

4

important are now regarded as inconsequential; problems which were recognized as unexplained but relatively unimportant now become critical. A new set of ways of conceptualizing, of relating data to each other, of ways of defining problems, or research techniques, usually accompanies such 'scientific revolutions'" (Warren, 1971: 470)

Criminology

The substantive area of criminology has increasingly become politicized with new paradigms arising to challenge the traditional perspectives. Ideology has been very important in the rise and subsequent changing focus in the study of crime. In a well presented sociohistorical analysis, Radzinowicz (1966) describes the rise of the "liberal" position in criminology as a concommitant of the enlightenment, with growing scientism, emphasis upon reason, and the revolt against unquestioning acceptance of tradition and authority. The system of criminal justice was subject to a great deal of attack. Montesquieu, Voltaire, and Beccaria, among others, condemned the legal institutions of the time for their arbitrairiness, secrecy, and cruel and oppressive nature. This Classical School of criminology arose as a reaction to the abuses of the time and its leaders called for reform (Vold, 1958).

Unlike the Classical School, the Positive School became committed to the thesis that any measure necessary to protect society (the accused and, of course, the convicted person are automatically excluded therefrom) is justifiable (Jeffery, 1959). The belief in the ability to use techniques of social control, e.g., law, to make a better society was productive of much legislation for the purposes of guiding man's morals. Thus, scientism and positivism as a panacea for man's ills led to increasing "overcriminalization" and the belief in the perfectability of "deviants" through the use of the social sciences and law.

The increasing divisiveness of the 1960's magnified the fact that different perceptions of criminality were vying for public attention. The consciousness of the younger generation may be producing a shift in perspective of societal wrongdoing (Reich, 1970). Increasingly, certain segments of society are viewing the brutal destruction wrought upon Indochina as a crime of unimaginable magnitude, the fraudulent dealing of large manufacturers and corporations suggest they are "ideal delinquents," the prosecution and persecution of political criminals, e.g., war protesters, is viewed as criminal, lawlessness of the law is an increasing problem of "law and order," e.g., Riots of 1967, Chicago, 1968, Kent State, Jackson State, Southern University, etc., and the increasing lawlessness of political leaders and their

5

accomplices, e.g., ITT, Watergate, surveillance of political "deviants." In recent years the erosion of the legitimacy of the state has been due to (1) a belief that the law and legal institutions are not only unresponsive but illegitimate, (2) a condemnation of the bureaucratic delays, judicial indifference and overt racism of courts, (3) a rejection, and in many instances, a contempt for Establishment officials—police, judges, and lawyers, and (4) an affirmation of individual rights and an identification with group, class, racial and sexual liberation (Lefcourt, 1971).

The evident divisiveness and conflict has brought about changing perspectives on crime and society among segments of the general public, and subsequently there is a growing realization among some criminologists of the importance of interest groups in determining what crime is, and which type of crime will be of major concern to law enforcement and administration of justice personnel, and thus of criminologists (Quinney, 1970; Turk, 1969; Hills, 1971; Chambliss and Seidman, 1971). Miller (1973) has recently presented a penetrating analysis of the contemporary influence of ideology upon criminal justice policy and personnel, including criminologists and criminal justice personnel.[1]

> The major contention of this presentation is that ideology and its consequences exert a powerful influence on the policies and procedures of those who conduct the enterprise of criminal justice, and that the degree and kinds of influence go largely unrecognized. Ideology is the permanent hidden agenda of criminal justice. (Miller, 1973: 142)

Increasingly, competing "world views" have influenced the methods and focus of criminologists. While criminology draws from various disciplines, it can be considered as a discipline unto itself:

> We are contending . . . that criminology should be considered as an autonomous, separate discipline of knowledge because it has accumulated its own set of organized data and theoretical conceptualism that use the scientific method, approach to understanding, and attitude in research." (Wolfgang, 1963:156)

The criminologist is:

> One whose professional training, occupational role, and fiduciary reward are concentrated toward a scientific approach, study, and analysis of the phenomena of crime and criminal behavior. (Wolfgang, 1963:160)

6

The voluminous amount of criminological research and writing may be placed into three major paradigmatic categories: (1) kinds of people, (2) kinds of environment, and (3) power/conflict. The increasing articulation of the last approach has brought about an intensification of conflict in society and among criminologists.[2]

Kinds of People. Criminology has historically been very imbued with the positivist spirit and paradigm.[3] This emphasis led to the discovery of the "causes of crime" within the individual. The differences of the criminal from the non-criminal was assumed and criminological research was devoted to finding the basis of this difference. This "kinds of people" approach has led from the measuring of skulls to psychic conflict, selfconcept, anomie, etc., with essentially the same results, no ultimate answers to the question of "cause" (Wilkins, 1968; Pap, 1962; Sjobert and Nett, 1968).

This search for the basic "causes of criminality" in the differentness of the criminal has been based upon a "correctional" perspective toward crime and the criminal (Matza, 1969). From biological, to psychological to sociological analysis of the offenders, the emphasis has been upon diagnosis, prognosis, and treatment. This "medical model" of criminality still largely pervades American criminological thought. Theoretically, the "kinds of people" paradigm assumes a basic difference between the criminal and non-criminal which can be discovered through scientific analysis. Methodologically, emphasis is placed upon case study and statistical verification of the differentness of criminals and the implication of such differences for "remedying" the crime problem. While the "kinds of people" paradigm has largely dominated American criminological thought in the Twentieth Century, a shift in the focus of determinism is evident in the "kinds of environment" paradigm.

Kinds of Environment. The circle of causality expanded with a change from focusing upon the individual to the conditions that "produced" the criminal. The conception that crime is a product of the social system is an increasingly widespread perspective in criminological circles. It appears in the nature of "kinds of environment" theories emphasizing differential opportunity structures, poverty, racism, etc., as important causal factors.

Social determinism is an important cornerstone of the "kinds of environment" approach. The early Chicago School's ecological work and social disorganization analysis found the "causes" of crime in the conditions of communities. The criminal was not a sick, pathological entity in an other wise healthy, stable environment. The "causes" of criminality transcended the individual and included the family, peer group, and community. Due to differential association, differential opportunity structures, cultural transmission, focal concerns, etc., the criminal was largely a "normal" product of abnormal

7

and pathological conditions. Thus, reformation of these causal conditions was indicated. Therefore, community rehabilitation projects, street-gang work, increased job training, community action programs and general social reform became the emphasis in criminological circles. This is particularly noticeable in the "community-based" correction movement.

Traditional correctional policies and practices have been based upon a "medical model" of deviancy, subscribing to an erroneous analogy to the physician's practice. Therefore, like a disease, an individual was to be diagnosed, prognosed, prescribed, treated, and cured of his "illness." This model has depended upon the "sick-well" dichotomy focusing upon the individual as both cause and effect of his illness (criminality). The basic legal concept of mens rea is predicated on individual responsibility for one's actions, and this concept of legal culpability has been transferred to treatment models in corrections. Therefore, like the leper, insane, and other "sick" people, the criminal must be isolated and treated for his "illness."

While the individual is legally culpable for his actions, it is acknowledged that many societal factors, e.g., economic, family, peer group pressure, racism, etc., impinge upon and effect everyone's behavior, including those who commit criminal acts and are officially labelled criminal. The circle of causality and thus treatment has broadened from the individual to the family, peer group and community. Therefore, community-based corrections, e.g., work-study release, furloughs, halfway houses, etc., have become the basis of new and innovative techniques of habilitation. This approach acknowledges the obvious fact that the offender, like the non-offender, is largely a product of his family, community, and society, and that the offender will have to reenter the community.

It is generally recognized that the concept of community-based corrections is desirable on both treatment and financial bases. The President's Commissions on Law Enforcement and Administration of Justice, and Violence (1969), point out the valuable aspects of community involvement in habilitation. It generally costs approximately ten times as much to incarcerate an individual as to put him on probation or parole. Many criminologists agree that a majority of those presently incarcerated could be dealt with in the community without excessive risk (President's Commission on Law Enforcement and Administration of Justice, 1967). The need for flexible alternatives in corrections is increasingly recognized among students and practitioners of criminology (Southern California Law Review, 1969). Such programs as work-training release, furloughs, probation, subsidy, and community based facilities attempt to provide alternatives to better meet the realities of a truly habilitative emphasis.

Power/Conflict. Increasing awareness regarding the political nature of crime has arisen with heightened conflict between traditionally powerless groups, e.g., students and youth, poor and nonwhite, and those in power (Lefcourt, 1972; Campbell, 1969; Skolnick, 1969; Tenbroek, 1966). Traditionally submerged in a consensus perspective of society, viewing the state as neutral, the criminologist has been recently struck by the increasing questioning of the legitimacy of specific laws and ultimately the authority of the state. Some criminologists have begun to critically investigate the origin, enforcement, and administration of laws within the context of interests, power, and conflict.

The viewing of law as an instrument of interests has become a growing area of concern among American criminologists. Quinney (1970) articulately presents what many dissident leaders of the 1960's suggested, that criminal law is made, enforced, and administered by interest groups for their own gains. A conflict perspective has become a paradigm of increasing usefulness in criminological study (Turk, 1966; Denisoff and McCaghy, 1973). Therefore, crime may be viewed as phenomena created by individuals in concerted action to have their definitions of rightness win out and become legitimated in public policy, i.e., laws and regulations.

Although Jeffery's article on the structure of American Criminological Thought was published in 1956, it still reflects the major thrust of criminologists (Jeffery, 1956). Jerome Halls' comment is still applicable: "The most serious criticism of 20th Century Criminology is that it has gone whole hog positivistic." While there are some recent excellent analyses of socio-legal development, these are quite the exception rather than the rule.[4] Most textbooks on criminology still place their emphasis upon "kinds of people" analysis of criminals arrested and confined. Emphasis remains upon "focal concerns," "opportunity structures," "self-concept," "drift," and "techniques of neutralization," "typologies," "labeling," etc., with relatively little emphasis upon the fact that crime is created, enforced, and administered in a politically organized society characterized by conflict, differential power and influence in such a process. In an intensive and extensive critical assessment of criminological theory, Dessaur points out that:

> Where the penal law is used to secure the norms of a debatable ideology, the only thing we can hope to detect by empirical research is what kind of conduct and/or what kind of people the adherents of this ideology should like to eradicate. We are getting information about the (ideological) interests the penal law is serving, not about the "psychological" causes of crime. . . . The logical and the empirical objection to dogmatic labelling of criminals (etiological criminology) imply that in traditional criminology (carefully jotting down all sorts of socio-graphic

9

and psychological variables about criminals without even looking critically at their raison-d' etre), we shall either draw from the hat what we put into it, or draw nothing at all. By this I mean the following: It is the penal law, its scope, its sub-divisions, the selection of deviant behavior that is made by it and the selective enforcement of it that determines whether the criminals tend to be rebels, psychopaths, or rational profit-seekers. (Dessaur, 1971)

The emphasis upon "good guy" and "bad guy" dichotomy is important because it still pervades "kinds of people" and "kinds of environment" thought. As Poveda has noted: "The image of the criminal in any given historical era emerges from those positions in the social structure which constitute a threat to the established power systems." (Poveda, 1960:61) As social, political and economic circumstances have changed so has the image of the criminal. The perpetuation of the imagery of the "dangerous classes" is apparent in the consistent and persistent attention given to the lower class criminal. This emphasis upon "common crime" and the "common criminal" helps to maintain our stereotypes of crime and the criminal.[5]

The social sciences accept the stereotype of the criminal as a given, for to challenge it would involve heavy penalties. The penalties are to be isolated from the main stream of professional activity, to be denied resources for research, and to be denied official patronage with its rewards in material and status.[6] (Chapman, 1968:23)

The "power/conflict" paradigm demystifies the traditional conception of criminal and noncriminal pervading criminology. By focusing upon the political nature of criminal definitions, their application and enforcement the "power/conflict" perspective asserts that crime is a product of current power differentials and conflicting world views. Crime is a definition of behavior made by officials of the state and not inherent in an act. Those behaviors which are offensive to the powers that be will be made crimes. Rather than focusing upon the "common crimes" of the "common criminals," emphasis is placed upon the lawless behavior of the state and those in positions of power. The Watergate Affair, ITT, increasing pervasive repression of political dissidents, government lawlessness in Indochina and at home, corporate and white collar crime, and the violence of continual hunger, impoverishment, poor housing, etc., are identified as "the crime problem" in the United States (Falk, Koko and Lifton, 1971; Liberman, 1973; Becker and Murray, 1971; Schur, 1969).
When attending to "common crimes" and "common criminals" emphasis is placed upon the oppressive, arbitrary and self-serving

nature of the criminal justice system and its injustices from the criminals perspective (Petersen and Truzzi, 1972; Irwin, 1970; Wright, 1973; Atkins and Glick, 1972). Wolfgang (1972:22) has recently suggested a change in criminological concern. "We have focused long enough on the offender and his weaknesses. It is time we look to ourselves—to this chaotic, decaying, degrading system and indict it for its failures." By calling for us to demystify the police department, district attorney's office, courts, probation, parole, and prison and make them accountable to various publics, he presents a potential powder keg to the student of crime. Such emphasis is necessary in order to revolutionize the criminal justice system. However, such analyses will not be easy given the traditional secrecy and paranoia of such agencies. Professor Wolfgang has taken an activist, potentially humanistic perspective of the criminologists' role. While such an inquiry may not elicit large grants, it is necessary, for "making the criminal justice system accountable means making it more responsible and more humane" (Wolfgang, 1972:22)

Conclusion

Three different paradigms (kinds of people, kinds of environment, and power/conflict) are vying to become "the paradigm" for criminologists. With the heightened conflict and divisiveness of the last decade the power/conflict paradigm has increasingly challenged the largely apolitical, antiseptic, and value-free paradigms previously dominant in American criminological thought. The future portends not a lessening, but an intensification of this competition and the further politicizing of crime and the criminologist.

When the researcher comes forward with certain ideas about man and society, and methods to approach those ideals, he leaves his sanctuary to confront politically opposing positions. Under these circumstances how can one hope that those responsible for administration will not look upon these researchers as a political pressure group whose weapon in the social struggle is called "scientific research". . . . We may conclude then that researchers, by becoming spokesmen for reform, are reagrded by administration as representatives of a pressure group who use 'scientific research' as a tool to disguise plans for a test of strength designed towards the exercise of power. (Szobo, Libbanc, and Normandeau)[7]

11

1. See Miller (1973). Miller uses ideology to refer "to a set of general and abstract beliefs or assumptions about the correct or proper state of things, particularly with respect to the moral order and political arrangements, which serve to shape one's positions on specific issues."

2. Edwin Schur (1973) has to a great extent delineated the "kinds of people" and "kinds of environment" approaches under the categories of "individual treatment" and "liberal reform". Since the "kinds of people" and "kinds of environment" paradigms should be readily recognized by the student of crime, emphasis will be placed upon an explication of the "power/conflict" paradigm.

3. The rise of positivism was to greatly influence the structure of criminological thought. The major characteristics of positive thought are that it (1) denies free will (2) divorces science and law from morals (3) proclaims the priority of science and believes in the existence of invariable social laws (4) emphasizes unity of the scientific method for social and natural sciences (5) emphasizes the criminal (6) emphasizes quantitative research, not qualitative, and (7) causality and determinism are paramount concerns to be pursued through observation. See Mannheim (1960). In an excellent discussion of positivism in criminology, Matza (1964) notes that while that all social science is deterministic, a distinction can be made between "hard" and "soft" determinism. The former has long been the major thrust of American criminological analysis and rigidly adheres to the characteristics of positivism noted above, while soft determinism allows for the incorporation of a degree of free will or choice in human behavior. In a later discussion of deviance, Matza (1969), notes that the positive school of criminology separated the study of crime from the workings and theory of the state and he suggests we take a naturalist perspective and deviance, including crime. While traditional positivist criminology views man as object the naturalist perspective sees man as subject. Much of positivistic criminology has been devoid of naturalist content.

4. While it is recognized by the author that attention has increasingly been given to the criminal justice system and its problems, much of this discussion provides technological and/or manpower remedies for the problems of the system which must be better coordinated to meet the needs of the "clients."

5. This is not to suggest that lower class "criminality" is not more prevalent in arrest, processing, and institutionalized statistics. A casual observation of drunk court will verify such "criminality." (Drunkenness makes up over 25 percent of our "crime."). However, the question is why are only poor people processed for drunkenness,

vagrancy, addiction, etc.? More analyses of statute formulation and differential processing are needed.

6. See Chapman (1968:244): "A theme in this essay is that of the contribution made by the sociologist and criminologist to the creation and maintenance of the stereotype of crime and the criminal. This stereotype asserts that crime is a distinctive kind of behavior and that criminals are created by special physical, psychic, social, or environmental factors. Such theories are maintained and diffused by researchers that are based on socially determined groups, generally chosen without controls, often by criteria which prejudge the issue."

7. Szabo, Libbanc, and Normandeau (1971) argue for the concept of criminology as an applied science. However, it remains to be resolved as to whom it is applied by whom, for what purposes, and with what results!

References

Atkins, B. M. and H. R. Glick
  1972   Prisons, Protest, and Politics. Englewood Cliffs, N.J.: Prentice-Hall.

Becker, T. L. and V. G. Murray
  1971   Government Lawlessness in America. New York: Oxford University Press.

Campbell, J. S., J. R. Sahid and D. P. Strong
  1970   Law and Order Reconsidered. New York: Bantam Books.

Chambliss, W. J. and R. B. Seidman
  1971   Law, Order, and Power, Reading, Mass.: Addison-Wesley.

Chapman, D
  1968   Sociology and the Stereotype of the Criminal. London: Tavistock Publications.

Dessaur, C. I.
  1971   Foundations of Theory-Formation in Criminology. The Hague: Moutan and Company.

Denisoff, R. S. and C. H. McCaghy
  1973   Deviance, Conflict and Criminality. New York: Rand-McNally and Company.

Falk, R. A., G. Koko and R. J. Lifton
  1971   Crimes of War. New York: Random House.

Hampden-Turner, C.
  1970   Radical Man. Cambridge: Schenkman.

Hills, S. L.
  1971   Crime, Power, and Morality. Toronto: Chandler.

Irwin, J.
  1970   The Felon. Englewood Cliffs, N.J.: Prentice-Hall.

Jeffery, C. R.
  1956   "The structure of American criminological thought."
           Journal of Criminal Law, Criminology, and Police Science
           46(January-February):648-672.

  1959   "The historical development of criminology." Journal of
           Criminal Law, Criminology, and Police Science 50 (May-
           June):3-19.

Kuhn, T. S.
  1970   The Structure of Scientific Revolutions. Second Edition.
           Chicago: University of Chicago Press.

Lefcourt, R. (ed.)
  1971   Law Against the People: Essays to Demystify Law, Order
           and the Court. New York: Random House.

Liberman, J. K.
  1973   How the Government Breaks the Law. Baltimore: Penguin
           Books, Inc.

Mannheim, H.
  1960   Pioneers in Criminology. Chicago: Quadrangle Books, Inc.

Matza, D.
  1964   Delinquency and Drift, New York: Wiley.

  1969   Becoming Deviant. Englewood Cliffs, N.J.: Prentice-Hall,
           Inc.

Miller, W. B.
  1973   "Ideology and criminal justice policy: Some current issues."
           Journal of Criminal Law and Criminology 64(June):141-62.

Pap, A.
1962   An Introduction to the Philosophy of Science, New York:
         The Free Press.

Petersen, D. M. and M. Truzzi
1972   Criminal Life: Views from the Inside. Englewood Cliffs,
         N.J.: Prentice-Hall, Inc.

Poveda, T. G.
1970   "The image of the criminal: a critique of crime and delin-
         quency theories." Issues In Criminology 5(Winter):59-83

President's Commission on Law Enforcement and Administration of
Justice
1967   Task Force Report: Corrections. Washington, D.C.: U.S.
         Government Printing Office.

President's Commission on Violence
1969   Law and Order Reconsidered. Washington, D.C.: U.S.
         Government Printing Office.

Quinney, R.
1970   The Social Reality of Crime. Boston: Little, Brown and
         Company.

Radzinowicz, L.
1966   Ideology and Crime. New York: Columbia University
         Press.

Reasons, C. E. and J. L. Kuykendall
1972   Race, Crime and Justice. Pacific Palisades: Goodyear
         Publishing Company.

Reich, C. A.
1970   The Greening of America. New York: Random House.

Schur, E. M.
1969   Our Criminal Society: The Social and Legal Sources of
         Crime in America. Englewood Cliffs, N.J.: Prentice-Hall,
         Inc.

1973   Radical Non-Intervention: Rethinking the Delinquency
         Problem Englewood Cliffs Prentice-Hall Inc.

Sjoberg, G. and R. Nett
1968   A Methodology for Social Research. New York: Harper and Row.

Skolnick, J. H.
1969   The Politics of Protest. New York: Ballantine Books, Inc.

Szaba, D., M. Libbanc and A. Normandeau
1971   "Applied criminology and government policy: future perspectives and conditions of collaboration." Issues In Criminology 6 (Winter):55-83.

Tenbroek, J.
1966   The Law of the Poor. San Francisco: Chandler Publishing Company.

Turk, A. T.
1966   "Conflict and criminality." American Sociological Review 31(June).

1969   Criminality and Legal Order. Chicago: Rand-McNally and Company.

1969   "Turn em loose toward a flexible corrections system." Southern California Law Review 42:682-700.

Vold, G. B.
1958   Theoretical Criminology. New York: Oxford University Press.

Warren, R. L.
1971   "The sociology of knowledge and the problems of the inner city." Social Science Quarterly 52(December):469-49

Wilkens, L. T.
1968   "The concept of cause in criminology." Issues In Criminology 3(Spring):147-165.

Wolfgang, M. E.
1963   "Criminology and the criminologist." Journal of Criminal Law, Criminology and Police Science 54(June):155-162.

1972   "Making the criminal justice system accountable." Crime and Delinquency 18(January):15-22.

16

Wright, O.

1973   The Politics of Punishment. New York: Harper and Row.

3

CROSS-CULTURAL
ASPECTS OF
DELINQUENT AND
CRIMINAL BEHAVIOR

Franco Ferracuti
and Simon Dinitz

The need for interdisciplinary research (and for fusion and cross-communication) in the study of deviant and criminal behavior, is an article of faith for most professionals in the field. Unfortunately, the call for a multidisciplinary perspective usually remains only a statement of principle and an exercise in wishful thinking. For this reason, any research effort which promotes interaction between disciplines is, regardless of specific results, an important achievement. It is all too obvious that future progress in our field depends primarily on teamwork and communality of concepts.

In this context, we intend to discuss some general points related to cross-cultural or comparative work in delinquency, and then to relate some recent findings from an interdisciplinary study on delinquents and controls from the metropolitan area of San Juan, Puerto Rico. This paper will not deal directly with violence, even though a large group of our delinquents was violent, but may serve the purpose of illustrating some selected general methodological problems, which have a bearing also on the study of violent criminal behavior.

It is self-evident to all professionals in the field of criminology that the major obstacles to the development of comparative research consist of: (1) a lack of available reliable data; (2) national legal differences; (3) differences in methodology and in methodological

---

The data presented in this paper are abstracted from a book in press: F. Ferracuti, S. Dinitz, and E. Acosta de Brenes, prepared under the joint sponsorship of the University of Puerto Rico, Social Science Research Center and United Nations Social Defence Research Institute. The authors gratefully acknowledge the continuing intellectual support and contributions of the late Eleanor Glueck and Professor Sheldon Glueck of Harvard University and Professor Walter C. Reckles of The Ohio State University.

emphasis; and (4) cultural variations in the identification and handling of offenders.

Similar difficulties, of course, exist in any kind of comparative work. For example, cultural differences in the definition and handling of schizophrenia still delay the development of valid cross-cultural concepts of psychosis, and the WHO is slowly and painfully struggling with the task of developing a valid international classification of mental diseases. The situation is even more complicated in the field of crime and delinquency. These cultural variations, on the other hand, also modify the perceptions by the public, no less than by the professionals involved, of the functioning of the criminal justice system. The perception of violence is a very different thing indeed in a country where civil protest and revolution are endemic, or under war conditions, or where a subculture of violence prevails, in comparison to a peaceful, traditional Swiss or mid-western village. A Pennsylvania Dutch rural adolescent will give a very different definition of violence-eliciting behavior from that offered, verbally or behaviorally, by a culturally deprived black youngster in an urban ghetto in a major U.S. city.

Yet, because of these obstacles, the need for comparative work is such that an effort must be made to overcome the existing difficulties inhibiting comparative research.

Criminal behavior, as a socio-psychological phenomenon, with occasional biological determinants or facilitating factors, is in essence, defined by legal and social norms. We consider criminal behavior which is either so defined by the law; or so defined by the prevailing social norm, or frequently, but not always, both. Since legal and socio-cultural elements are fundamental to the definition of crime and delinquency, cross-cultural, comparative research is essential to our understanding of the etiology of the phenomenon of crime.

Existing etiological theories, particularly when single-discipline oriented, have conspicuously failed to achieve a level of "proof," that we can consider satisfactory for explanation, prediction, and more dramatically, prevention and control. As in other behavioral fields, the question of "why", implied in explanatory and etiological studies, does not overlap exactly with the question of "how", implied in prediction, prevention and control. Also, a basic fallacy led early criminologists to study crime as if they were dealing with a physical phenomenon and not with a legally or socially defined behavior which cannot be framed in our existing biological-science oriented nosographies. There is no valid reason why crime and delinquency should follow the distribution, the etiological aspects, and the normal-abnormal dichotomies of, say, mental deficiency or epilepsy.

Cross-cultural research cannot but facilitate a sharing of concepts, data and experiences which will allow theory testing and validation of tactics, results, and programs. Just to cite one example, the assessment of the incidence of crime and delinquency in countries at different points of the developed-underdeveloped continuum will permit the testing of theories which relate crime to socio-economic development, and to urbanization and industrialization.

Confrontations between Western and Soviet data (when and where available) will, in the light of convergent theory, make it possible to assess factors such as level of expectations and anomie, in a context where such concepts are sharply defined and reasonably different.

Replication in different legal setting and in contrasted cultural milieux, will allow us to focus on these factors which constitute the essential, hard-core set of cross-culturally valid crime related variables.

It is, therefore, in this direction that our efforts should be directed. An interdisciplinary comparative criminology is a major priority in our research efforts.

In this context, we will present some interesting findings from our recently completed Puerto Rican study. The milieu under study was the San Juan metropolitan area, a large, rapidly increasing Latin (and yet North-American in laws and partially in culture) megalopolis which has a serious crime and delinquency problem. Yet, even though criminality, especially by juveniles, is a major concern in San Juan, many of the characteristics associated with juvenile delinquency in U.S. mainland cities are absent. To cite the two most evident differences, gangs as a way of life, and gang warfare are almost totally unknown in San Juan, and the color problem has not poisoned the atmosphere in the San Juan slums. The population of the slum areas is composed, of course, of multi-problem families, but color-determined isolation is not a factor for entering, or remaining, in the slum culture. Economic and mobility factors prevail in assigning a subject or a family into a caserio (low income public housing quarter) or arrabal (natural slum area, Latin style), the Puerto Rican equivalents of the inner city ghetto. Consequently, our delinquency data are "color-free," and may provide an interesting element of comparison with similar studies in the "noncolor-free" mainland high delinquency areas.

The Research Design

As in many projects which originate out of a variety of inputs and expectations, several design and methodological decisions were made which did not necessarily optimize the feasibility of this investigation. Since so little was known of Puerto Rican delinquency, for example, a multifactor approach was employed as a research strategy in designing the study and collecting data.

The research design was limited to an operational plan for data gathering on matched pairs of delinquents and non-delinquents. Our design included careful checking of the delinquency and non-delinquency status of the matched subjects. This made our non-delinquents as free as possible from hidden delinquency involvement.

The following general objectives were accepted as basic in our study: (1) to assess the medical, neurological, psychiatric, psychological and social patterns prevailing in Puerto Rico juvenile delinquents as compared to non-delinquents; (2) to establish the relationship, if any, between these factors and anti-social behavior; (3) to draw from the analysis indications for control and treatment policies to be based simultaneously on general theoretical knowledge about juvenile delinquency in other cultures and on specific data on Puerto Rican delinquency.

The total group of subjects included in the study was composed of 202 males varying in age between 11-17 years, all resident in one of the several slum areas in the city of San Juan. Of the 101 pairs, 20 percent were living in arrabales and the remainder in caserios. The subjects were divided into two groups. Each subject in the delinquent group was carefully matched with a non-delinquent subject. The delinquent group was composed of 101 juveniles with a case pending in the juvenile court in San Juan. They were selected from all cases on the Court list, year by year, between 1966-1969. Each year a certain number of cases were selected, following the procedure of choosing every 25th name from the court listing until the predetermined number of cases for that year had been reached. If for any reason the 25th, 50th, etc. subject was not available, the preceding or following name was chosen.

The control group was composed of a number of juveniles comparable to that of the experimental group. Each member of the control group was individually matched with a member of the experimental group on the following variables: sex (all males), area of residence, socio-economic level, family income, and age (with a six-month tolerance margin in both directions). Each member of the control group had no known criminal history. This was checked not only in the court records, but also in the police records for "police contacts" which might have occurred without leading to court proceedings. If any evidence of criminal behavior appeared subsequently while taking the social history of the case, the subject was dropped and replaced with another one. The controls were located by the social workers attached to the project from the universe of juveniles attending public schools in the areas where the experimental group subjects were residing. Whenever possible, they were attending the same class as the delinquent match. In many cases the delinquents were not attending school and in these instances the control group subjects were selected from the classes that the delinquents would have been attending had they not dropped out. Automatically, this meant that no control group subject was a drop-out. The population characteristics are presented in Table 3.1.

For each subject the following data were collected; (a) Social History, including educational history and criminal history (for the experimental group); (b) Psychiatric Examination; (c) Psychological Test Battery; (d) Physical Examination; including laboratory tests; (e) Neurological Examination and (f) Electroencephalogram.

The 42 page social history was taken from the subject himself, his available relatives and his neighbors; it was checked against available records from the school, courts, police and public welfare. Taking the social history involved a minimum of two to a maximum of eight visits by the social worker to the family.

The psychiatric examination was conducted in an interview which lasted approximately one hour. The interview was conducted in the

TABLE 3.1

Population Characteristics*

Item	Delinquent Group	Non-Delinquent Group
Number of Subjects	101	101
Sex	Male	Male
Age Range (percents)		
11-14 years	43	43
15-17 years	57	57
Selected From	1966-1969 Court List	Same neighborhood schools as delinquents
Type of Residence (percents)		
Arrabales	20	20
Caserios	80	80
Average Height	61.7 inches	62.8 inches
Average Weight	105.4 pounds	111.1 pounds
Skin Color (percents)		
Light	49	55
Medium	25	29
Dark	27	25

*Subjects selected from San Juan, Puerto Rico metropolitan area.

psychiatrist's office and, as was the case in all other examinations, the subject was accompanied to the office of the examiner by the social worker. The psychiatrist was aware of the delinquent/non-delinquent status of the juvenile. The results of the interview were summarized in a psychiatric descriptive report and a final diagnosis was formulated following the APA Diagnostic and Statistical Manual of Mental Disorders, 1968 edition.

The psychological examination consisted of the administration of a battery of tests over a period of two sessions. The battery included the following:

(1.) Wechsler-Bellevue Intelligence Scale for Children (WISC) or Wechsler Adult Intelligence Scale (WAIS), depending on the age of the subject (the cut-off point for using the WAIS was 15 years of age and above). The Puerto Rican standardization of the WAIS was used; in the case of the WISC, the scores were adjusted for the Puerto Rican population.

(2.) Bender-Visual-Motor-Gestalt Test.

(3.) Draw-A-Person Test.

(4.) Rorschach Test.

(5.) Five plates from the Make-A-Picture-Story Test. The five plates were the following: "Dream," "Street", "Bedroom," "Medical," and "Shanty."

The psychological tests were administered by a qualified psychologist who had knowledge of the delinquency/non-delinquency status of the subjects. However, the protocols were neither scored nor interpreted by him. They were sent to another clinical psychologist who interpreted them without any information on the subjects. The interpretation was scored on a psychological report blank which listed different areas of intellectual functioning, personality characteristics and modalities of reaction.

The physical examination was administered by a physician following standard procedures. The laboratory tests included the following: urinalysis, complete blood count (CBC), Venereal Disease Serology (VDRL) and stools examination for parasites. The neurological examination included standard testing of cranial nerves, motor areas, coordination, sensation, reflexes and station. The electroencephalogram was administered under standard conditions, and included hyperventilation and photic drive.

The data yielded in these several protocols—medical, neurological, encephalographic, psychological and social history—were analyzed in two principal ways: by univariate and multivariate techniques. First, the two groups were compared on every variable in a straightforward chi square analysis. Second, after eliminating all but 184 variables on statistical and theoretical grounds, each of the 101 delinquents was compared with his control across each variable in a sign test analysis. The purpose of the sign test was to address the question whether the matched pairs differed significantly from each other and if so, on which items. In contrast, the chi square indicated whether the two groups differed from each other at an acceptable level of confidence. Third, all 184 items were subjected to a factor analysis and seven separate clusters of variables emerged accounting for more than a third of the total variance. Fourth, using a multidiscriminant function analysis approach, the identification of delinquents and non-delinquents in terms of small subsets of variables was compared with their actual status. Eventually, perfect discrimination was obtained using only 13 variables taken together and treated as one.

Findings

The following results were obtained using the two univariate and two multivariate methods described briefly above.

1. Medical, neurological, and encephalographic variables derived from physical examinations, laboratory tests and carefully taken histories generally failed to distinguish the delinquents from the non-delinquents. A few specific health findings did differentiate the two groups. There was, for example, a curious but explainable hematological finding. Our delinquents have more eosinophils (and consequently fewer neutrophils and basophils) than the non-delinquents. This appears to be related to chronic repeated and more frequent parasitic infections in the delinquent group. More important than the specific items were the clinical impressions. On this grosser interpretive level, the non-delinquents predictably were rated as being in better overall health and having fewer organic signs and symptoms.

2. The psychological and psychiatric evaluations were highly discriminating. The data point to a rather serious degree of maladjustment in the delinquents. Whether antecedent, concomitant or consequence of delinquent behavior, interpersonal and emotional problems are clearly associated with delinquency in court derived cases. This association, of course, tells us nothing very definite about the etiological implications of disturbance for delinquency. (See Tables 3.2 and 3.3).

3. The major specific distinctions between the matched groups occurred on the family and school items. Interpolating from individual item differences, the families of the controls were more cohesive and stable in every respect. The economic aspirations were greater, the religious interests more firm. (See Table 3.4). On nearly every

24

TABLE 3.2

Significant Psychological Findings
(X^2 Analysis)

Item	Delinquent Group	Non-Delinquent Group
Verbal I.Q.		
Normal and Above	24	40
Low-Normal and Above	77	61
Performance I.Q.		
Normal and Above	37	58
Low-Normal and Above	64	43
Prognosis		
Unconditionally Good	0	16
Conditionally Good	1	43
Uncertain	45	39
Unfavorable	55	3

Significant Traits

Creativity
Other-Oriented Thinking
Reality Orientation
Fantasy Control
Stereotyped Thinking
Perseveration
Memory Recall
Speed of Mental Processes
Organic Signs
Maturity
Emotional Instability and
  Impulsivity
Extroversion/Introversion
Conformity (Family)
Aggression (Family)
Capacity to Relate (Family)
Hostility (Family)
Suspiciousness (Family)

Aggression (Environment)
Capacity to Relate (Environment)
Hostility (Environment)
Suspiciousness (Environment)
Feelings of Rejection
Overt Homosexuality
Latent Homosexuality
Capacity for Heterosexuality
Prognosis
Assertiveness
Defiance
Suspiciousness
Destructiveness
Emotional Responsibility

TABLE 3.3

Psychiatric Diagnoses

Classification	Delinquent Group	Non-Delinquent Group
Neuroses		
Anxiety	1	2
Obsessive-Compulsive	0	1
Neurasthenic	0	1
Hypochondriacal	0	3
Other	1	0
Sub-Total	2	7
Personality Disorders		
Cyclothymic	0	1
Schizoid	2	2
Explosive	2	0
Hysterical	0	1
Asthenic	0	1
Anti-Social	10	0
Passive-Aggressive	16	5
Inadequate	2	1
Other (Specified)	1	0
Sub-Total	33	11
Homosexuality	2	0
Drug Dependence (Non-Psychiatric)		
Opium (Heroin)	9	0
Other	2	0
Sub-Total	11	0
Psychophysiologic Disorders		
Cardiovascular	0	1
Transient Situational Disturbances		
Adjustment Reaction of Adolescence	18	24
Behavior Disorders		
Hyperkinetic Reaction	0	1
Overanxious Reaction	0	1
Unsocialized Aggressive Reaction	1	0
Group Delinquent Reaction	3	0
Sub-Total	4	2
Mental Retardation		
Borderline	10	10
Mild	13	3
Moderate	6	1
Sub-Total	29	14
Dyssocial Behavior	2	0
Total Impaired	101	59
Total No Mental Disorder	0	42

TABLE 3.4

Significant Family Items
(X^2 Analysis)

Item	Delinquent Group	Non-Delinquent Group
Size of Household: (Not Significant)		
5 or Fewer Persons	20	15
6-9 Persons	63	70
10 or More Persons	18	16
Mother's Birthplace:		
Rural	34	58
Urban	67	43
Father's Birthplace:		
Rural	37	65
Urban	64	36
Father's Education:		
None-9th Grade	71	55
10th-12th Grade	29	42
Vocational or Other	1	4
Father's Occupation:		
Permanent	59	81
Temporary	13	6
Disabled, Unemployed	29	14
Vertical Mobility of Family:		
Rising	0	50
Stable	19	19
Declining	82	32
Mother's Church Attendance:		
Never	54	26
Holidays	25	29
Weekly	22	45
Children's Church Attendance:		
Never	61	2
Holiday	22	79
Weekly	11	20

major measure of school performance and attitudes toward school, the controls showed to great advantage. The policy implications here are evident. (See Table 3.5). With regard to the specific school, family, and psychological-psychiatric variables, it is important to note that the results obtained in Puerto Rico corroborate the findings obtained in mainland city slums. This augurs well for comparative criminology in that inter-cultural generalizations may be possible under certain circumstances.

4. On the sign test, the matched pairs differed significantly on 29 of the 184 variables. Nearly all of these 29 differences occurred on the psychological and school behavior items. However, and at least as important, on 183 of the 184 items the matched pair difference fell in the expected direction. Thus, no matter what the items, the delinquents were not performing as well as their individually matched controls.

5. The principal axis factor analysis yielded seven clusters or patterns of variables which totally accounted for more than 34 percent of the variance. These seven patterns were named and identified as follows: (1) Personal and Social Pathology (34 items), (2) Psychological Traits (12 items), (3) School Misconduct and Problem (14 items), (4) Competent Housekeeping (11 variables), (5) Broken Home (11 items), (6) Interpersonal Hostility and Incompetence (17 items), and (7) Physical and Intellectual Maturity (11 items). Weighted factor scores were computed on each of these seven clusters or patterns and an analysis of variance yielding F ratios was run on each cluster. All seven patterns of items significantly differentiated the delinquents from the controls. In addition, the 101 delinquents and 101 controls, as pairs, were compared on these seven factors with the result that the discrimination was even more pronounced within these pair sets than within the groups.

6. The most significant achievement of this research was the retrospective identification of all 202 subjects as either delinquents or controls. This altogether unique outcome was achieved in a stepwise multidiscriminant function analysis. It need only be noted that the variables used in the univariate analyses and others, principally of a historical and clinical nature, were grouped logically and theoretically into the following subsets of items: medical, psychological-psychiatric, home-family, school and other performances, and electro-encephalogric. Each subset was then used to retrospectively identify the subjects. The optimal medical subset misidentified 18 of the 202 boys, erring on 11 delinquents and seven nondelinquents. The optimal clinical subset misclassified 12 boys calling seven delinquents controls and five controls delinquents. The family variables subset was markedly more accurate. Only three of the delinquents and one control were mistakenly classified. The school subset was even more

TABLE 3.5

Significant School Items
(X^2 Analysis)

Item	Delinquent Group	Non-Delinquent Group
Dropped Out of School	63	NA
School Conduct and Learning Problems:		
(Significant Items)		
Fighting	18	0
Lying	13	0
Cheating	10	0
Disrespectful	26	0
General Misconduct	21	0
Domineering	14	3
Temper Tantrums	21	0
Instigator/Provoker	14	1
Too Talkative	20	14
Uncooperative	13	1
Isolated	38	26
Slow Learner	44	31
Inattentive	20	2
Quiet	19	69
Sensitive	12	36
Attitudes of Subject Re School		
Like School to Some Degree	28	98
Good Relations w/ Classmates	69	100
Good Relations w/ Teacher	65	99
Family Encourages Subject To Stay in School	72	100
Mother Wants Subject in School	72	100
Father Wants Subject in School	52	89
Subject Feels School Important to Life	57	98
Subject's Peers Feels School Important to Life	44	100
Truant	17	7
Homework Difficult	95	50

TABLE 3.6

Classification after First Thirteen Variables of SDFA

Actual Groups	Predicted	
	Delinquent	Non-Delinquent
Delinquents	101	0
Non-Delinquents	0	101

U=0.12671—Degrees of Freedom=
(14,1,20)
F=99.67148—Degrees of Freedom=
(13,188)
p<<0.001

Optimal Classification
(with 39 Variables)

	Delinquent	Non-Delinquent
Delinquents	101	0
Non-Delinquents	0	101

U=0.8412—Degrees of Freedom=
(39,1,200)
F=45.22392—Degrees of Freedom=
(38,162)
p<<0.001

accurate. No controls were misidentified and six delinquents were called controls. In contrast, the EEG-neurological subset was of no use at all. Nearly as many subjects were misplaced as were identified correctly.

In view of the success with the first four subsets, a final analysis was done using as discriminators the first ten variables from each of medical, psychological-psychiatric, home-family, and school analyses. Error free classification of all 202 subjects was accomplished with only thirteen variables including two from the medical, three from the clinical, five from the family and three from the school subsets. These variables are the first 13 in the total list of best discriminators in Table 3.7.

7. The stepwise discriminant function analysis also yielded something never before reported in delinquency research: a paradoxical effect phenomenon. This phenomenon explains, in part at

TABLE 3.7

The Complete List of Best Discriminators from the
Stepwise Discrimination Function Analysis

Items

37. Subject is a Truant (Yes)
39. Subject Steals (Yes)
 7. Suspiciousness (High)
14. Vertical Mobility
28. Children's Church Attendance (Seldom)
27. Father's Church Attendance (Often)*
 3. Emotional Instability (High)
13. Birthplace of Father (Urban)
21. Subject Smokes (Yes)
 2. Complete Blood Count (Abnormal)
24. Home Has Dining Room Set (Yes)
33. Subject Participates in Social Group Activities (Yes)
12. Psychological Diagnosis 318—No Mental Disorder (No)
16. Family Pays Social Security (No)
30. Family Encourages Subject to Stay in School (Yes)*
40. Subject's Family Members Have Police Contact for Type I Offenses (Yes)
31. Subject Likes School (No)
38. Subject Lies (No)*
 8. Destructiveness (High)
29. Teacher Reports Subject Steals in School (Yes)
15. Subject Has Left Home (Yes)
25. Subject's Home Has a Television (No)
 5. Guilt Feelings (Low)
32. Subject is a Dropout (Yes)
 4. Suspiciousness (High)
22. Relatives Had Mental Illness (Yes)
18. Subject has High Blood Pressure (Yes)
19. Subject has History of Infections (No)
26. Area Surrounding the Home was Clean (Yes)
20. Subject has been Treated for Alcoholism (Yes, or needed but not obtained)
35. Subject's Bedwetting (Less than age 3)
23. Subject has a Mental Defect (Yes)
17. Subject has Ulcers (Yes)
 1. Health Status (Fair)
11. Diagnosis 304.0—Drug Dependence (Opium) (No)*
 9. Diagnosis 300.1—Hysterical Neurosis (No)
34. Subject Participates in Church Group Activities (No)
10. Diagnosis 301.82—Inadequate Personality (yes)
36. Subject Sleeps Out (Yes)

*Paradoxical effect phenomenon.

31

least, the seemingly erratic patterns obtained from social history data in previous prediction studies. The implications for diagnosis and outcome research are, therefore, of marked importance. In the paradoxical effect phenemenon, variables which operate in one direction when analyzed separately, may reverse direction when included as part of a broader function. This reversal is reflected in the relative weight as well as the sign (direction) of the coefficient attached to the item. In our analysis, "father's church attendance" proved to be paradoxical in the context of children's church attendance and 11 other concurrent variables which resulted in perfect discrimination. These paradoxical items have an asterisk before them in Table 3.7.

8. In the San Juan arrabales and caserios, juvenile delinquency in the index cases appears to be only one element of a multiproblem family syndrome. This is evident in the item clusters (broken home and competent housekeeping) obtained in the factor analysis. It is also evident in the lengthy case histories of each of the subjects. It is even more obvious in the repeated visits to the homes and in interviews with the parents or adults in the households. Of the three principal family patterns characteristic of mainland families—the truncated extended (Jewish, Italian), the nuclear-atomistic, and the mother-children—the latter, the female based household, devoid of a significant father figure, or at least a stable one, best describes the index families. This instability is coupled with a subsistence standard of living, physical and mental disabilities of every discription, and a retreatist philosophy which makes coping with external problems and realities difficult. Social agency intervention, geared to alleviating specific problems, has failed to enable these household units to reach the critical mass stage from which achievement and mobility are possible. The band-aid approach has merely reinforced the coping inadequacies of these households and created hardcore families without the resources—inner or outer—to alter their destinies.

Thus, mainland and island are not so very different in respect to the multiproblem family origins of court adjudicated delinquents.

9. A very careful analysis of police and court records and the 42 page social history suggests that mainland and island patterns of delinquency do differ in two very important respects. First, Puerto Rico delinquent index cases are largely loners; gang involvement is minimal. Second, the personal violence so endemic in Hispano-American culture is effectively reflected in the aggravated assaults and simple assaults which dot the records of the index cases. This propensity to violence, some 33 violent episodes resulting in court action were found, may well account for the deaths of 11 and 101 index cases since the study was completed just a few years ago.

10. Although Puerto Rico has very high rates of heroin use and addiction the data regarding drug use in the delinquent group are

still astonishing. A careful check of police and court records revealed that 11 delinquents were either hard drug users or addicts. Interviews revealed 15 others who were also hooked—26 out of 101 cases in all. Three observations are in order on this matter. First, official records grossly underestimated the problem of hard drug use. Clearly there is need for other procedures to estimate the prevalence of the problem in order to determine the effectiveness of drug prevention and control programs. Second, the 26 delinquents with serious drug problems were found to be even more seriously disadvantaged and impaired, in relation to their controls, than the other 75 delinquents studied. Whether cause or effect, this special group aged 11-17 at the point of study, needs something more than the present institution can offer if they are to survive and settle down. Third, no nondelinquent subject was even suspected—officially or in the interviews—of experimenting with narcotics.

Cross-cultural studies such as the one herein presented hopefully will do much to encourage better designed and better aimed prevention and treatment programs.

In our view, apart from the obvious methodological and theoretical differentiation of delinquents and non-delinquents, our study contributes to underscoring three relatively important points which are relevant for criminological research and action regardless of cultural and legal national boundaries:

1. In a setting which is relatively free of racial bias, color does not appear to be significantly related to delinquency. In view of the current conflict over genetically induced racial differences, especially in intelligence and in view of the long statistical association between crime and racial minorities in U.S. research, our color free findings may help bury this recurrent thesis. Race in a non-race oriented culture has nothing to do with crime.

2. The operative link between delinquency prevention and the school has been self-evident for a long time in criminology everywhere. Our study reinforces this link adding the notion that the socializing effect of the school in the slum areas is equally or more important than its pedagogical function. When family socialization fails, only the school offers the child a path to non-deviant maturation. If the school also fails, the commitment to delinquency becomes almost inevitable.

3. Our study may help convince adherents of unilateral disciplinary orientation that viable answers can be found only in hard facts painfully and slowly sifted from the full existential reality of delinquent and non-delinquent adolescents. No politically or ideologically derived shortcuts exist to the integration of clinical and

sociological findings in the framework of a modern statistically grounded, value free, positivistic behavior science perspective.

CHAPTER

4

**TYPE OF HOMICIDE
AND PATHOLOGIES AMONG
HOMICIDE OFFENDERS:
SOME CULTURAL PROFILES**

Simha F. Landau

Since the early days of Criminology, homicide has been, and still is, one of the most attractive topics for social scientists interested in criminal and deviant behaviour.[1] A great contribution to the scientific study of this phenomenon was made by Wolfgang (1958) in his work on criminal homicide in Philadelphia, the influence of which is seen in a number of studies published since then (among them Jayewardene and Ranasinghe, 1963; Pokorny, 1965; Voss and Hepburn, 1968, etc.).[2]

In a previous paper on this topic (Landau, Drapkin and Arad, in press) we investigated several factors related to homicide victims and offenders in Israel, namely, sex and ethnic origin of victim and offender, the victim-offender relationship and motives involved in the criminal homicide. In that study we analyzed all the known and solved cases of criminal homicide perpetuated in Israel between January 1, 1950 and December 31, 1964. We excluded cases of homicide caused by infiltrators from neighbouring Arab countries. 279 offenders and 311 victims were involved. The source of information was data from Police files and files of the Prison Service. Comparisons were made between Oriental Jewish, Western Jewish and Non-Jewish (mainly Arab) offenders. The reason for these comparisons stemmed from our basic hypothesis that the influence of cultural norms and traditions on behaviour will be reflected in a clear way in the crime of homicide in Israel. This hypothesis was strongly supported by our findings. Along all the variables, very striking differences were found between offenders and victims of the three ethnic groups.

The Study

The present study was conducted on the same population of offenders, using the same sources of information as the previous one.

35

The topics investigated in this study include the type of homicide as well as the pathologies of the offenders prior to their capital crime: type of first known disturbed or deviant behaviour, previous physical illness or handicap, and hospitalization for physical and mental disorders.

Here again, comparisons will be made between the same three ethnic groups, defined as follows:

1. Oriental Jewish offenders: Those born in Asia or Africa or born in Israel to parents whose origin is in Asia or Africa.

2. Western Jewish offenders: Those born in Europe or America, or born in Israel to parents whose origin is in Europe or America.

3. Non-Jewish offenders: Most of the offenders in this group are Moslem Arabs while some are Christian Arabs or Druzes. Culturally speaking, these three groups have much in common and are organic elements of the oriental native society of the Middle East.

It is important to mention that the great majority of both Oriental and Western Jewish offenders were immigrants (86.5% and 87.9%) as was the majority of the Jewish population in Israel during the period covered by the study.[3]

Our aim in this study is to find out whether the clear distinction between the three ethnic groups found in the victim-offender interaction, will also be reflected in the type of homicide as well as in some background variables in the past of the offender. Thus, what we are aiming at is to create some cultural profiles as regards criminal homicide in the Israeli society.[4]

Type of Homicide

Table 4.1, presenting the distribution of offenders by ethnic origin and type of homicide, shows that 74 percent of the total number of offenders were convicted for either murder or manslaughter.[5] The rate of homicide offenders who subsequently killed themselves is 11 percent, while 12 percent of the offenders were declared insane. The least frequent category of homicide is that of infanticide which is three percent.

The study of West (1965) provides some comparative data on homicide followed by suicide. The rate of offenders of this kind out of the total number of homicide offenders is: in Denmark, 42 percent; in England and Wales, 33 percent; in Australia, 22 percent and in the U.S.A., four percent. In Denmark this rate is 3.8 times higher than in Israel, in England and Wales three times higher, in Australia, twice as high, while in the U.S.A. this rate is 2.75 times lower than in Israel.

TABLE 4.1

Type of Homicide by Ethnic Origin of Offender
(in percents)

	Oriental Jews	Western Jews	Non-Jews	Total
Murder	35.2	30.8	51.7	41.2
Manslaughter	31.8	20.0	41.4	32.7
Homicide-Suicide	11.0	27.7	1.7	11.0
Insane	17.6	20.0	2.6	11.8
Infanticide	5.5	1.5	2.6	3.3
Total	101.1	100.0	100.0	100.0
N	(91)	(65)	(116)	(272)

$G = 57.1787$; d.f. $= 8$; $p < .001$

As to homicide offenders declared insane, this rate in Phila-delphia (2.7 percent, Wolfgang, 1958) is 4.4 times lower than the corresponding rate among homicide offenders in Israel. The picture in England and Wales is completely different: Morris and Blom-Cooper (1964) report that over the period of 1900-1949 as many as 21.4 percent of persons brought to trial were found either unfit to plead or guilty but insane, a rate which is 1.8 times higher than in Israel. However, since 1957 the precentage of apprehended homicide offenders found unfit to plead or guilty but insane fell to 13 percent which is about the same rate as that found in our study. Those successfully pleading diminished responsibility formed an additional 14 percent of the total number indicated for capital or non-capital murder. The introduction of the Homicide Act, 1957, in England and Wales is, as presented above, a good example of how changes in the law affect the criminal statistics.

As regards infanticide, Wolfgang (1958) reports that 1.9 percent of victims in his study were infants under one year of age. There is no information in his study as to the number of offenders involved in these cases of infanticide.

Table 4.1 shows that the distribution of the three ethnic groups differ significantly as regards the type of homicide. Non-Jews are almost exclusively concentrated in the murder and manslaughter groups, the other types being very rare among them. Homicide followed by suicide is especially characteristic of Western Jews: it comprises more than a quarter of all homicide offenders in this ethnic group, and as seen, the rate of this type among Western Jews is 2.5 times higher than among Oriental Jews and 14 times higher than among Non-Jews.

It is of interest to note that considering the four countries mentioned above (Denmark, England and Wales, Australia and the U.S.A.), there is an inverse relationship between the rate of suicide cases among homicide offenders and homicide death rates in these countries. In a table presented by Wolfgang and Ferracuti (1967), we find the following homicide death rates per 100,000 population: in Denmark, 0.5; in England and Wales, 0.6; in Australia, 1.6 and in the U.S.A., 4.5. In order to explain this relationship, another variable has to be taken into consideration, namely the suicide death rate in these countries. Stengel (1964) presents these rates per 100,000 population for the years 1951, 1955, 1959 and 1961. Computing the average suicide death rate for these years we obtain the following rates: in Denmark, 21.4; in England and Wales, 11.75; in Australia, 10.7 and in the U.S.A., 10.4.

All the data presented above lead to three main conclusions:

1. There is an inverse relationship between homicide death rates and suicide death rates. This conclusion is by no means a new or original one and is discussed and studied by numerous researchers, among them Henry and Short (1954), and Gold (1958).

2. There is a direct relationship between the suicide death rate and the rate of homicide offenders committing suicide after their crime.

3. There is an inverse relationship between homicide death rates and the rate of homicide offenders committing suicide after the crime. This conclusion is, of course, a logical outcome of the two previous ones.

Now let us examine whether the above conclusions are applicable when comparing the three ethnic groups in Israel with each other. The mean annual rate of homicide offenders per 100,000 population in Israel is[6]: For Non-Jews, the rate is 4.00, for Oriental Jews, 1.07, and for Western Jews, 0.59. No precise information is available as yet regarding the differential suicide death rates of these ethnic groups. However, a recent study on suicide (Drapkin et al., in press) provides us with the ethnic distribution of all persons who committed suicide in Israel during the years 1962-1966. Although this period is not identical to that of our homicide cases, it may nonetheless help us to test the applicability of the above conclusions to the situation in Israel. The ethnic distribution of suicide cases in the study of Drapkin et al. is as follows;[7]

Western Jews	67.8%
Oriental Jews	25.6%
Non-Jews	6.6%
Total	100.1% (N=854).

These figures, together with those of our study, provide full support to all the three above-mentioned conclusions: Western Jews show the lowest homicide rate, the highest suicide rate and also the highest rate of homicide followed by suicide (Table 4.1). On the other hand, Non-Jews show the highest homicide rate and the lowest rate of suicide and homicide followed by suicide. Oriental Jews fall in-between these two extreme groups on all the three variables: their homicide rate is higher than that of Western Jews but lower than that of Non-Jews, while their suicide and homicide-suicide rates are lower than that of Western Jews and higher than those of Non-Jews.

Thus, we may conclude that the relationship between homicide, suicide and homicide followed by suicide among the main ethnic groups in Israel is essentially similar to the findings in other countries.

The rate of insane offenders in the present study is almost equal among Western and Oriental Jews and is more than six times higher than among the Non-Jews. With regard to infanticide, the numbers are much too small for empirical generalizations.

It is quite justifiable to look at the first two types of homicide (murder and manslaughter) as representing the "normal" example of homicide, while the third and fourth type (i.e. homicide-suicide and offenders declared insane) as cases in which some basic psychopathology is involved. Taking this viewpoint, we may conclude that almost all (93 %) Non-Jewish offenders are normal persons (at least from the legal point of view) who commit "normal" or "classic" homicides. Among Oriental Jewish offenders this part comprises about two-thirds (66 %), while among Western Jewish offenders it goes down to only half (51 %) of the offenders. Almost half (49%) of the Western Jewish offenders belong to the "psychopathological" classification as compared to less than one-third (29%) among Oriental Jewish offenders. Again, and as will be shown on other variables as well, the two extreme ethnic groups are on the one hand the Western Jews, on the other, the Non-Jews, with the Oriental Jews located between these two extremes.

The Problematic History of the Homicide Offender

By problematic history we include here physical as well as mental disorders, deviant behaviour (i.e. previous convictions), and previous hospitalizations.[8]

Table 4.2 shows that of the 200 offenders about whom information was available, only 30 percent did not show any kind of previous disturbed or deviant behaviour. This finding means that the homicide offender is in most cases a person who previously showed clear overt signs of maladjustment. The most frequent type of maladjustment is found in offenders who have committed previous offences (55%), while mental and other disturbances are found in only 16 percent of the offenders. As seen, the distributions of the ethnic groups differ significantly: Among Oriental Jews we find the highest rate of cases (36%) in which no disturbances occurred previous to the homicide; among Western Jews the highest rate of mental and other disturbances (32%) is found while among Non-Jews there is the highest rate of cases is for previous offences (67%) as the first known disturbance. The extremely low rate of Non-Jewish offenders showing mental disturbances has already been mentioned. It is worth pointing out the fact that half of the Western Jewish offenders started their maladjustment career by a clash with the law.

In Table 4.3, various pathologies related to the homicide offender are presented. With regard to severe physical illness or handicap previous to homicide (such as tuberculosis, ulcer, heart desease, serious accidents etc), the data on Table 4.3 (category one) show that 32 percent of all the offenders on whom information was available, did suffer at some time previous to their capital crime from such illness or handicap. Again, there are significant differences between

TABLE 4.2

Distribution of Offenders by Ethnic Origin and
the Type of First Known Disturbed or
Deviant Behaviour
(in percents)

	Oriental Jews	Western Jews	Non-Jews	Total
The Homicide	36.4	18.4	29.2	29.5
Other Offences	40.9	50.0	66.7	55.0
Mental Disturbance and others	22.7	31.6	4.2	15.5
Total	100.0	100.0	100.1	100.0
N	(66)	(38)	(96)	(200)

G = 25.8821; d.f. = 4; p < .001

TABLE 4.3

Distribution of Offenders by Ethnic Origin and
Various Pathologies Prior and/or After the Homicide
(in percents)

	Oriental Jews	Western Jews	Non-Jews	Total
1. Physical Illness or Handicap Any Time Prior to the Homicide[a]	42.1	54.3	15.9	32.2
Total N	(57)	(35)	(82)	(174)
2. Bad Health Condition Immediately Prior to the Homicide[b]	28.0	35.0	7.6	19.4
Total N	(50)	(31)	(79)	(160)
3. Hospitalization for Physical Disorders Before or After the Homicide[c]	19.5	50.0	9.0	18.4
Total N	(41)	(22)	(78)	(141)
4. Hospitalization for Mental Disorders Only After Homicide[d]	20.6	29.3	2.4	14.4
Total N	(63)	(41)	(83)	(187)
5. Hospitalization for Mental Disorders Only Before or Before and After Homicide[d]	22.2	22.0	3.6	13.9
Total N	(63)	(41)	(83)	(187)

[a]$G = 21.0691$; d.f. $= 2$; $p < .001$
[b]$G = 15.2327$; d.f. $= 2$; $p < .001$
[c]$G = 16.7208$; d.f. $= 2$; $p < .001$
[d]$G = 42.9655$; d.f. $= 4$; $p < .001$ (This G value applies to both
categories 4 and 5 as they were both part of one table. The third
category in that table was "No mental hospitalization")

Note: Percentages for each ethnic group were computed using
as the base the total number of subjects in that group about whom information was available. The percentages in each column, therefore
do not sum to 100.0 percent.

the ethnic groups: while among Non-Jewish offenders the rate of those who suffered in this manner is only 16 percent, among Western Jewish offenders this rate is 3.4 times higher (54%) and among Oriental Jewish offenders this rate is 2.6 times higher (42%).

Another related variable within our field of interest is the offender's general health condition immediately prior to the homicide. This variable is basically different from the previous one which referred to events any time in the past of the offender. Category two in Table 4.3 shows that only 19 percent of all offenders were defined as not healthy immediately prior to the homicide. Among Western Jews this rate (35%) is 4.4 times higher than among Non-Jews (8%) while among Oriental Jews (28%) it is 3.5 times higher than among Non-Jews. This finding is consistent with out previous findings which indicate than in general the Non-Jewish offenders suffered less than the Jewish from previous physical as well as mental difficulties. This conclusion is strongly supported by the findings of categories three to five in Table 3 which provide information about hospitalization for physical as well as mental disorders. In category three we find that in general, only 18 percent of the offenders were hospitalized for physical disorders before or after the homicide. However, among Western Jews this rate is much higher and amounts to 50 percent which is 5.6 times higher than among Non-Jewish offenders (9%), and 2.5 times higher than among Oriental Jewish offenders (20%). As to hospitalization for mental disorders, we find in category four that 14 percent of our offenders were hospitalized only after the homicide. Another 14 percent were hospitalized for mental disorders either only before, or before and after the homicide (see category five). As we know already from our previous findings, cases of mental disturbance are extremely rare among Non-Jewish homicide offenders. Table 4.3 provides further support to this conclusion. On the other hand, this table indicates that among Western Jews, 51 percent of the offenders were hospitalized for mental disturbances before and/or after the homicide. The corresponding rate among Oriental Jews is only a little lower, (43%). This high frequency of mental disorder among Jewish homicide offenders as compared to the Non-Jews is of very great importance in the distinction between these two main ethnic groups as regards the crime of homicide.

Some findings obtained by Palmer (1960) are of special relevance to our findings about the offender's problematic history. Palmer compared murderers with their brothers and arrived at the conclusion that the murderers apparently experienced physical and psychological frustrations which were significantly greater in number and intensity than those experienced by their control brothers. Among the murderers there was a significantly higher rate of severe visible physical defects from birth as well as extreme physical defects after birth.

These physical defects, in effect, social stigmata, together with some additional psychological frustrations, "swelled their reservoirs of aggression to a point where the aggression eventually would, and finally did, burst its confines violently" (Palmer, 1960:99).

Comparing our findings with those of Palmer, we see that the Jewish offenders in our study (especially Western Jews) show a relatively high frequency of physical illness, handicaps and hospitalizations. The same is true as regards mental disorders. Thus, Palmer's hypothesis of physical and psychological frustration as important contributing factors to homicidal behaviour can be carefully applied to our Jewish offenders. However, this does not apply to the Non-Jewish offenders in our study. In comparison with both Palmer's murderers and to the Jewish offenders in our study, they seem to be significantly more "normal" more adjusted and less frustrated physically as well as psychologically.

Conclusions

The findings of the present study provide additional evidence to the distinct differences found in our previous study (Landau et al. in press) between the three ethnic groups investigated. Again, the two extreme profiles are those of Western Jews and Non-Jews, while the Oriental Jews are located in between these two extremes.

Western Jews are lowest as regards outward directed personal violence (lowest homicide rate), and the highest as regards inward directed violence (suicide and homicide-suicide cases). This group exhibits also the highest proportion of insanity among offenders, and of physical and mental problems prior to the homicide.

Non-Jews, being the highest as regards acting-out violent behaviour (highest homicide rate) are lowest as regards inward-directed violence (suicide and homicide-suicide). Among this group there is also the lowest proportion of insanity and of physical as well as mental problems prior to the homicide. Oriental Jews are located in-between these two extremes. They exhibit more acting-out violent behaviour than Western Jews but much less than Non-Jews. On the other hand, they are much higher on inward directed violence than Non-Jews In other words, the prevalence of suicide and homicide-suicide among them is much higher than among Non-Jews but far lower than that of Western Jews. As regards insanity among homicide offenders, as well as physical and mental problems prior to the homicide, the characteristics of this group are generally closer to those of Western Jews rather than to those of Non-Jews.

These findings support the interpretation of the findings of our previous study. In the case of Western Jewish offenders, homicide might be interpreted as a result of pathology on the individual-person level, as suggested by Palmer, 1960, 1972. Among Non-Jewish offenders this phenomenon should be approached rather from the cultural point of view, that is, these offenders are part of the Arab culture of the Middle East in which reliance on violence is in many cases a social norm or even a cultural-prescribed behaviour.[9]

As to the Oriental Jewish offenders, special attention should be paid to the factor of culture conflict (Shoham, 1962). It is true that most Jewish offenders in both groups are immigrants (as was the majority of the Jewish population in the country during the period covered by the study). However, there is no doubt that Western Jews, although being affected by their immigration, were initially better equipped for the re-adjustment into the Western oriented Israeli society than were the Oriental Jews. The disruption of the traditional family-structure and the need for a quick adaptation to an achievement-oriented society constitute sources of tension both in the inner system of the immigrant of this ethnic group and in his surrounding social environment. This tension may be considered as an important factor in a variety of behavioural pathologies, homicide being one of them.

Interpreting the findings in terms of general criminological theory, it seems that the most relevant one is the theory of subculture of violence (Wolfgang and Ferracuti, 1967). Some propositions of this theory could be clearly applied to the Non-Jewish homicide offenders, or rather to segments of the Israeli society from which they stem. Moreover, support this theory from another direction is provided also by the profiles of the Western Jewish offenders who are part of a culture of non-violence. Their profiles are in accordance with one of the hypothesis included in the propositions of the subculture of violence theory which were put forward as suggestions for further research. This hypothesis (no. 6) states as follows:

> Persons not members of a subculture of violence who nonetheless commit crimes of violence have psychological and social attributes significantly different from violent criminals from the subculture of violence; i.e. violent criminal offenders from a culture of non-violence have more psychopathological traits, more guilt, and more anxiety about their violent behaviour. (Wolfgang and Ferracuti, 1967: 315).

However, at this point it should be stressed that the analysis of the profiles of the three ethnic groups as regards the crime of homicide is done in the specific setting of the Israeli society. It would be undesirable to draw conclusions which are too general from this specific framework of place and time. In this context it is important to mention that the period of time covered by this study (1950-1964), being the first years of the State of Israel was characterized by a vast mass immigration of Jews into the country, especially during the late forties and fifties. Therefore, it would be of great interest to conduct a follow-up study to discover possible changes in the ethnic patterns of homicide in this society as a result of the social and political developments in this country in recent years. In such a study, as well as in other studies on violent behaviour, efforts should be made to test further hypotheses derived from the theory of the subculture of violence in the special setting of the Israeli society.

Notes

1. This paper presents some findings from a larger study on criminal homicide in Israel. The project was supported in part by a grant from the Ford Foundation and is being conducted by the Institute of Criminology, Hebrew University, Jerusalem, in cooperation with Professor I. Drapkin.

The author is indebted to Commander A. Shur, Head of the Investigation Branch of the Israeli Police and Mr. A. Nir, Prison Commissioner and his Staff, for their willing cooperation and assistence without which this study would not have been possible. Thanks are due to S. Arad for his assistance in all stages of the research, to Mrs. Z. Peled for her assistance with the statistics and to B. Beth-Hallahmi, I. Elan and Miss I. Fishman, who took part in the various stages of the study.

2. For an extensive bibliography see Wolfgang (1958) and Wolfgang and Ferracuti (1967).

3. The mean percentage of immigrants in the total Jewish population during this period was 61%. The discrepancy between this figure and the percentage of immigrants among the Jewish homicide offenders is due to the fact that here all age groups are included while among the offenders, the low age groups are obviously not included. (Source: Publication No. 215 of the Central Bureau of Statistics, Jerusalem, 1967, Table 1.)

4. For the statistical analysis of the data, Wilks' G Independence Test was utilized (Wilks, 1962: 423-424). $G \sim \chi^2$ $(r-1)(s-1)$.

5. Five Non-Jewish offenders were neither Christian nor Moslem Arabs nor Druzes. These were not included in the tables dealing with the variable of ethnic origin. Thus, the total number of cases in Table 1 and the other subsequent tables is less than 279.

6. The rates were computed from the figures in <u>Statistical Abstracts of Israel</u>, 1966, 17, Table B/1, and from Publication No. 215 of the Central Bureau of Statistics, Jerusalem, 1967, Table 1.

7. The following percentages do not represent the suicide rate of the three ethnic groups. However, it should be stressed here that the proportion of Western Jews in the general population is much lower than their contribution to the population of suicide cases. On the other hand, the percentage of Oriental Jews and Non-Jews in the general population is much higher than their share among the suicide cases.

8. The information as regards these variables was collected from the files of the Prison Service. Therefore all homicide-suicide cases (as well as other offenders who were not sent to prison) are not included in the following tables.

9. For details about subcultures of violence in the history of the Middle East and other Mediterranean countries, see Gibbens and Ahrenfeld (1966).

References

Central Bureau of Statistics
   1966   Statistical Abstracts of Israel, Vol. 17. Jerusalem.

   1967   Development of the Jewish Population in Israel 1948 to 1964, Part A. Special Series No. 215. Jerusalem.

Drapkin, I., Z. Peled, and Y. Hassin
         Suicide in Israel. Tel Aviv: Gomeh Publishing House. (in press)

Gibbens, T.C.N. and R.H. Ahrenfeld (eds.)
   1966   Cultural Factors in Deliquency. London: Tavistock Publication.

Gold, M.
   1958   "Suicide, homicide and the socialization of aggression." The American Journal of Sociology 63 (May): 651-661.

Henry, A. F. and J. F. Short
   1954   Suicide and Homicide. Glencoe, Illinois: The Free Press.

Jayewardene, C. H. S. and H. Ranasinghe
   1963   Criminal Homicide in the Southern Province. Colombo: The Colombo Apothecaries Co.

Landau, S. F., I. Drapkin, and S. Arad
    "Homicide victims and offenders: An Israeli study."
    Journal of Criminal Law and Criminology. (in press)

Morris, T. and L. Blom-Cooper.
1964   A Calendar of Murder: Criminal Homicide in England
        since 1957. London: Michael Joseph.

Palmer, S.
1960   A Study of Murder. New York: T. Y. Crowell.

Palmer, S.
1972   The Violent Society. New Haven: College and University
        Press.

Pokorny, A. D.
1965   "A comparison of homicides in two cities." The Journal
        of Criminal Law, Criminology and Police Science 56
        (December):479-487.

Shoham, S,
1962   "The application of the 'culture conflict' hypothesis to the
        criminality of immigrants in Israel." Journal of Criminal
        Law, Criminology and Police Science 53 (June):207-214

Stengel, E.
1964   Suicide and Attempted Suicide. Penguin Books.

Voss, H. L. and Hepburn, J. R.
1968   "Patterns in criminal Homicide in Chicago." The Journal
        of Criminal Law, Criminology and Police Science 59 (De-
        cember):499-508.

West, D. J.
1965   Murder Followed by Suicide. London: Heinemann.

Wilks, S. S.
1962   Mathematical Statistics. New York: John Wiley.

Wolfgang, M. E.
1958   Patterns in Criminal Homicide. Philadelphia: University
        of Pennsylvania Press.

Wolfgang, M. E. and Ferracuti, F.
1967   The Subculture of Violence. London: Tavistock Publications.

CHAPTER

5

MURDERS IN
A DRUG USING
POPULATION
Margaret A. Zahn
and Mark Bencivengo

Murder has long attracted the attention of criminologists. A classic study conducted by Wolfgang in Philadelphia determined, as have other studies (Gastil, 1971; Bohannon, 1967; Iskrant and Joliet, 1968) that certain populations are more likely to be victims of homicide attacks or involved in situations where homicide is a likely result than are other populations. Black males, for example, are more likely to be involved in such occurrences. A subculture of violence has been posited to help explain this fact (Wolfgang, 1958, 1967). Whether such an explanation is adequate for explaining the dramatic increase of homicides among drug using populations is one object of this paper. We contend that other notions must be used to augment the "subculture of violence" explanation when explaining violent death among those who use illicit drugs in this society.

Data from the Medical Examiner's Office and Philadelphia Police indicate that homicide among drug users increased appreciably in Philadelphia from 1969 to 1972. In 1972, it was the leading cause of death among drug users. In Philadelphia, there was a total of 286 homicides in 1969, 382 in 1970, 453 in 1971 and 468 in 1972. This represents an increase of 33.5 percent from 1969-1970; and 18.6 percent increase from 1970-1971, and a 3.3 percent increase from 1971-1972. Drug users show an even more dramatic rate of increase. There were 13 homicides among drug users in 1969, 27 in 1970, 87 in 1971 and 144 in 1972. These represent a 107.7 percent increase from 1969-1970; a 222.2 percent increase from 1970-1971; and 65.0 percent increase from 1971-1972. Further, homicide among drug users accounts for an increasing percentage of the total number of homicides. In 1969, 4.5 percent of the homicides involved drug users, in 1970 it was 7.1 percent in 1971, 19.2 percent and in 1972., 30.9 percent. In 1972, then, approximately one of every three homicides in Philadelphia involved a drug user. The question is why? What accounts for such high rates of homicide among this population.

Our hypotheses are twofold. First, since drug users, especially heroin users, are likely to be young black males, the high rate of homicide in drug using populations reflects the fact that heroin users are part of the "subculture of violence" postulated by Wolfgang (1958, 1967). Second, in addition to this, the style of life of a drug user, in a society where drug use is illicit, involves behaviors which ultimately may prove lethal. One such behavior is frequent involvement in theft which may result in deadly confrontations with law officers or other citizens who are the victims of thefts; another is involvement in arguments relating to securing and maintaining a supply of drugs in a highly competitive market. These two sets of behavior we refer to as transactional risks. Homicide among drug users, in other words, is related to explanations dealing with the relation of homicide to other forms of crime and to the risks attending the buyer-seller transaction in the drug culture. Further elaboration of these two explanations occur in the paper.

Methodology

Data for the study were drawn from the records of the Medical Examiner's Office of the City of Philadelphia.[1] Sections of records used included:

1. A face sheet which contained demographic information on the victim. A medical investigator was responsible for completing this form and for conducting interviews with the family and/or friends of the victim.
2. An autopsy report completed by a doctor on the staff of the Medical Examiner's Office. Of special interest to us was the physician's determination of cause of death and the toxicology findings. The toxicology report, based primarily on thin layer chromatography, was used to determine if drugs were present in the victims system at the time of death. If a victim had track marks as a result of narcotics use, it was also reported in the autopsy section.
3. A report filed by the Philadelphia Police Department. This section was completed by the officers at the scene of the homicide incident and by the members of the Homicide Unit subsequently assigned to the case. This report included a description of the surroundings at which the homicide event occurred. It also contained witnesses' statements when available. Most importantly, it included a description of and statement from the defendant in the event that an arrest was made. The description of the offender included his age, sex, race, and number of previous police contacts, if any. The section provided by the Police Department also included the arrest

record of the victim. From this it was possible to determine the type and extent of criminal involvement on the part of the victim.

Definition of Major Variables

It was obvious from the outset that a point of careful consideration would be the definition of a drug user for the purposes of this study. It was not possible to rely on toxicology reports alone. Sometimes toxicology findings were negative. The most frequent reason for negative toxicology findings was that death occurred after drugs had passed out of the victims' system. It was necessary, therefore, to employ additional criteria to determine if the victim was a drug user. Discussions with a medical investigator who was involved in investigations of homicides among drug users and analysis of the records suggested additional ways of defining the population in question.

Criteria for inclusion in the drug using population included:
1. Positive toxicology.
2. Two or more arrests for illegal possession of narcotics during the five year period prior to death.
3. Drugs or drug related paraphenalia found on or near the body at the time of death.
4. Admission by the victim's family that the homicide victim was a drug user.
5. Track marks.

For purposes of this study homicides included both unjustifiable and justifiable killings. The Medical Examiner's Office does not exclude justifiable homicides from its records. These would include, for example, cases in which the victim was killed by a police officer, storekeeper or homeowner while attemptimg to commit a felony. Because of the inclusion of these cases, the total number of homicides for each year exceeds figures submitted by the Philadelphia Police Department.

The additional cases, however, were seen as being important because a question we sought to answer concerned the number of individuals who were killed while committing or attempting to commit a felony. These cases were included since we were also interested in determining if drug users were more likely than non-drug users to be killed during the commission of a felony.

Sample

The population consisted of all homicide victims who were drug users in the years 1969-1972. The years 1969-1972 were selected for analysis since there was a dramatic increase over that four year period. The population also consisted of a random sample of homicide victims who were not drug users. The sample was selected by listing all homicides for each of the four years by case number. After homicides involving drug users had been identified, a random sample was chosen from each year from the remaining homicides. The number of cases selected for the sample was based on the percentage of drug user homicides in a given year. For example, drug user homicides made up five percent of the total number of homicides in the year 1969; therefore, five percent of the remaining homicides were selected for study. This technique was used for each of the four years. The number of non-use cases for each year was as follows: 14 in 1969; 25 in 1970; 73 in 1971; and 93 in 1972. The final sample included the universe of drug user homicides (N-271) and a random sample of non-user homicides (N=205).

Findings

The first part of the analysis deals with sex, race, age and marital status of drug using homicide victims versus non drug using homicide victims.

Sex and Homicide. Males in both drug using and non-using populations were more likely than females to be the victim of a homicide; they were, however, even more likely to be so among drug using populations. Among drug users 88.7 percent (N=236) of the victims were male while only 11.3 percent (N=30) were female. Eighty percent (N=163) of the homicide victims who do not use drugs were male, while 20 percent of the victims were female. These differences are significant at the .01 level.

Race and Homicide. Previous research (Wolfgang, 1958) reveals findings similar to those found in the present study. Blacks are decidedly more likely to be homicide victims than are whites. Eleven percent (N=53) of the homicide victims were white while 89 percent (N=410) were black.

In addition, black drug users were more likely to be the victims of homicide than either white drug users or black non-users. Ninety-five percent (N=249) of the drug users were black while only five percent were white. Black non-users accounted for 39 percent (N=161) of the black population while black users made up 61 percent (N=249) of that racial group.

The converse is true of whites. Twenty-seven percent of the white victims were drug users while 73 percent (N=39) were non-users. For blacks, at least, the attribute of race and being a drug user substantially increases the risk of death through murder. These differences are significant at well beyond the .0001 level.

51

Age, Drug Use and Homicide. While not significant (t=.492, p >.05) the differences in the mean ages of the two groups was 8 years. Among drug users the $\bar{x}$ age at death was 25.8 years. The $\bar{x}$ age for non-users was 33.5.

Marital Status and Homicide. The two populations also differ somewhat in terms of marital status. Table 5.1 indicates that for both drug using and non-using homicide victims the single person is more likely to be killed than the married, divorced or widowed; however, the drug user who is single is even more likely than his single non-using counterpart to be a murder victim. It would appear that being single means being on the street more, in bars more frequently, and for the single drug user "hustling more". All of these may create conditions which increase the likelihood of being a homicide victim.

The foregoing analysis indicates that the attributes of being single, young, black, male and a drug user are significantly associated with homicide. One reason for this is that in order to sustain their habits drug users, especially young black males, resort to a series of illegal acts i.e., primarily robbery, to obtain necessary funds. This action substantially increases their chances of being killed either by the police, a guard, or a person who may be the object of the robbery attempt. Second, the use of illegal drugs itself requires involvement in activities to obtain and maintain a drug supply. This may be accomplished by purchasing or stealing drugs from someone who has them; by dealing in drugs, or by other underworld activity. While a full scale analysis of the buying and selling transaction cannot be undertaken here, it is fair to assume that in any such transaction there will be some dissatisfied customers, some people who are trying to reduce competition by eliminating other sellers in the market and so forth. Where a commodity is scarce and highly in demand (as is the case with drugs) extreme measures of control i.e., homicide, may be involved.

To test the effect of involvement in illegal activities on the likelihood of being murdered the data were examined to determine, first, who the decedent was killed by (spouse, family member, friend, police officer on duty, off-duty police officer, a guard, a storekeeper or barowner, a homeowner, other or unknown). Second, whether or not the decedent was killed while committing or attempting to commit a felony. Finally, the data were analyzed in relation to whether the decedent had a police record for other than narcotic offenses and if so, if they were for property crimes (burglary, larceny, auto theft, robbery); crimes against persons (homicide, assault, rape) or other crimes (gambling, intoxication, prostitution).

In both groups there was a high percentage of cases in which the killer was unknown or the relationship could not be determined from the records. For both groups, then, a high percentage of cases

52

TABLE 5.1

Drug Using and Non-Using Homicide Victims
by Marital Status

| | Drug Use | | Non-Use | | |
	Number	Percent	Number	Percent	Total
Single	167	61.9	99	48.7	266
Married/					
Common Law	74	27.4	77	37.9	151
Divorced/					
Separated/					
Widowed	29	10.7	27	13.3	56
Total	270	100.0	203	100.0	473

Note: $X^2 = 7.89 \leq .05$

involve assailants who are other than a primary relation or someone
formally (police) or informally (storekeeper) trying to protect against
theft or assault. When the unknowns and the category of "other" are
removed from the analysis there are, however, significant differences
in the assailants of drug users vs. non-users.

Table 5.2 indicates a higher percentage of non-users were killed
by a spouse (11.5%) or other family member (14.1%) than were drug
users, 6.8 percent for spouse and 3.4 percent for other family member
respectively. Furthermore, in both cases a friend is frequently likely
to be the assailant (in 51.2 percent of the drug using cases and in
64.6 percent of the non-using cases). The police are the assailants
in 20.5 percent of the cases of a drug user's homicide, but only 5.3
percent of the cases in non-users. Furthermore, drug users were
killed by storekeepers in 12 percent of the cases and by a homeowner
in six percent of the cases in contrast to non-users who were killed
by storekeepers and homeowners in only five cases (4.4%). This
suggests that drug users are more likely than non-users to be killed
by an officer of the law or a person being attacked by the decedent
in some way.

Data on decedents being killed while committing a felony further
supports the conclusion, as does data on offense records of both types
of victims. Assessments of whether the decedent was killed while
committing a felony were made by reading through the records supplied by the medical examiner's investigative staff. For purposes
of this study a felony was considered to be a burglary or robbery

TABLE 5.2

Drug Using and Non-Drug Using Homicide Victims by Known Assailants*

| | Drug User | | Non-User | | |
	Number	Percent	Number	Percent	Total
Spouse	8	6.8	13	11.5	21
Family Member	4	3.4	16	14.1	20
Friend	60	51.2	73	64.6	133
Police	24	20.5	6	5.3	30
Storekeeper	14	11.9	5	4.4	19
Homeowner	7	5.9	0	0.0	7
Total	117	100.0	113	100.0	230

*Unknowns and others have been excluded from this table.

Note: $X^2 = 30.76$ $p \leq .05$

attempt in which the offender was killed either by the victim of the attempt, by a police officer, or private security guard.

Eighteen and one-half percent (N=48) of the drug using victims were killed while committing a felony, while only 9.1 percent (N=18) of the non-drug using victims were so killed. These differences are significant at less than the .01 level. Thus, while most homicides were not the result of "being caught" in a felonious act, many more drug users are victims in these situations than non-users.

Arrest Records of Homicide Victims. Analysis of the arrest records for both groups further points to the likelihood that drug use is related to other criminal activity, especially crimes against property, and that criminal activity is associated with increased risks of being a homicide victim. In terms of arrest records we found that 83.5 percent (N=187) of the drug users have a record for a non-narcotics offense, while the corresponding figure for non-users is 45.7 percent (N=90). This latter figure is comparable to the one found by Wolfgang (1958) in his original study of homicide. Differences between drug users and non-drug users in terms of arrest records were significant at beyond the .001 level ($x^2 = 64.86$). The vast majority of drug using victims, it appears, have an arrest record. The nature of their arrest record however, is different from the arrest records of others who are homicide victims.

Arrest records for each group were coded into three categories; arrests for crimes against property (burglary, robbery, larceny); crimes against persons (assault, rape, and homicide); and other crimes (e.g., intoxication, gambling, and flim-flam games). The data indicates there were no significant differences between drug users and non-users in arrests for assaultive crimes. Fifty-four percent of the drug using homicide victims had been arrested for person crimes while 50.6 percent of the non-users with arrest records had been arrested for such a crime. Some of both drug users and non-users who end up as homicide victims have been involved in violent behavior before; for these, the homicide act is the terminal point in a career of violent activity.

Both users and non-users are likely to have been arrested for gambling, intoxication, etc.; however, non-users who have been arrested are much more likely to have had police contacts for these crimes than are users. Eighty-six percent (N=77) of the non-users with arrest records have been arrested for these crimes, while 62 percent (N=121) of the drug users with arrest records had been so arrested. Differences were significant at the .001 level (x^2 = 14.57).

In regard to property crimes the expected association between arrest for such crimes and being a drug user homicide victim did hold. Table 5.3 shows that 78.5 percent of the drug users have been arrested for crimes against property while only 50.6 percent of the non-users who have been arrested have been so for property offenses. These differences are significant at beyond the .0001 level. This fact seems to indicate that the involvement of drug users in robbery, burglary, etc. is the additional risk in their lives; for many the risk ultimately proves fatal.

Generally, the data indicate that more drug using homicide victims than non-drug using homicide victims have been involved in some kind of crime. While the drug using homicide victim is involved in crime against the person and "other crimes," he is much more likely to be involved in crimes against property. Such activity, because it is more frequent among drug users, is likely to increase the chance of an altercation leading to death. This may help account for the high rates of homicide among the drug using group.

Difficulties stemming from these kinds of involvements are not the only kinds of risks entered into by drug users. They also run an increased risk of being killed because they have an additional area in which disagreements may arise. Any situation in which limitations are placed on scarce goods is likely to evoke mechanisms to ensure access and/or control of these goods. This may be true at the organizational level (Thompson, 1967) as well as the individual level. The mechanisms involved may include homicide as a way of securing goods. Homicide may also be a byproduct of other attempts to secure

TABLE 5.3

Drug Using and Non-Drug Using Homicide Victims
by Arrests for Property Crimes

	Drug Users		Non-Users		
	Number	Percent	Number	Percent	Total
Arrest for Property Crimes	146	78.5	45	50.6	191
No Arrest for Property Crimes	40	21.5	44	49.4	84
Total	186	100.0	89	100.0	275

Note: $X^2 = 22.67$ $p \leq .001$

drugs e.g., fights. While we do not have data to sufficiently test this notion, we do have some preliminary data. The records used in this study describe the transaction between victims and offenders prior to the homicide act. In many cases the transaction was witnessed by a number of people and their descriptions of the event were transcribed into the records. Data of this type, of course, were not always avaliable. Wherever the records indicated clearly a description of the circumstances surrounding the homicide act, however, they were coded. Coded categories emerged from the data itself and included; victim of a robbery attempt; gang slaying; drug related argument; killed during a holdup; killed in other illegal act; accidental death; argument in a bar; domestic quarrel; other reason; and unknown (Table 5.4).

Drug related arguments, which are of special importance here, were arguments where witnesses clearly indicated that the decedent had been angry about a drug related event, such as getting "bad" drugs, or where the type of killing indicated a strong likelihood that it was drug related. For example, in one case a man came into a bar, put a gun to a user's head, indicated his anger for not getting paid, and then shot him. Eleven percent, the second largest category of homicides among drug users, involved drug related arguments. In only one case among non-drug users was this the case, and in this instance the non-user was arguing with a user about his use of drugs and the non-user lost the argument. Drug related arguments, then, serve as a basis for risk of homicide among drug users, although it does not appear to be as salient a factor as involvement in illegal activity.

TABLE 5.4

Drug Using and Non-Drug Using Homicide Victims
by Reason for Death*

| | Drug User | | Non-User | | |
	Number	Percent	Number	Percent	Total
Victim of Robbery Attempt	7	4.0	25	20.8	32
Gang Killing	17	9.7	13	10.8	30
Drug Related Argument	30	17.2	1	.8	31
Killing During Holdup by Police, etc.	63	36.2	7	5.8	70
Killed in Other Illegal Act	26	14.9	4	3.3	30
Accident	8	4.6	9	7.5	17
Argument in Bar	6	3.4	22	18.3	28
Domestic Quarrel	17	9.8	39	32.5	56
Total	174	100.0	120	100.0	294

*Unknowns and others have been excluded from this table.

Note: X^2 = 126.83 $p \leq .01$

The data reveal other interesting differences. Non-drug users
are more likely than users to be victims of robbery attempts; more
likely to be killed in an argument in a bar; or in a domestic quarrel.
Drug users are more likely than non-users to be a victim of homicide
as a result of drug arguments and as a result of all forms of illegal
activity. Both groups are equally likely to be slain in a gang related
incident (6.3 percent of both groups die this way); are equally likely
to be a homicide victim by accident (in these cases usually the victim
had tried to intervene in an argument and was accidentally killed as
a result or else was sitting near an intended victim when someone
attempted to slay him). Furthermore, there are in both groups a
relatively high percentage in which the precipitating circumstances
remains unknown, although the unknowns are greater in the case of
the drug using victim. Conceivably many of those unknowns might
involve drug related matters, however, that is impossible to tell.
In any event, while death by homicide is an act which is similar in

57

some respects for users and for non-users, there are significant differences in the circumstances of their death. For drug users the death is more likely to be a result of his involvement with drugs, attempts to secure them or attempts to secure money for them. Taking drugs then constitutes a risk toward homicide. If drug use increases in a society which makes it illegal to take drugs, we might then expect that robbery will increase as will homicides among drug using populations.

Note

1. We found the records used for this study to be complete, orderly and thorough. We would like to thank Dr. M. E. Aronson Medical Examiner of Philadelphia, for his gracious cooperation in making these excellent records available to us.

References

Bohannan, P.
1967   African Homicide and Suicide. New York: Atheneum.

Gastil, R. D.
1971   "Homicide and a regional culture of violence." American Sociological Review 36 (June):412-427.

Iskrant, A. P., and P. V. Joliet
1968   Accidents and Homicide. Cambridge, Massachusetts: Harvard University Press.

Thompson, J. D.
1967   Organizations in Action. New York: McGraw-Hill.

Wolfgang, M. E.
1958   Patterns in Criminal Homicide. Philadelphia; University of Pennsylvania Press.

Wolfgang, M. E. (ed.)
1967   Studies in Homicide. New York: Harper and Row.

6

HOMICIDE AND A REGIONAL CULTURE OF VIOLENCE: SOME FURTHER EVIDENCE

William C. Bailey

In a recent publication, Gastil (1971) presents an interesting analysis of the transmission of "Southern Culture" throughout the United States and rates of homicide. Building upon the observations of numerous scholars of the South, he attributes the high homicide rate for this part of the country to a "regional culture of violence." He further argues that with the mingling of the American population through migration, the Southern tendency to violence has diffused; differences in homicide rates for sections of the country reflects the degree of Southerness of the populations.

To test this notion, Gastil constructs a quantitative index of southern migration for each state based upon the proportion of each state's population of southern origin. He next fit these data along with nine additional variables associated with homicide (percent Negro, percent population age 20-34 years, median income, percent urban population, physicians per 1000 residents, hospital beds per 1000 residents, median years of school completed, population, percent population living in cities over 300,000) into a multiple correlation analysis. This analysis revealed the association between Southerness and homicide (1960) to be $r = .86$. Combining the effects of Southerness and the nine additional independent variables resulted in a multiple correlation (R) of .946, indicating an increment of about 15 percent of additional explained variance by considering these factors. Due to the high intercorrelation between Southerness and percent nonwhite ($r = .71$) Gastil next "forced" Southerness last in the regression analysis to test its independent effect. Here, of the total variance in homicide explained by all ten independent variables ($R^2 = .89$) 66 percent could be attributed to percent nonwhite, 12 percent of population 20-34 years, and 11 percent to the remaining eight variables. Forced last, Southerness only accounted for approximately four percent of independent variance in rate.[1]

Although Gastil presents an interesting and creative examination of the diffusion of the southern tradition of violence and homicide rates, his analysis suffers from a difficulty that has plagued many homicide investigations: his use of U.S. Public Health Service figures as an index of criminal homicide.

Periodically the Public Health Service (1967), in its series on mortality, issues figures on homicide as cause of death. Homicide is defined by this agency as "a death resulting from an injury purposely inflicted by another person" (U.S. Public Health Service, 1967: 9). Intent to kill is not required to classify a death as a homicide. Unfortunately, the Public Health Service does not report figures separately for different types of killing nor has anyone been successful in separating out of these figures important types of homicide, such as first degree murder (Sellin, 1967).[2]

In short, the "catch-all" nature of the definition of homicide used by the Public Health Service would clearly seem to limit the use of these data in scholarly investigations of criminal homicide. The research reported here is an attempt to move beyond the limitations of these statistics and examine the factor of Southerness with alternative homicide figures.

The Present Investigation

The research reported here is similar to that of Gastil's with one important exception; we examine here the association between Southerness and rates of: (1) first degree murder, (2) second degree murder and (3) murder and nonnegligent manslaughter. While Public Health statistics may provide an adequate general index of lethal violence, they do not permit a more refined analysis of the effect of Southerness on legally and theoretically distinct types of murder.

First and Second Degree Murder. To obtain figures on first and second degree murder, a survey was conducted of all state bureaus of corrections throughout the United States. Inquiries were made of each agency requesting figures on the number of first and second degree murderers referred to penal institutions in 1967 and 1968. For states without a central corrections authority, individual inquiries were made to penal institutions requesting the needed information. Admissions data were only requested for these two years because: (1) initial inquiries revealed that referral statistics for prior years were not available, in many cases and (2) this investigation was initially launched late in 1970, and referral statistics for 1969 in many cases had not yet been compiled. In total, figures were received from 41 states and the District of Columbia, with Mississippi, Arkansas, Georgia, South Carolina, Missouri, Pennsylvania, Arizona and Alaska either unwilling or unable to supply the required data.[3]

Due to variation in homicide statutes across the country, definitions of murder in the first and second degree were provided with our requests to assure comparability of data. Only for the state of Florida was it found impossible to "break down" homicide referrals by degree. Consequently, this state was dropped from the analysis.

Limitations of the Data. It should be kept clearly in mind that the first and second degree murder figures reported here refer solely to persons convicted of first and second degree murder and referred to penal institutions. The data may not be interpreted as reflecting: (1) the total number of first and second degree murders committed in a state, (2) the number of persons accused of murder in the first or second degree, or (3) the number of persons tried for first and second degree murder. One additional possible limitation of the data should also be noted. It is well recognized that many homicide suspects initially charged with first degree murder are later recharged with second degree murder or manslaughter in exchange for "copping a plea." As important as this consideration may be, it is not possible to state in the absence of hard evidence how this practice might have affected our data. Most authorities, however, suggest that plea bargaining has the effect of underestimating the "true" first degree figures and overestimating the "true" second degree figures (Sellin, 1954).

Murder and Nonnegligent Manslaughter. In addition to first and second degree murder, figures were also gathered from the Uniform Crime Reports for the offense of murder and nonnegligent manslaughter. This offense is defined by the Federal Bureau of Investigation (1970: 61) as, "all willful felonious homicides as distinguished from deaths caused by negligence." These F.B.I. data, although subject to many difficulties, are examined here for two reasons: (1) Gastil refers both to murder and homicide (a more inclusive offense) as consequences of Southerness, and (2) F.B.I. figures for homicide along with data for first and second degree murder permit both a comprehensive as well as a more refined analysis of Southerness and lethal violence than found in Gastil's investigation.

Index of Southerness. Gastil's (1971: 425-426) index of Southerness is used for the states examined in this investigation. An index value ranging from 5 to 30 is assigned each state depending upon the influence of southern migration for the jurisdiction. To illustrate, values of 30 are assigned the most southern states (Virginia, West Virginia, Kentucky, Tennessee, etc.) while those experiencing the least southern migration (North Dakota, South Dakota, Minnesota, Wisconsin, etc.) are assigned index scores of 5.[4]

Data Processing. Data processing consisted of fitting figures for each offense and Southerness along with a number of additional independent variables similar to those considered by Gastil into a multiple correlation analysis: The variables were: (1) median

61

educational attainment, (2) median family income, (3) percent of population 18-44 years of age, (4) percent of population nonwhite, (5) percent of population in metropolitan areas, (6) population density, (7)
physicians per 1,000 population, and (8) hospital beds per 1,000 population.[5] To avoid needless confusion, the offenses of first degree
murder, second degree murder and murder and nonnegligent manslaughter will be referred to as Murder I, Murder II and homicide in
the discussion to follow.

Results

First Degree Murder (Murder I). Table 6.1 reports simple,
partial and multiple correlations for Murder I admissions for the
states and years surveyed.

Inspection reveals that for both years Southerness proves to
be the factor most strongly associated with rate, permitting approximately 46 percent ($r = .676$, $P < .001$) and 28 percent ($r = P < .001$),
respectively, of explained variance in the dependent variable.[6] After
Southerness, median education and hospital beds per 1,000 population
prove to be the next most important variables, but not in the same
order each year. Although the zero order correlations between each
of these variables and Murder I are significant, these two factors
combined only contribute a total of about five percent additional explained variance in rate each year. The remaining variables, including
percent nonwhite only contribute slightly to the total explained variance
in Murder I. Median income (1967), population 18-44 years (1968)
and physicians per 1,000 population (1968) are excluded from Table
6.1 due to low F levels (not to be confused with significance level);
their inclusion in the correlation equation would add little of value.
This procedure of excluding variables whose F value falls below .01
will be followed throughout the analysis.

To test the independent effect of Southerness on Murder I, after
controlling for the effects of other independent variables, Southerness
is "forced" last in the multiple correlation. Results are presented
in Table 6.2. Table 6.2 shows median education to now be the factor
most strongly associated with Murder I. The second variable of
entry for both 1967 and 1968 is hospital beds per 1,000 population
which allows an increment in explained variance of 19 percent for
1967 and 12 percent for 1968. With the exception of Southerness,
the remaining variables provide little assistance in accounting for
Murder I. This is reflected by the slight increments in R^2 values
from the second order multiple correlations downward.

In Gastil's investigation, he attempts to account for a similar
small increase in explained variance when comparable variables are

TABLE 6.1

Relation of State Murder I Admission Rates to Selected Independent Variables, 1967 and 1968

Variables	Simple r	Partial r at Entry	Cumulative Exp. Variance (R^2)
1967			
Southerness	.676[c]	.676	.457[c]
Mdn. Education	-.480[c]	-.057	.476[c]
Hospital Beds/1000	-.406[b]	-.270	.514[c]
Percent Urban	.113	.140	.524[c]
Population Density	-.175	-.131	.532[c]
Percent Nonwhite	.456[c]	-.098	.536[c]
Percent 18-44 years	.281[a]	-.073	.539[c]
Physicians/1000	-.294[a]	-.034	.539[c]
1968			
Southerness	.533[c]	.533	.284[c]
Hospital Beds/1000	-.349[a]	-.182	.308[b]
Mdn. Education	-.394[b]	-.189	.333[b]
Mdn. Income	-.159	.194	.358[b]
Percent Nonwhite	.348[a]	-.109	.365[b]
Percent 18-44 years	.255	-.078	.369[c]
Population Density	-.124	-.029	.370[c]

[a] p < .05
[b] p < .01
[c] p < .001

63

TABLE 6.2

Relation of State Murder I Admission Rates and Selected Independent Variables,
1967 and 1968; Southerness Forced Last

Variables	Simple r	Partial r at Entry	Cumulative Exp. Variance (R^2)
1967			
Mdn. Education	-.481[c]	-.231	.231[c]
Hospital Beds/1000	-.406[a]	-.495[b]	.420[c]
Percent Metropolitan	.113	.165	.436[c]
Population Density	-.175	-.285	.481[c]
Physicians/1000	-.294[a]	-.084	.485[c]
Percent 18-44 years	.281[a]	.049	.486[c]
Percent Nonwhite	.456[c]	.028	.487[b]
Southerness	.676[c]	.320[b]	.539[c]
1968			
Mdn. Education	-.394[a]	-.394	.155[a]
Hospital Beds/1000	-.349	-.379[a]	.277[b]
Mdn. Income	-.159	.190	.303[b]
Population Density	-.124	-.117	.312[a]
Percent Metropolitan	.116	.058	.314[a]
Physicians/1000	-.187	-.070	.318[a]
Percent 18-44 years	.255	.045	.319
Percent Nonwhite	.348[a]	-.090	.365
Southerness	.533[c]	.258[a]	.370

[a] $p < .05$
[b] $p < .01$
[c] $p < .001$

64

added to the analysis by arguing that Southerness may well be "causally prior" to factors like percent nonwhite, median education and income, etc. To illustrate, he reports Southerness to be significantly correlated with percent nonwhite (r = .71), and when Southerness is forced last in the analysis, nonwhite accounts for 66 percent of the total variance (89 percent) accounted for in homicide. For our Murder I data, however, when Southerness is forced last (Table 1a), percent nonwhite is not the variable of first entry, but rather the second to last variable to enter both years accounting for only one percent (1967) and five percent (1968) of additional explained variance.

Second Degree Murder (Murder II). Table 6.3 reports zero order, partial and multiple correlations between Murder II admission rates and selected independent variables. Like Murder I, the largest bivariate correlations are between rate and percent nonwhite and rate and Southerness for both years. Here, however, percent nonwhite is more strongly associated with Murder II than Southerness, permitting approximately 29 percent (1967) and 37 percent (1968) of variance in rate to be accounted for. Southerness, the second variable of entry for 1967, only permits an additional four and one-half percent of explained variance while for 1968 it allows less than one percent of additional explained variance.

Table 6.3 also reveals that the inclusion of the remaining independent variables adds little to the explanation of Murder II, averaging only about one percent each of additional explained variance. For 1968, with the exception of hospital beds per 1,000 population, the remaining independent variables also only contribute slightly.

Following the procedure used with Murder I, percent nonwhite is forced last in the multiple correlation to test its independent effect on Murder II. Results are reported in Table 6.4. Forcing percent nonwhite last in the multiple correlation, Southerness is the first variable of entry for both years, allowing approximately 26 percent (r = .514) and 32 percent (r = .566) of explained variance in rate for 1967 and 1968, respectively. The next six variables to enter the analysis permit an additional eight percent (1967) and 14 percent (1968) of variance to be accounted for in Murder II. The final variable of entry-percent nonwhite-individually contributes most to the multiple correlation adding an increment of over five percent of additional variance each year. The importance of percent nonwhite is further reflected by the significant partial correlations between this factor and Murder II.

To more closely examine the independent effect of Southerness on Murder II, controlling for its presumed indirect effect through education, income, medical services, etc., Southerness is now excluded from the multiple correlation. Results of this analysis (not shown here in table form) yield multiple correlations of R^2 = .408

TABLE 6.3

Relation of State Murder II Admission Rates and Selected Independent Variables, 1967 and 1968

Variables	Simple r	Partial r at Entry	Cumulative Exp. Variance (R^2)
1967			
Percent Nonwhite	.542^c	.542	.294^c
Southerness	.514^c	.254	.339^c
Percent Metropolitan	.006	-.134	.351^c
Hospital Beds/1000	-.235	-.151	.366^b
Mdn. Income	-.190	.159	.382^b
Mdn. Education	-.411^b	-.130	.392^b
Percent 18-44 years	.314^a	.123	.401^c
1968			
Percent Nonwhite	.611^c	.611	.373^c
Hospital Beds/1000	-.336^a	-.345^a	.448^c
Mdn. Education	-.458^c	-.175	.465^c
Mdn. Income	-.141	.158	.478^c
Physicians/1000	-.261^a	-.217	.503^c
Southerness	.566^c	.091	.507^c
Percent Metropolitan	.196	.025	.507^c
Percent 18-44 years	.320	.023	.507^b

^{a}p = < .05
^{b}p = < .01
^{c}p = < .001

TABLE 6.4

Relation of State Murder II Admission Rates and Selected Independent Variables, 1967 and 1968; Percent Nonwhite Forced Last

Variables	Simple r	Partial r at Entry	Cumulative Exp. Variance (R^2)
1967			
Southerness	.514[c]	.514	.264[c]
Mdn. Education	-.411[b]	-.184	.289[b]
Percent 18-44 years	.314[a]	.138	.303[b]
Physicians/1000	-.246	-.103	.310[b]
Mdn. Income	-.190	.136	.323[a]
Percent Metropolitan	.006	-.105	.330[a]
Hospital Beds/1000	-.235	-.151	.346[a]
Percent Nonwhite	.542[c]	.292[a]	.402[a]
1968			
Southerness	.566[c]	.566	.321[c]
Mdn. Education	-.458[c]	-.193	.346[c]
Percent Metropolitan	.196	.250	.387[c]
Physicians/1000	-.261[a]	-.227	.419[c]
Hospital Beds/1000	-.336[a]	-.180	.437[c]
Mdn. Income	-.141	.186	.457[b]
Percent 18-44 years	.320	.059	.459[b]
Percent Nonwhite	.611[c]	.300[b]	.507[b]

[a] $p = < .05$
[b] $p = < .01$
[c] $p = < .001$

and R^2 = .506 for 1967 and 1968, respectively. Comparison of these R^2 values with those reported in Table 6.4 (R^2 = .402, 1967; and R^2 = .507, 1968) shows Southerness to have little to no independent effect on rates of Murder II.

Murder and Nonnegligent Manslaughter (Homicide). Table 6.5 reports zero order, partial and multiple correlations for the offense of homicide. These data show homicide rates to be strongly associated with both percent nonwhite and Southerness, reaching statistical significance at beyond the .001 level. Like Murder II, percent nonwhite proves to be more strongly associated with rate than Southerness which enters second in the multiple correlation both years. Percent nonwhite permits approximately 61 percent and 59 percent of explained variance in rate respectively, with Southerness permitting an increment in variance of 11 percent (1967) and five percent (1968). The remaining seven independent variables only contribute very slightly to an explanation of rates each year.

As with Murder II, percent nonwhite is forced last in the multiple correlation to test its independent effect on homicide. Results are presented in Table 6.6. With percent nonwhite forced last in the analysis, Southerness becomes the first variable of entry allowing approximately 59 percent (r = .765) and 46 percent (r = .678) of variance to be accounted for, respectively, for 1967 and 1968. The next seven variables to enter the multiple correlation only contribute slightly to the cumulative R^2 values, with percent nonwhite—the variable forced last—permitting the largest increment in explained variance each year; 9.1 percent for 1967 and 10.2 percent for 1968.

In sum, Tables 6.5 and 6.6 indicate that Southerness and percent nonwhite account for much common variance in homicide. Like Murder II, however, the overlap in variance accounted for by these two factors is not perfect.

To better examine the independent effect of Southerness on homicide controlling for its presumed indirect effect through education, income, etc., Southerness is next excluded from the multiple correlation. This analysis (not shown here in table form) yields multiple correlations of .720 for 1967 and .671 for 1968. These compare to R^2 values of .761 and .689 for 1967 and 1968, respectively, when Southerness is included in the analysis. In sum, like Murder II, these results indicate that Southerness does not have a substantial independent effect on rates of homicide.

Summary and Conclusion

The investigation reported here is a further examination of homicide and the Southern tradition of violence. Our analysis is

TABLE 6.5

Relation of State Homicide Rates and Selected Independent Variables, 1967 and 1968

Variables	Simple r	Partial r At Entry	Cumulative Exp. Variance (R^2)
1967			
Percent Nonwhite	.784[c]	.784	.614[c]
Southerness	.765[c]	.543[c]	.728[c]
Mdn. Education	-.483[c]	.194	.738[c]
Percent 18-44 years	.483[c]	.121	.742[c]
Physicians/1000	-.263[a]	-.156	.748[c]
Mdn. Income	-.179	.146	.754[c]
Population Density	-.105	-.108	.758[c]
Hospital Beds/1000	-.241	.079	.759[c]
Percent Metropolitan	.197	.081	.761[c]
1968			
Percent Nonwhite	.768[c]	.768	.590[c]
Southerness	.678[c]	.350[a]	.640[c]
Hospital Beds/1000	-.034	.264	.666[c]
Physicians/1000	-.322[a]	-.218	.682[c]
Population Density	-.097	-.098	.685[c]
Mdn. Education	-.605[c]	-.090	.687[c]
Percent 18-44 years	.341[a]	.061	.688[c]
Percent Metropolitan	.005	.046	.689[c]

[a] $p = < .05$
[b] $p = < .01$
[c] $p = < .001$

69

TABLE 6.6

Relation of State Homicide Rates and Selected Independent Variables, 1967 and 1968;
Percent Nonwhite Forced Last

Variables	Simple r	Partial r At Entry	Cumulative Exp. Variance (R^2)
1967			
Southerness	.765[c]	.765	.586[c]
Percent Metropolitan	.197	.248	.611[c]
Hospital Beds/1000	-.241	.178	.623[c]
Physicians/1000	-.263[a]	-.234	.644[c]
Percent 18-44 years	.483[c]	.202	.659[c]
Mdn. Education	-.483[c]	-.092	.661[c]
Mdn. Income	-.179	.117	.666[c]
Population Density	-.105	-.114	.670[c]
Percent Nonwhite	.784[c]	.524[c]	.761[c]
1968			
Southerness	.678[c]	.678	.460[c]
Mdn. Education	-.605[c]	-.353[c]	.527[c]
Hospital Beds/1000	-.034	.261	.560[c]
Percent Metropolitan	.005	.120	.566[c]
Physicians/1000	-.322[a]	-.170	.578[c]
Percent 18-44 years	.341[a]	.123	.585[c]
Population Density	-.097	-.078	.587[c]
Mdn. Income	-.292	.027	.587[c]
Percent Nonwhite	.786[c]	.496[c]	.689[c]

[a] p = < .05
[b] p = < .01
[c] p = < .001

70

similar to that of Gastil's with the exception that we examine the association between Southerness on rates of: (1) first degree murder (2) second degree murder and (3) homicide.

For all three offenses our analysis reveals a somewhat similar pattern. First, for each offense, for both years, the zero order correlations between Southerness and rate and nonwhite and rate are quite substantial and highly significant. Second, of the remaining independent variables examined—income, percent urban population, population density, population 18-44 years, education, physicians per 1,000 population, hospital beds per 1,000 population—only the latter four prove significantly associated with rates for all offenses for both years. The size of the correlations, however, are much less substantial than those for Southerness and percent nonwhite. Third, to examine the independent effect of Southerness and percent nonwhite on rate, controlling for socioeconomic and demographic factors, both variables were forced last in the multiple correlation analysis. Results are summarized in Table 6.7. These figures show that for Murder I, percent nonwhite has little to no independent effect on rate, with Southerness only contributing slightly to this offense for one year (1967). In contrast, for Murder II, Southerness has little to no independent effect on rate with percent nonwhite only having a slight independent effect each year. For homicide, the effect of Southerness is similar to that for Murder I, but the independent effect of percent nonwhite is roughly twice that for Murder II.

As noted above, in attempting to explain the rather small amount of variance accounted for in rate by Southerness, after controlling for socioeconomic and demographic factors, Gastil argues that one could well "imagine that Southern culture caused them all," thus reducing the zero order correlations between Southerness and rate.

TABLE 6.7

Percent of Independent Explained Variance
in Offense Rate Accounted for by Southerness
and Percent Nonwhite, 1967 and 1968

Offense	Year	Southerness	Nonwhite
First Degree⎱	1967	5.2	.004
Murder ⎰	1968	.005	.005
Second Degree⎱	1967	.006	5.6
Murder ⎰	1968	.001	4.8
Homicide (Murder and Non-⎱	1967	4.1	9.1
Negligent Manslaughter) ⎰	1968	1.8	10.2

71

He also notes, however, that in such a case if the residual were small, "a separate regional cultural trait of homicide, and the claim of Southern cultural influence on the rate would be much harder to make convincing" (Gastil, 1971: 419). It thus seems odd that Gastil concludes Southern culture to be a major contributor to homicide for by his own reasoning (with Southerness only accounting for approximately four percent of independent variance in rate) this conclusion would seem ruled out both in his investigation and ours.

Although there is a conspicuous absense of literature on first and second degree murder, and none to this writer's knowledge relating percent nonwhite to these offenses, our findings for nonwhites are essentially consistent with the views of most writers,

There would appear to be a consensus that nonwhites, primarily Negroes, are greatly overrepresented in the homicide statistics. Most are quick to point out, however, that differences in Negro-white rates reflect social class and not racial differences. As reported by the President's Commission, the difference in white and black involvement in crime becomes very small when comparisons are made between rates for whites and Negroes living under similar conditions.

Our findings for percent nonwhite are only partially consistent with this assessment. The data show percent nonwhite to account for very little independent explained variance in Murder I (.004 percent, 1967; .005, 1968) after controlling for education, income, etc. For Murder II, however, a more substantial percent of independent explained variance (5.6 percent and 4.8 percent) can be accounted for by percent nonwhite after controlling for socioeconomic and demographic factors. The increment in explained variance in homicide allowed by percent nonwhite is even more substantial, averaging nearly ten percent each year.

Although these data are far from conclusive, they suggest that the greater Negro involvement in certain forms of homicide cannot be simply accounted for by social class differences, at least not as operationalized here. Clearly, however, additional research is needed to more closely examine the relationship between: (1) race and forms of homicide, controlling for additional socioeconomic factors, and (2) Southerness and forms of homicide examining smaller, more homogeneous geographic units. Research of this sort is currently underway by this writer in the hope that such cumulative investigations will shed a more comprehensive light on the etiology of homicide.

Notes

1. Gastil accounts for this by the high correlation between Southerness and the other independent variables (percent nonwhite,

r = .71; median education, r = .52; hospital beds per 1,000 population, r = .61; physicians per 1,000 population, r = .48, etc.).

2. To illustrate, causes of death ranging from premeditated murder to legal executions are combined into one overall homicide rate by this agency.

3. For Virginia, New Jersey, Oregon, Minnesota and Connecticut statistics were only available for the fiscal years 1967 and 1968. These cases were included in the analysis.

4. For a more detailed discussion of the procedure used to assign Southerness index scores to states, see Gastil (1971: 425-426).

5. Source: Statistical Abstracts of the United States; 1968: 12; 1969: 12, 25, 66, 68, 320; 1970, 27, 69; 1971: 18, 25, 110, 425-26. For both 1967 and 1968 estimates of median education, percent non-white, and population residing in urban areas were derived from interpolating figures for 1960 and 1970.

6. Both r^2 and R^2 will be given explained variance interpretations because: (1) Gastil uses this interpretation and it will better allow us to compare our findings with his, and (2) it would seem the most clear cut interpretation of both zero order and multiple coefficients of determination.

References

Federal Bureau of Investigation
    1970   Crime in the United States: Uniform Crime Reports—1970.
            Washington: U.S. Government Printing Office.

Gastil, R. D.
    1971   "Homicide and a regional culture of violence." American
            Sociological Review 36 (June):412-427.

President's Commission on Law Enforcement and Administration of
            Justice
    1967   The Challenge of Crime in a Free Society. Washington:
            U. S. Government Printing Office.

Sellin, T.
    1954   "Minutes of proceedings of evidence." No. 17 (January 1-2).
            Joint Commission on the Senate and the House of Commons
            on Capital Punishment and Lotteries. Ottawa, 669.

    1967   Capital Punishment. New York: Harper & Row, Publishers.

U.S. Bureau of the Census
  1967   Statistical Abstracts of the United States, 88th Edition.
          Washington, D.C.: U.S. Government Printing Office.

  1968   Statistical Abstracts of the United States, 89th Edition.
          Washington, D.C.: U.S. Government Printing Office.

  1969   Statistical Abstracts of the United States, 90th Edition.
          Washington, D.C.: U.S. Government Printing Office.

  1970   Statistical Abstracts of the United States, 91st Edition.
          Washington, D.C.: U.S. Government Printing Office.

  1971   Statistical Abstracts of the United States, 92nd Edition.
          Washington, D.C.: U.S. Government Printing Office.

U.S. Public Health Service
  1967   Homicide in the United States, 1950-1964. Washington, D.C.:
          U.S. Government Printing Office.

7

AN INVESTIGATION OF THE EFFECT OF PARENTAL AND PEER ASSOCIATIONS ON MARIJUANA USE: AN EMPIRICAL TEST OF DIFFERENTIAL ASSOCIATION THEORY

Marvin D. Krohn

The investigation of adolescent drug use, especially marijuana use, has received much attention from social scientists in the past five years.[1] Most of these efforts have been directed toward collecting and analyzing a variety of data concerning the characteristics of drug users. The two volume study by Blum (1969a, 1969b) is, perhaps, the most ambitious undertaking of this kind. However, to date, there has been little effort in analyzing these data in terms of a theoretical explanation of drug use as a form of deviant behavior. Notable exceptions to this tendency are the works by Howard S. Becker (1963) and Ronald L. Akers (1973). However, Becker does not explain the initial use of marijuana and Akers simply attempts to apply a theoretical explanation to data which has previously been collected.

Previous research has indicated that relationships exist between an adolescent's use of drugs and his interaction with both his parents and peers. The present study will examine the utility of a theoretical model incorporating the adolescent's interaction with parents and peers in the explanation of adolescent marijuana use.

Review of the Literature

Much of the research concerning adolescent drug use has implicitly assumed that drug-taking behavior is learned. As Blum has stated, "It would appear that normal processes such as learning and social interaction must be considered in the development of use patterns" (Blum, 1969a:275). Having made this assumption, the task is to analyze the adolescent drug-taker's learning experience. Studies have, therefore, investigated the two groups which traditionally have been considered to be most influential in the adolescent's socialization process: the family and the peer group.

The research relating the family situation to drug use has consistently been based on the thesis that the adolescent is dissatisfied with his parents and, in rejecting them, turns to drugs. It has been found that there is more disagreement between parents and adolescent drug-users than there is between parents and non-users (Blum, 1969b) and that users report more family conflict and unhappiness in their family life (Blum, 1969b; Brotman et al, 1970; Matchett, 1971; Suchmann, 1968). Nechama Tec (1970), in a comprehensive study assessing the effects of family life on the differential involvement of adolescents with marijuana, reported that the degree of involvement with marijuana is negatively associated with the availability and quality of parental models; the amount of recognition and the level of evaluation received within the family; the perception of the family as being warm; and the subjective feeling of satisfaction and involvement with, as well as the ability to rely upon, the family as a unit.

The second source of social interaction and learning for the adolescent which has been extensively investigated in relation to drug use, is his peer group. It has been found that friends are the major source of the adolescent's drug supply (Blum, 1969b; Cohen, 1970; Pearlman, 1968) and that adolescents are initially "turned on" by friends (Cohen, 1970; Sutter, 1970). The act of turning someone on is of particular significance as a symbolic act expressing friendship:

> To turn someone on means to introduce him to a drug,
> usually marijuana. It is an expression of trust, friend-
> ship and acceptance. Most lower-strata youth were in-
> troduced to drugs in the normal course of living by a
> close friend or relative. After they learned to use drugs
> for pleasure, being turned on and luring others on becomes
> established social practice, similar to the convention of
> buying a friend a drink or offering a drink to a guest when
> he comes to your home. (Sutter, 1970:77)

The adolescent's peer group not only is the major supplier of drugs and instigator of drug use, but also exerts social pressure on the adolescent to use drugs. Studies have indicated that adolescents' initial motivation for using drugs was either social pressure from peers or an attempt to facilitate social interaction (Blum, 1964; Blum, 1969b; Brotman, 1970; Chapel and Taylor, 1970; Cohen, 1969; Steffenhagen et. al., 1969; Sutter, 1970).

Blum (1969b) has suggested that the best method of predicting future use of drugs by adolescents is to examine the behaviors of the adolescent's friends. Specifically, the variables shown to be the best predictors were the adolescent's drug sources, friends' and leaders' actual drug use, and friends' and leaders' willingness to use drugs.

Tec (1972) has also found that association with friends who use marijuana increases the likelihood that an adolescent will use marijuana.

Research on drug use among adolescents has found that the drug user has poor relationships with his family and that he is supplied with and turned on to drugs by his friends or close relatives. Given these two general findings, a theoretical framework consistent with them can be introduced.

Theoretical Framework

The theory of differential association, as developed by Edwin Sutherland and later explicated by Donald Cressey analyzes deviant behavior from a learning perspective, and on that account, provides a theoretical framework for the study of adolescent drug use. The final statement of differential association theory consists of nine basic tenets, which may be briefly summarized. Most importantly, criminal behavior is learned in interaction with others, and to the extent that the quantity and quality of these interactions vary, so will the criminal or deviant behavior vary. A major component of what is learned in these interactions are attitudes, values, or "definitions" regarding lawful as well as unlawful behaviors. In the context of differential association then, a person behaves in a deviant manner because of "an excess of definitions favorable to violations of law over definitions unfavorable." (Sutherland and Cressey, 1970:75).

Much of the research investigating hypotheses derived from Sutherland's theory have been limited to analyzing the extent to which adolescents interact with deviant others (Hardt and Peterson, 1968; Reiss and Rhodes, 1964; Short, 1957; Voss, 1964). The study by James A. Short is illustrative of this type of research. Short developed a scale intended to operationalize Sutherland's seventh proposition which states: "Differential associations may vary in frequency, duration, priority and intensity." (Sutherland and Cressey, 1970:76). He correlated this scale with scores on a self-reported delinquency scale and found a strong relationship between these variables for adolescent boys. (Short, 1957)

Although Short's research apparently supports Sutherland's theory, it must be regarded as incomplete because it has ignored the potential impact of primary associations other than those of a delinquent's or deviant's peers. Specifically, the present study is interested in including the effect of the parent-adolescent relationship,[2] as well as the adolescent-peer interaction, in the explanation of marijuana use.

The crucial element in the parent-adolescent relationship for differential association is the interaction between the two. If the adolescent does not interact with his parents, his opportunity to learn definitions favorable or unfavorable to deviant behavior will be limited If it is assumed that parents typically do not condone the use of drugs, it can be suggested that the adolescent who does not associate with his parents may not learn definitions unfavorable to drug use.

Sutherland and Cressey have considered the issue of poor parent child relationships and conclude that such relationships may promote delinquency only if they result in "increasing the frequency and intimacy of associations with delinquent patterns or the prestige of those patterns or in isolating the individual from the patterns of anti-crimina behavior" (Sutherland and Cressey, 1970:28). This is quite consistent with Hewitt's (1970) notion that if parents do not assist the adolescent in the task of building self-esteem, the adolescent will depend upon his peers for self-esteem. In the company of his peers the adolescent is "likely to become involved in situations in which deviant behavior is precipitated and tolerated." (Hewitt, 1970:47).

It is possible that the parent-adolescent relationship will not only result in the increased association with peers but will also affect the types of peers with whom the adolescent interacts. Stanfield (1966) investigated the relationship between family variables and gang-membership variables, and found that satisfying experiences at home lead to greater acceptance of the family culture which in turn leads to greater selectivity toward peers. Unsatisfactory experiences at home lead to the selection of peer groups who do not support the family culture. In the latter case, the effect of the family relationship will be to enhance the adolescent's chances of establishing a deviant identity.

As a consequence of interactions within two arenas, the family and the peer group, the adolescent can be taught definitions favorable and unfavorable to drug use. The role of the parent-adolescent relationship is conceived of being one which has the potential to both limit the adolescent's opportunity to learn definitions unfavorable to the deviant behavior and to encourage the adolescent to seek more contact with his peer groups. The peer groups, in turn, may teach the adolescent definitions favorable to deviant behavior. Thus, the following temporal sequence is suggested:

Poor family relationships ———→ association with deviant peers ———→ deviant behavior.

Jensen, in a recent study, has analyzed this temporal sequence in relation to delinquent behavior. He found that although there was a relationship between parental supervision and affection and delinquent behavior, and between association with delinquent peers and delinquent behavior, the parental variables were independently related to delinquent behavior. He thus concludes that doubt is cast on the temporal sequence suggested by differential association theory (Jensen 1972).

The purpose of the present study is to examine the relationships between parents, peers and marijuana use, being particularly concerned with examining the temporal sequence suggested by differential association theory. On the basis of the foregoing, several hypotheses can be suggested:

Hypothesis 1: The adolescent who is less willing to associate with his parents will associate more with drug-using friends than the adolescent who is willing to associate with his parents.

Hypothesis 2: The less willing the adolescent is to associate with his parents, the more likely he is to use marijuana.

Hypothesis 3: The greater the association with drug users, the more likely the adolescent is to use marijuana.

Hypothesis 4: Adolescents who use marijuana will have been "turned on" by friends or close relatives rather than by pushers or casual acquaintances.

Hypothesis 5: The temporal sequence of the three variables is: poor family relationships ———→ association with drug users ———→ marijuana use.

The first and second hypotheses presume, of course, that less frequent association with parents will provide more opportunity to associate with potentially drug-using peers, while the third and fourth hypotheses make explicit the logical consequences of "differentially associating" with the two sources (parents and peers) of definitions concerning drug use. The fifth hypothesis examines the temporal sequence suggested by differential association theory.

Methodology

The sample for this study was drawn from a population of in-coming freshmen participating in a summer orientation program which was being conducted by the Counseling Center at the University of Maryland. A total of 525 students were sampled, of which 9 were eliminated due to failure to complete the questionnaire, or due to unusual responses which make the questionnaire highly suspect. The final sample was composed of 236 males and 279 females (one did not respond). There were 35 blacks, 469 whites and 10 who reported being in the "other" category, (2 did not respond), represented in the sample. The survey was conducted in three one-hour sessions.

The data used to test the foregoing hypotheses were generated from responses to two separate scales which were part of a much larger questionnaire. The first scale is an adaptation of Short's (1957) "specific differential association scale," and consists of four items designed to measure the frequency, duration, priority and intensity of association with delinquent peers. Slight changes in wording were necessary to accomodate the present focus upon association with drug users.

The second scale is composed of seven items intended to measur the degree to which adolescents enjoy associating with their parents. This scale represents a portion of the items included in the Bowerman and Kinch Family-Peer Group Orientation Questionnaire (1959). Student responses to the Bowerman and Kinch scale (association with parents) were divided into "High" and "Low" categories, with the former reflecting greater willingness to associate with parents. Similarly, responses to the Short specific differential association scale (association with drug-using peers) were categorized as "High" and "Low."

Data concerning the use of marijuana by the adolescent was acquired by asking the respondent to indicate the level of his marijuan use. The use of the self-report technique required that steps were taken to insure the respondent's anonymity and to assure the respondent of this.

The gamma measure of association, appropriate for an ordinal level of measurement, is used to assess the relationship between the variables. Significance tests based on gamma are employed to test the hypotheses (Weiss, 1968).

Results

The first hypothesis suggested that the adolescent who is least willing to associate with his parents, will be most likely to associate with drug-using peers. Table 7.1 summarizes the relationship betweer the variables included in the model. The data support the hypothesis, in that the gamma measure of association is statistically significant. However, it is evident that the relationship is not very strong. It can therefore be said that there is a tendency for adolescents who are least willing to associate with their parents to associate with drug-using peers.

The result of the investigation of the first hypothesis tentatively supports Sutherland's notion that the effect of parent-adolescent relationships is to increase the probability that adolescents will associate with deviant peers. However, the question of temporal order, whether parent-adolescent relationships do lead to adolescent association with deviant peers, has not, as yet, been answered.

It was also hypothesized that adolescents who are least willing to associate with their parents will be most likely to use marijuana. The gamma measure of association indicates that there is a

TABLE 7.1

Zero-Order Gamma Measures of Association
Between Variables Included in the Model

	Willingness to Associate with Parents	Association with Drug-Users	Experience with Marijuana
Willingness to associate with parents	1.00	-.27* (N = 445)	-.23* (N = 476)
Association with drug-users		1.00	.74* (N = 472
Experience with marijuana			1.00

*p < .05

statistically significant difference in the use of marijuana between those adolescents who are less willing to associate with their parents and those who are more willing to associate with their parents. The relatively weak relationship indicated by the size of the gamma is not surprising. In fact, if, as hypothesized, the willingness to associate with parents variable is an antecedent variable, it would be expected that its relationship with the dependent variable would be relatively weak since, in terms of temporal order, it is removed from the dependent variable.

The results of the first two hypotheses indicate that parent-adolescent interaction is related to both adolescent association with drug users and the likelihood that the adolescent will use marijuana. It is now necessary to investigate the third hypothesis which concerns the relationship between the adolescent's drug-using friends and his use of marijuana. It would be expected that adolescents who associate highly with drug-using friends would be more likely to use marijuana than those who have a low degree of association with drug-users. The results strongly indicate that the hypothesis is tenable.

The question of whether adolescents associate with drug users after having tried drugs or whether the association with drug-users affect their subsequent drug-using behavior, must be addressed in order to support the differential association theory. As was hypothesized it would be expected that a good friend or close relative (assuming that a close relative is considered to be a good friend) would have "turned on" the adolescent to drugs. Table 7.2 reports the percentages of who introduced the respondents to the use of drugs. The results indicate that 65 percent of those who have used marijuana were introduced to drugs by a good friend and that 14 percent were turned on by a close relative. These data suggest that associations with drug users influenced the respondent's behavior regarding drug use rather than the respondent's drug-taking behavior influencing his choice of friends. This result provides evidence refuting the criticism of differential association theory which was based on the contention that it was behavior which led to association rather than associations leading to behavior (Glueck, 1956).

Having reported data which support the hypotheses that there is a relationship between marijuana use and associations with both parents and drug-using peers, it is appropriate that the temporal order among these variables be considered. Based upon Sutherland's logic, it was hypothesized that (poor) association with parents is antecedent to association with drug-using peers, which is then productive of drug use. In this model, drug use may be regarded as the dependent variable, with parental associations and peer associations regarded as the antecedent and independent variables, respectively. Rosenberg (1968) has provided a three step process by which the temporal order of these variables can be addressed statistically.

The first step has already been performed, indicating that all the variables are related to one another (Table 7.1). The second step entails controlling for association with parents and investigating the relationship between associations with drug-using friends and marijuana use. The relationship obtained should not be greatly affected by this procedure.

As the results in Table 7.3 indicate, the relationship between association with drug-users and marijuana use does not differ within the two categories of the antecedent variable. Since the relationship between the independent and dependent variable was not greatly reduced, the results are supportive of the model.

The third step in the process investigates the relationship between the antecedent variable and the dependent variable controlling for the independent variable. It is expected that the relationship found in Table 7.1 will be greatly reduced.

In examining the gammas (Table 7.3), a curious result appears. Whereas the relationship between willingness to associate with parents and marijuana use is significantly reduced within the moderate and low categories of associations with drug-users, the gamma appears to be greater within the high category. However, this is quite misleading for the gamma is not statistically significant. The small N

TABLE 7.2

Percentage of "Who Turned On" Drug Users

Who turned you on	Number	Percent
A good friend	136	65
A relative	29	14
A youthful acquaintance	36	17
An adult acquaintance	8	4
A pusher	0	0
Total	209	100

coupled with the disproportionality of the marginals (Table 7.4) inflate the size of the relationship. If the criterion of statistical significance is employed, it can be said that the relationship between willingness to associate with parents and marijuana use has been reduced.

The results of the above statistical procedures have provided evidence for Sutherland's contention that (poor) parent-adolescent relationships increase the probability of the adolescent interacting with drug-using peers who, in turn, increase the likelihood that the adolescent will use marijuana. Although the statistical requirements to test this model were met, a note of caution should be interjected. It is evident that when the independent variable was controlled the relationship between the antecedent and dependent variables was reduced. However, whether the reduction in the relationship reported within the three categories of the independent variable is sufficient to verify the model, is not known. Therefore, a conservative interpretation of the data would suggest that the hypothesized model can tentatively be entertained; however, more convincing data is needed.

Summary

This study has investigated the application of differential association theory to the explanation of adolescent marijuana use. The findings have indicated that Sutherland's theory is useful in providing a model to partially account for adolescent marijuana use. Specifically, the study focused on two variables: willingness to associate with parents and association with drug users. It was found that both variables are related to adolescents' experience with marijuana.

Of particular theoretical interest were the findings which served to tentatively answer questions which have been raised concerning

TABLE 7.3

Gamma Measures of Association Examining the Causal Order
of the Model by Controlling on the Test Factor

Control variable: willingness to associate with parents	Relationship between experience with marijuana and associations with drug users	
	Gamma	Significance Level
1. Less willing	.74	p < .05
	(N = 259)	
2. Willing	.72	p < .05
	(N - 186)	

Control variable: associations with drug users	Relationship between experience with marijuana and willingness to associate with parents	
	Gamma	Significance Level
1. High	-.30	p > .05
	(N = 40)	
2. Moderate	-.01	p > .05
	(N = 110)	
3. Low	-.15	p > .05
	(N = 295)	

TABLE 7.4

Experience with Marijuana by Willingness to Associate
with Parents for Respondents who Associate Highly with
Drug Users

| | Willingness to Associate | | | |
| | High | | Low | |
Experience with Marijuana	Number	Percent	Number	Percent
Still Using	6	75.0	27	84.4
Tried but Quit	1	12.5	4	12.5
Never Tried	1	12.5	1	3.1
Total	8	100.0	32	100.0

Note: Gamma = -.30, p > .05

differential association theory. Sutherland's theory had been criticized because it was contended that the delinquent boy would seek association with other delinquents after having committed the delinquent behavior. Data were presented which suggests that not only was association with drug users related to marijuana use, but also association with drug users typically preceded the use of marijuana.

Although both the influence of parents and peers had been investigated previously and found to be related to deviant behavior, the temporal relationship between these variables was in question. The logic of Sutherland's theory would suggest that the association with parents was an antecedent variable to the independent variable of association with drug users. The results of statistical procedures utilized to examine the temporal order provided data which supported the model derived from Sutherland's theory. However, this support was not overwhelming and more research is needed to investigate the relationship between parents, peers and deviant behavior.

One question which must be addressed is why did Jensen's (1972) results suggest that the parental variable had an independent effect on delinquent behavior, whereas the present study found data which suggests that the parental variable affects marijuana use in that it increases the probability that the adolescent will associate with drug users? Although Jensen operationalized the parental and peer variables differently than the present study, the most important distinction between the two studies is the dependent variable examined. It is suggested that for the use of marijuana, supply and the learning of the proper technique are more important than similar needs for various types of delinquent behavior. Therefore, the adolescent, regardless of his relationship with his parents, needs to associate with other users in order to obtain marijuana and to learn the proper techniques to use it. Hence, for the marijuana user, the importance of parental relationships is in whether they increase the probability that the adolescent will associate with drug users.

It is hoped that this investigation will elicit theoretical and research efforts to substantiate, refine, or refute the interpretation of adolescent marijuana use presented in this study. Of particular interest would be longitudinal studies to assess the effects of parents and peers on deviant behavior.

Notes

1. I would like to express my appreciation to Peter R. Maida for his advice and assistance. The computer time for this project was provided by the Computer Science Center of the University of Maryland under the support source, HI-RGOA.

2. An aspect of the parent-adolescent relationship which will not be investigated in the present study is the potential effect of parental drug-using behavior on the adolescent's marijuana use. Cressey (1965) states that contradictory definitions in reference to legal codes can be presented by a person at different times and in different situations. Data supporting the hypothesis that a relationship exists between parental use of legal drugs and adolescent use of illegal drugs has been presented by Blum (1969a) and Tec (1970).

References

Akers, R. L.
1973   Deviant Behavior: A Social Learning Approach. Belmont, California: Wadsworth Publishing Company, Inc.

Becker, H. S.
1963   Outsiders. New York: The Free Press.

Blum, R. H. and Associates
1964   Utopiates: The Use and Users of LSD 25. New York: Atherton Press.

1969a   Society and Drugs. San Francisco: Jossey-Bass, Inc.

1969b   Students and Drugs. San Francisco: Jossey-Bass, Inc.

Bowerman, C. E. and J. W. Kinch
1959   "Change in Family and peer orientation of children between the fourth and tenth grades." Social Forces 37 (March): 206-211.

Brotman, R.
1970   "Adolescent substance use: a growing form of dissent." Pp. 66-70 in John H. McGrath and Frank R. Scarpitti (ed.), Youth and Drugs: Perspectives on a Social Problem. Glenview: Scott, Foresman and Co.

Brotman, R. I. Silverman and F. Suffet
1970   "Some social correlates of student drug use." Crime and Delinquency 16 (January):67-74.

Chapel, J. L. and D. W. Taylor
1970   "Drugs for kicks." Crime and Delinquency 16 (January): 1-35.

Cohen, A. Y.
1969   "Inside what's happening: Sociological, psychological, and spiritual perspectives on the contemporary drug scene." American Journal of Public Health 59 (November):2092-2095.

Cohen, H.
1970   "Principal conclusions from the report 'Psychology, Social Psychology and Sociology of Illicit Drug Use.'" British Journal of Addiction 64 (May):39-44.

Cressey, D. R.
1965   "Social psychological foundations for using criminals in the rehabilitation of criminals." Journal of Research in Crime and Delinquency 2 (July):49-59.

Glueck, S.
1956   "Theory and fact in criminology." British Journal of Delinquency 7 (October):92-109.

Hardt, R. H. and S. J. Peterson
1968   "Arrests of self and friends as indicators of delinquency involvement." Journal of Research in Crime and Delinquency 5 (January):44-51.

Hewitt, J. P.
1970   Social Stratification and Deviant Behavior. New York:
        Random House.

Jensen, G. F.
1972   "Parents, peers and delinquent action: A test of the dif-
        ferential association perspective." American Journal of
        Sociology 78 (November):562-575.

Matchett, W. F.
1971   "Who uses drugs? A study in a suburban public high
        school." Journal of School Health 41 (February):90-93.

Pearlman, S.
1968   "Drug use and experience in an urban college population."
        American Journal of Orthopsychiatry 38 (April):503-514.

Reiss, A. and L. A. Rhodes
1964   "An empirical test of differential association theory."
        Journal of Research in Crime and Delinquency 1 (January):
        5-18.

Rosenberg, M.
1968   The Logic of Survey Analysis. New York: Basic Books,
        Inc.

Short, J. F.
1957   "Differential association and delinquency." Social Problems
        4 (January):233-239.

Stabfield, R.
1966   "The interaction of family variables and gang variables
        in the aetiology of delinquency." Social Problems 13
        (Spring):411-417.

Steffenhagen, R. A., C. P. McAree and L. S. Zheatlin
1969   "Social and academic factors associated with drug use on
        the University of Vermont campus." International Journal
        of Social Psychiatry 15 (Spring):92-96.

Suchman, E. A.
1968   "The 'hang loose' ethic and the spirit of drug use." Journal
        of Health and Social Behavior 9 (June):156-164.

Sutherland, E. H. and D. R. Cressey
1970   Criminology. Philadelphia: J. B. Lippincott Co.

Sutter, A. G.
1970   "Worlds of drug use on the street scene." Pp. 74-86 in
        John H. McGrath and Frank R. Scarpitti (ed.), Youth and
        Drugs: Perspectives on a Social Problem. Glenview:
        Scott, Foresman and Co.

Tec, N.
1970   "Family and differential involvement with marihuana: A
        study of suburban teenagers." Journal of Marriage and the
        Family 32 (November):656-663.

1972   "The peer group and marijuana use." Crime and Delinquency
        18 (June):298-309.

Voss, H. L.
1964   "Differential association and delinquent behavior." Social
        Problems 12 (Summer):78-85.

Weiss, R. S.
1968   Statistics in Social Research: An Introduction. New York:
        John Wiley & Sons, Inc.

CHAPTER

8

THE DRUG AND
CRIME ASSOCIATION:
A TEST OF THREE
EXPLANATORY MODELS

Donald B. Wallace,
Seymour J. Rosenthal,
and James E. Young

In this study we assess the explanatory power of three competing explanations of the manner in which illicit drug use and illegal
behavior vary together.[1]

In spite of an extensive literature in which narcotic drug use
is examined, and a voluminous accumulation of sociological thought
and findings on crime and criminality, it is noteworthy that researchers
have only recently become interested in the correlation between drugs
and crime. This fact is an indication that much of the relevant work
has been exploratory in nature, and has proceeded without theoretical
guidelines or an accumulation of documented facts. Admittedly, our
own work is exploratory. We have posed general theoretical questions,
but these must be considered preliminary and tentative at this time,
since the resolution of one set of questions inevitably suggests additional "problem" areas which remain unexplored.

Theoretical Guidelines

We pose three plausible explanations of the drug and crime
association:

Drug Causation. Is there a correlation between narcotic drug
use and crime, whereby drug users are shown to engage in illegal
acts during the time of their drug involvement? Further, can the onset of drug use be shown to increase, or exaggerate, the illegal behavior which preceded drug use? We have designated this set of
questions the "drug causation" hypothesis, whereby a linear cause-
and-effect association between narcotic drug use and crime is postulated.[2]

Crime Continuities. Is there evidence that narcotic drug users
have committed illegal acts prior to drug involvement? This question

90

is derived from the proposition that illegal behavior in evidence during the drug career is plausibly attributable to behavior patterns which are independent of narcotic drug use. In this regard, we draw a conceptual distinction between illegal behavior and illegal drug-seeking activity. Phrased as a hypothesis, can it be shown that drug users' social deviance patterns are continuous throughout the career, regardless of illicit drug involvement?[3]

Social-Structural Background Factors as a Common Cause. Can it be shown that narcotic drug use and crime are related to social "background" factors such that social deviance per se (including illicit drug use and criminal activity) is attributable to variables such as socioeconomic status and ethnicity? Generally, if there is an association between drug use and crime, should such a correlation be attributable to a cluster of other explanatory variables which can be termed the "common cause" of both forms of social deviance?

A review of the sociological literature relating drug use and crime reveals a theoretical tradition incorporating two interrelated concepts: (1) culture (value systems external to individuals), and (2) social structure (patterned relations among roles). In this regard, a pervasive feature of the sociology of crime and drugs is the concept of the lower-class peer group, sometimes seen as a subculture whose values emphasize a preoccupation with "toughness," "maleness," and "excitement".

This theoretical tradition, incorporating elements of culture, and social structure, has generated much of the thought and empirical work concerning the "common cause" effect of social "background" factors on illicit drug use and crime.[4]

Such a theoretical approach implies that the prevalence of social deviance can be attributed to the social context in which it occurs, and provides a convenient method for organizing the analysis which follows. That is, we begin our investigation by examining the effects of social structure (ethnicity, education, sex, and age) on the crimes which our respondents report for the twelve month period prior to their entry into treatment. We then examine the explanatory utility of two additional sets of variables: measures of pre-drug crime and drug use variables. Our research problem then becomes one of testing the importance of each of these three variable sets as they relate to our sample's adult crime activities.[5] Each variable set speaks to one of the theoretical questions under consideration. Thus, the effects of social structure, drugs, and pre-drug crime, as they relate to the variables we wish to explain (crimes which take place during the year prior to our respondents' entry into treatment) can be assessed with respect to their importance as empirical, and theoretical, correlates of our sample's criminal activities.

Method and Measurement

We focus our research on the examination of a 16 variable "multistage-multivariate" path model (Land 1969:24-29) which includes four sets of variables and attributes arranged in a temporally-ordered sequence.

The variables and attributes of the model's four stages are detailed in Table 8.1.

Social-Structural Background Factors. Ethnicity (white-black), sex, education, and age, are the social-structural predetermined ("exogenous") variables in the first stage.

Pre-drug Crime. Illegal activities which our respondents report for the period up to but not including opiate use onset are: burglary, robbery, prostitution, and shoplifting. The frequencies of these activities are coded into rank-ordered categories, but are considered continuous variables for purposes of statistical treatment.

Drug Variables. Measures of drug use, appearing in the model's third stage, are: age of first opiate use; frequency of opiate use at the time of maximum use; the number of drugs used (multiple-drug-pattern) during the year prior to our respondents' entry into the drug treatment programs in which they were interviewed; and, heroin versus non-heroin drugs of choice during the pre-treatment year.

Illegal Activity Subsequent to Opiate Onset. As with the pre-drug stage, we examine the burglary, robbery, prostitution, and shoplifting frequencies which our respondents report for the year prior to entry into treatment.

TABLE 8.1

Multistage-multivariate Path Model*
Relating Social Structure, Delinquency,
Drug Use, and Crime

Social Structure	Delinquency	Drug Use	Crime
Ethnicity	Burglary	Age 1st opiate	Burglary
Sex	Robbery	Max. f opiate	Robbery
Education	Prostitution	Multiple-drug	Prostitution
Age	Shoplifting	Heroin	Shoplifting

*Model generates 96 possible paths (not shown), relating social structure (exogenous variables) to delinquency, subsequent drug use, and crime, in a temporally-ordered sequence.

With the exception of race and sex, all of the information under consideration was collected through self-reports in interviews with respondents.

Results

Statistical Treatment: The Relation Between Research and Theory. The quantified estimates (path coefficients) relating each variable or attribute to each variable subsequent to it in time yielded the result that 14 out of the 96 temporally-ordered paths (see Table 8.1) were "significant" according to the following criterion: a path coefficient is defined as significant if its magnitude exceeds twice its standard error.

A model "trimming" procedure yielded the results reported in Tables 8.2 and 8.3. This technique has generated the model which most closely approximates the empirical, and theoretical, relations among the social, pre-drug crime, drug, and crime variables under consideration.

In this section we examine the 14 empirical relations ("significant" paths) which our model "trimming" procedure indicates are of the greatest utility in explaining the association between drug use and crime, for our respondents. The quantified estimates (path coefficients) of the direct associations of interest are reported in Tables 8.2 and 8.3. We discuss, in sequence, relevant associations within each of the path models' stages.

Social Structure and Social Deviance:
Drug Use and Crime

The Prevalence of Illegal Pre-Drug Behavior. Blacks are over-represented in robbery (a person crime) in the pre-drug stage (Table 8.2). Prior to drug use onset, burglary is a masculine activity (Table 8.2). There are no "significant" associations between age and education, and pre-drug crime (delinquency).

Drug Epidemiology. Our older respondents began using opiates at a relatively late period, in career terms, and seem to be "heavier" opiate users, relative to their younger counterparts, during the time of maximum opiate use.

Whites are over-represented in multiple-drug use during the year prior to entry into treatment, as are our relatively poorly-educated respondents. The sex of the respondent appears to be related to drug use.

93

TABLE 8.2

Significant Paths Relating Social Structure to Delinquency, Drug Use, and Crime

	Social Structure	Ethnicity	Sex	Education	Age
Delinquency*	Burglary	—	—.18 (Male)	—	—
	Robbery	.27 (Black)	—	—	—
	Prosti-tution	—	—	—	—
	Shop-lifting	—	—	—	—
Drug Use	Age 1st opiate	—	—	—	.61
	Max.f opiate	—	—	—	.24
	Multiple-drug	.45 (White)	—	.18	—
	Heroin	—	—	—	—
Crime†	Burglary	—	—	.18	—
	Robbery	—	—	—	—
	Prosti-tution	—	.33 (Female)	—	—
	Shop-lifting	—	.16 (Female)	—	.09

*Designated crime self-reported to have occurred prior to drug use onset.

†Designated crime self-reported to have occurred during 12 months prior to entry into drug treatment.

It is noteworthy that no social factors are related to heroin use (during the pretreatment year). We interpret this result as an artifact of the manner in which we asked our respondents to indicate their drug of choice: preferences were indicated for the year prior to entry into treatment rather than for the best characterization of the drug use career.

The Prevalence of Adult Crime. Relatively low educational attainment is associated with burglary during the year prior to entry into treatment.

TABLE 8.3

Significant Paths Relating
Delinquency to Adult Crime

	Delinquency	Burglary	Robbery	Prostitution	Shoplifting
Adult crime {	Burglary	.17	—	—	—
	Robbery	—	.30	—	—
	Prostitution	—	—	.20	—
	Shoplifting	—	—	—	—

*Designated crime self-reported to have occurred prior to drug use onset.
†Designated crime self-reported to have occurred during 12 months prior to entry into drug treatment.

No social-structural variable or attribute is significantly associated with robbery during the pretreatment year. Unlike the pre-drug stage, in which prostitution was not shown to be directly linked to a particular sex category, its occurence in the pretreatment year is a female activity (Table 8.2).

Shoplifting activities tend to be female crimes (Table 8.2) during the year prior to entry into treatment. Further, our older female respondents are associated with this type of property crime.

Pre-Drug Crime and Drug Use. There are no significant relations between the pre-drug crime variables and measures of drug use. In fact, none of our hypotheses call for such associations because the social-structural "common cause" theory implies that observed relations among drug and crime activities are "spurious" with respect to underlying social factors.

Pre-Drug Illegal Behavior in Relation
to Adult Crime: A Test of the
"Crime Continuities" model

Table 8.3 reveals a dramatic association between pre-drug illegal behavior and similar crime activity following drug onset. Three of the four adult crimes under consideration are directly linked to counterpart behaviors in the pre-drug stage. Property crime (burglary, p = .17), robbery (p = .30), and "victimless" crime (prostitution, p = .20) are "continuous" with respect to our respondents' illegal behavior careers, independent of drug use. This finding provides a compelling argument in favor of the crime "continuities" model of the drug and crime association.

Illicit Drug Use and Adult Crime:
A Test of the "Drug Causation" Model

Only heroin is significantly and directly related to property crime (burglary, p = .32). No other drug variable displays such an association, nor does heroin relate to any other crime.

Discussion

These findings provide a measure of support for each of the hypothesized explanations. However, the degree of confirmation varies. From this point forward, our inquiry takes a new form. The issue now is not whether illicit opiate use is related to property crime; we have seen that it is. In combination with heroin, what else is associated with heroin users' behavior patterns?

Our results show that six of eight non-drug factors are directly implicated in at least one of the crimes reported for the year prior to our respondents' entry into treatment. This result contrasts to the single drug effect (heroin), which now becomes one element in a larger framework in which social structure, culture, and delinquent (pre-drug illegal) behavior overshadow heroin use as the explanation of crime which takes place during the drug career.

Property Crime (Burglary). Three antecedent variables directly relate to burglary: education (p = -.18), pre-drug burglary (p = .17), and heroin (p = .32). Given these results, it is apparent that non-drug factors are as important in the understanding of our respondents' burglary crimes as is the fact of heroin use. Low educational attainment (a social-structural variable)[6] and a pre-drug history of prior burglary, which is in turn linked, theoretically (via the concept of the "lower class peer group"), and empirically (Table 1), to masculine behavior, are factors with which a linear "drugs-cause-crime" theory can be supplemented.

Robbery. A theoretical interpretation of our respondents' robbery activity of necessity must place the fact or frequency of opiate use, as it relates to robbery, in a social-structural perspective. The important relation with robbery is the fact of a pre-drug history of this type of person crime, (p = .32, Table 8.2). In addition, we have seen that blacks are over-represented in robbery which occurs prior to opiate use onset, implicating a social-structural factor, ethnicity, independent of opiate use. Since the ethnicity factor is independent of educational attainment, which is not significantly related to robbery, we are left with the interpretation that the serious person crime committed by our sample during the period of drug use is more highly related to the prevalence of this type of illegal activity as it occurs within minority groups, than to the fact of opiate use, which emerges as a relatively more useful component in a theory of property crime, but not robbery.

Prostitution (victimless crime) and Shoplifting. Our results do not indicate that prostitution and shoplifting, both relatively less serious than burglary and robbery, are directly implicated with heroin use. Therefore, the issue again becomes one of incorporating the explanation of these activities into a series of propositions in which heroin use is but one element. For our sample, prostitution and shoplifting tend to be female activities. Additionally, pre-drug prostitution is related to its counterpart behavior following drug use onset. Age is related to shoplifting, suggesting that our older female respondents, with a history of this type of activity, engage in shoplifting independent of drug-taking behavior.

Social-structural "Common Cause" as an Explanation of Illicit Drug Use and Illegal Behavior. Our evidence argues in favor of a comprehensive model which includes propositions relating the prevalence and incidence of social deviance to its social-structural location and cultural context. Our line of reasoning is straightforward: social "background" factors make a difference in rates of drug-taking and crime.

On balance, we conclude that illicit drug use and illegal drug-seeking can, and should, be isolated for empirical, theoretical, and policy science reasons. But, we would caution the medical practitioner and the policy-maker that the differential prevalence of deviant behavior, within identifiable social categories, requires understanding of the social context in which it occurs.

Notes

1. Research reported herein was supported by the Governor's Justice Commission, Commonwealth of Pennsylvania, Grant #DS-248-72A. We are indebted to Mr. Ross Koppel, Center for Social Policy and Community Development consultant; Prof. Thomas Keil, Gettysburg College; Mr. Yoav Santo and Ms. Susan Katzanelson, University of Pennsylvania; the staff of the Center for Social Policy and Community Development, Temple University; and the data reduction staff of the Institute for Survey Research, Temple University, for their assistance in the preparation of this report.

2. Early theory and findings tended to suggest that "addicts" were turned into "criminals" in order to support their "habits." We see this suggestion in Schur's (1966) concept of "enforced criminality." Refer also to Lindesmith (1947), Atlas (1961), Ball and Snarr (1969), Robins et al. (1970), Dupont (1973), and Brown and Silverman (1973).

3. For findings and discussion questioning the utility of a "causal" drug and crime theory, from a "crime continuities" frame of reference, see Markham (1973), Vaillant (1973), Lukoff (1973), Kolb (1962), Rosenberg Foundation (1967), Rogers (1970), DeFleur, Ball, and Snarr (1969), Stanton (1969), and Johnson (1970). Refer to Schrag (1971) for a comprehensive review of sociological theories of crime.

4. See Wilner et al. (1957), Roebuck (1967), Stephens and Levine (1971), Ausubel (1958), Klein and Phillips (1968), D. Glaser et al. (1968), Ball, Chambers and Ball (1967), Bean (1967), and Kavaler, Krug, Amsel, and Robbins (1968). The "anomie" tradition (Cohen, 1955; Miller, 1958; Cloward and Ohlin, 1960), has had an unmistakable impact on recent theories of crime and drug use. See Feldman (1968) and Johnston (1973).

5. The sample (N=216) was drawn from drug treatment programs in and around Philadelphia and interviewed during the Spring of 1973. A detailed discussion of sampling and related methodology appears in Rosenthal et al. (1973, Appendix I) from which the findings reported herein are derived. The validity and reliability of self-reported social deviance is a major methodological concern. With respect to non-drug illegal behavior, Schrag (1971: 116-117) lists 22 references of relevance to the self-report method in delinquency and crime research. One review of the literature (Hardt and Bodine 1965) concludes that there is relatively little knowledge of the "frankness" or "truthfulness" in self-report delinquency studies. However, a review of self-reported drug use findings (Whitehead and Smart 1972) concludes that there is reason to have confidence in self-reported drug use information. For an expanded discussion of these issues, see Rosenthal et al. (1973, Appendix II). We have concluded (based on empirical work) that our results are highly reliable. Further, we have no evidence that our findings are systematically biased.

6. It is conceivable that our relatively poorly-educated respondents' education was terminated by involvement in delinquency or drug activities. Recall, however, that, for our sample, education is not directly linked to pre-drug crime, nor is pre-drug crime directly related to drug behavior.

References

Atlas, G.
1961   "The clinical approach." Key Issues 1:34-36.

Ausubel, D.
1952   "An evaluation of recent adolescent drug addiction." Mental
        Hygiene 36 (July):373-382.

Ball, J. and W. Snarr.
1969   A test of the maturation hypothesis with respect to opiate
        addiction. Bulletin on Narcotics 21:9-13.

Ball, J., C. Chambers and M. Ball.
1968   "The association of marijuana smoking with opiate addiction."
        Journal of Criminal Law and Criminology 59 (June):171-
        182.

Bean, P.
1971   "Social aspects of drug abuse: a study of London offenders."
        Journal of Criminal Law and Criminology 62 (March):
        80-86.

Brown, G. and L. Silverman.
1973   The Retail Price of Heroin: Estimation and Applications.
        Drug Abuse Council, Inc. MS-4 (May).

Cloward, R. A. and L. E. Ohlin.
1960   Delinquency and Opportunity. Glencoe, Ill.: The Free
        Press.

Cohen, A. K.
1955   Delinquent Boys. New York: The Free Press.

DeFleur, L., J. Ball and R. Snarr.
1969   "Long-term social correlates of opiate addiction." Social
        Problems 17 (Fall) 225-234.

Dupont, R.
1971   "Profile of a heroin-addiction epidemic." New England
        Journal of Medicine 35:320-324.

Feldman, H.
1968   "Ideological support to becoming and remaining a heroin
        addict." Journal of Health and Social Behavior 9 (June):
        131-139.

Glaser, D. et al.
1969   "Later heroin use by marijuana-using, heroin-using and non-drug using adolescents in New York City." NACC Reprints 3:1-11.

Hardt, R. and G. Bodine.
1965   Development of Self-report Instruments in Delinquency Research. Syracuse University.

Johnston, L.
1973   Drugs and American Youth. Ann Arbor, Mich.: Institute for Social Research, University of Michigan.

Kavaler, F., D. Krug, Z. Amsel and R. Robbins.
1968   "A commentary and annotated bibliography on the relationship between narcotics addiction and criminality." New York Municipal Reference Library Notes 42:45-63.

Klein, J. and D. Phillips.
1968   "From hard to soft drugs: temporal and substantive change; in drug usage among gangs in a working-class community." Journal of Health and Social Behavior 9 (June):139-145.

Kolb, L.
1962   Drug Addiction: A Medical Problem. Springfield, Ill.: Chas. C. Thomas.

Lindesmith, A. R.
1947   Opiate Addiction. Evanston, Ill.: Principia Press.

Lukoff, I.
1973   Heroin Use and Crime in a Methadone Maintenance Treatment Program: a Two-Year Followup of the Addiction Research and Treatment Corporation Program. Washington D. C.: Law Enforcement Assistance Agency.

Markham, J.
1973   "Heroin hunger may not a mugger make." The New York Times Magazine (March 18):39-42.

Miller, W. B.
1958   "Lower class culture as a generating milieu of gang delinquency. Journal of Social Issues 14 (August):5-19.

Robins, L. et al.
1970   "Long-term outcome for adolescent drug users: a followup
        study of 76 users and 146 non-users." Pp. 159-178 in
        J. Zubin and A. Freedman (eds.) The Psychopathology of
        Adolescence. New York: Grune and Stratton, Inc.

Roebuck, J.
1962   "The Negro drug addict as an offender type." Journal of
        Criminal Law and Criminology 53 (March):36-43.

Rogers, A.
1970   "Narcotic addiction among young people." Federal Pro-
        bation 34 (June):34-41.

Rosenberg Foundation and the California Youth Authority.
1967   A Follow-up Study of the Juvenile Drug Offender. Institute
        for the Study of Crime and Delinquency: Rosenberg Foun-
        dation.

Rosenthal, S. J., J. E. Young, D. B. Wallace, R. Koppel, and G. B.
Gaddis.
1973   A Report on Illicit Drug Use and its Relation to Crime: A
        Statistical Analysis of Self-reported Drug Use and Illegal
        Behavior. Report to the Commonwealth of Pennsylvania's
        Governor's Justice Commission prepared by the Center
        for Social Policy and Community Development, School of
        Social Administration, Temple University, Philadelphia,
        Pennsylvania.

Shrag. C.
1971   Crime and Justice American Style. Publication No 1 HSM -
        72 - 9052. Washington, D. C.: National Institute of Mental
        Health.

Schur, E. M.
1966   Narcotic Addiction in Britain and America. London:
        Associated Book Publishers.

Stanton, J.
1969   Lawbreaking and Drug Dependence. State of New York
        Parole Division.

Stephens, R. and S. Levine.
1971   "The street-addict role: implications for treatment."
        Psychiatry 34 (November):351-357.

Vaillant, E. G.
  1973   "A twenty year followup of New York narcotic addicts."
          AMA Archives of General Psychiatry 29:237-241.

Whitehead, P. C. and R. G. Smart.
  1972   "Validity and reliability of self-reported drug use."
          Canadian Journal of Criminology and Corrections 14
          (January):83-89.

Wilner, D. et al.
  1957   "Heroin use and street gangs." Journal of Criminal Law
          and Criminology 48 (September-October):399-409.

CRIMINOLOGICAL ASPECTS OF
INTERNATIONAL TERRORISM:
THE DYNAMICS OF THE
PALESTINIAN MOVEMENT
Gideon Fishman

Despite profound fear and genuine resentment against all forms
of violence—individual, group, national and international—there is a
new and interesting phenomenon of political violence which has cap-
tured the imagination and the sympathy of many otherwise nonviolent
persons.

From skijacking to kidnapping, from extortion to the planting
of mines, from the blowing up of planes to the massacre of scores
of uninvolved or innocent persons, the world has watched in utter
fascination the unfolding of one violent drama after another.

This paper addresses itself to one specific aspect of this worldwide phenomenon of political violence: Arab terrorism since the
1967 war. Our concern is with terrorism as a criminological rather
than a political issue.

Criminologists, particularly those who have attempted to investigate the phenomenon of violence, have been hard pressed to understand and integrate in their theories such recent mass forms of violence
as the black ghetto and student upheavals in the last ten years. Less
yet have they been able to understand the activities of the urban,
ethnic and national terror groups. The activities of these groups,
involving mass violence, cannot be adequately conceptualized in
traditional criminological terms. Individual violence has been accounted for by a wide variety of explanations. Some theories discuss
violence as psychopathological (Alexander and Healy, 1935; Aichhorn,
1936; Redl and Wineman, 1951) or the offender as a psychotic or
sociopathic (Cleckley, 1950); other resort to subcultural conceptions
(Wolfgang and Ferracuti, 1967).

Little, if any, insight can be gained by those explanatory attempts
to understand the problem of international terrorism. The question
is whether there is any set of coherent hypotheses or any conceptual
framework that can incorporate the more conventional form of vio-
lences as well as this new type of international violence and terror.

One plausible hypothesis that seems to relate to various forms of violence, including international terrorism, is rooted in the rather simplistic notion of frustration-aggression. This hypothesis suggests that aggression—in the form of overt violence and other manifestations—is the direct result of frustration. Frustration itself is perceived as the effect produced by any interference with the attainment of goals, aspirations, or expectations.

One variant of the frustration-aggression hypothesis is the concept of systemic frustration (Feierabend, et. al., 1969). The latter refers to frustration that is experienced simultaneously and collectively within societies. It is our contention that international terrorism as experienced by the Palestinian liberation movement can be understood in the context of the frustration experienced by the Palestinians as a result of their inability to attain their goals by more traditional means. This frustration is multiphasic since the social system of the Palestinians is also under other stresses occasioned by the rapid and intensive social changes now taking place. In addition, there are the external pressures induced by the host Arab countries. This systemic frustration induces continuous unrest and tension within the Palestinian camp—as is indicated by the variety of rival terror groups and organizations.

While a theoretical statement can thus be offered for Palestinian terrorism, completely lacking is any organizing framework for examining these emergent and seemingly effective forms of mass violence committed in the name of political goals.

Arab terrorism since the 1967 war offers an ideal-typical model of a guerrilla-terrorist movement which self consciously defines violence as an acceptable mean to legitimate goals. While revolutionary movements self consciously employing violence for political ends are hardly unusual, recent Arab terrorism represents a new departure in the following respects: current guerilla-terrorists are not bound by locale; third parties, as often as not, are the victims; outside nationals are often used as the perpetrators of the violent events; the modus operandi consists of achieving maximum public visibility and of creating an atmosphere of perpetual and escalating terror. The latter is reinforced by the presentation of the perpetrators as "true believers" to the point that their actions are deliberately made to appear irrational and incomprehensible to outsiders in order to heighten the fear.

Arab group violence since 1967, particularly that perpetrated by the PLO, the Black Septemberists, and various splinter groups within the general Palestinian liberation movement, not only fulfills all the criteria of typical political terrorism, but contains certain other ideal-typical elements. For example, these terror groups have succeeded in enlisting world sympathy, almost to the point where the role of perpetrators and victims are reversed. Heros at home, these groups are able to inculcate in their members self images as freedom fighters and not as violent men and premeditated killers. It is one thing for individuals to neutralize (Sykes and Matza, 1957) their violent acts, and quite another for public opinion to sustain and even to glorify such activity. In the case of the Arab terrorist movement, the dream of many criminologists of reducing stigma has succeeded to the point that the perpetrator is honored and his act legitimized by many. Lastly, the Arab governments reaction to these groups is in itself worthy of serious study. Thus, despite approval by the public at home and sympathizers abroad, these groups have not had the support of many of the governments in the name of whose people they often speak.

This paper will proceed to examine the Palestinian terrorist-guerrilla movement in its historical context as well as in its present manifestations. Hopefully, the sources for the unique support this type of violence enjoys will be more apparent once the "anatomy" of the movement is sketched.

The Development of Arab Terrorism

Recent terrorist activities committed by Arab guerrilla groups such as Black September are another development in the evolutionary chain of terrorist activities beginning in the second decade of this century. What has changed, though, since 1967 are the short range objectives of the violence, the modus operandi of the guerrillas, the locale of the terror, the victims involved, and the number of other parties dragged into the conflict.

Arab terrorism existed for many years in the form of loosely organized gangs operating against Jewish settlers in Palestine. The purpose of these actions, in addition to maintaining ethnic tensions, was to eventually gain control over all of Palestine. The terror activities were conducted within the geographic limits of what was then Palestine, and was directed only against those perceived by the Arabs as the direct enemy. Most of the gang members were local people who were supported morally and financially by their Arab brothers in the neighboring Arab countries. Such terrorist activities continued long after the establishment of the state of Israel in 1948. However, the military bases, the planning, training, exit, and return points of the terrorists shifted across the ceasefire lines into Arab territory. The major targets became military installations as well as civilian settlements located near the borders. The motives for the raids were a mixture of hatred and revenge nurtured in the refugee camps and encouraged by the various Arab governments.

In spite of scattered successes, most of the terrorist activities were
contained by the Israeli army, and these efforts failed to create any
significant change in the geo-political situation. As a matter of fact,
the terrorists failed to gain much recognition and support outside
the Middle East. These attacks and other acts of violence were usually
perceived as an outgrowth of the border disputes between Israel and
its neighbors. This terrorism was, to a significant extent, limited
only to the parties directly involved.

It was only after June 1967, or even a year later, that the Arab
terrorists achieved international reknown, and attracted the attention
of millions all over the world. This sudden fame occurred largely
because the locale of operations changed. Although local terrorists
activities still continue in the pattern of the early decades of this
century, the conflict can no longer be perceived as a border dispute
between Israeli soldiers and Arab saboteurs. The loosely organized
gangs have been transformed into a terrorist-guerrilla movement
composed mostly of Arabs of Palestinian descent, operating mainly
in European cities. With this dramatic shift of locale, there was
inevitably a change in the victimized population, the methods of
operation, and the rationalization of the terror activities.

The intensive activity of international terrorism by Arab groups
which began in 1968 and has continued to the present, has had its
fluctuations depending on the internal situation in the liberation movement, the cooperation extended by Arab countries, and the intensity
of the counter-measures applied.

To systematically analyze the present terrorist approach it
is necessary to classify and type guerrilla activities since 1967. In
order to develop such a classification scheme it was necessary to get
a rather comprehensive picture of these terrorists activities longi-
tudinally. Titles in the New York Times Index were examined, and
all the major events listed under the term Middle East conflict, that
appeared to be relevant to our topic, were recorded. The information
was then tabulated along the following dimensions: The incident,
the location of the act, the victims (persons and property), and the
reasons or objectives given for the action by the commandos.[1]

Types of Violence

The new terrorism specifically documented in our table involves
a variety of violent forms of action of unprecedented scale. This
paper attempts to classify 30 major incidents. This taxonomy which
focuses on the offender, victim, location, and assuming responsibility
for the violent act, can later be expanded to include the nature of the
violent act as well.

TABLE 9.1

Types of Violence by Offender, Victim, Location, and
Assumption of Responsibility for the Act

| | Types of Violence | | |
	I	II	III
Offender	Arabs	Non-Arabs	Arabs
Victim	Israelis	Israelis	Israelis
Location	Israel	Israel	Out of Israel
Responsibility	Assumed	Assumed	Assumed
	IV	V	VI
Offender	Arabs	Non-Arabs	Arabs
Victim	Non-Israelis	Israelis	Non-Israelis
Location	Out of Israel	Out of Israel	Out of Israel
Responsibility	Assumed	Assumed	Denied

Type I Consists of acts committed by Arabs against Israelis[2] on Israeli soil. This type includes instances such as the planting of explosives in the Jewish market in Jerusalem (Nov. 23, 1968) in which 11 Israelis were killed. These acts represent the residual and older forms of terrorism that have been perpetrated virtually from the start of the conflict.

Type II refers to acts committed by non-Arabs against Israelis on Israeli soil. This type includes cases such as Lod Airport massacre (May 30, 1972) where three Japanese killed 25 and injured 72 in a shooting attack.

Type III refers to acts committed by Arabs against Israelis on non-Israeli soil. It includes cases such as the bombing of the residence of the Israeli ambassador to Cyprus (April 9, 1973), or the murder of the Israeli air attache in Washington, D. C. (June 30, 1973). This activity represents the international terrorism variant of the conflict and is by far the most spectacular and visible. It is also the most widely shown on T.V. Type III is probably now, as of this writing, the modal and most persistent form of Arab terrorism.

Type IV refers to acts committed by Arabs against non-Israelis on non-Israeli soil. The cases included in this category are represented by numerous hijackings of international airliners, or the killing of two American and one Belgian diplomats in Khartum (March 2, 1973). This variant also has created world alarm, concern, and horror. In consequence, it has elicited strong police reaction around the world.

Type V refers to non-Arabs committing acts of terrorism against Israelis on non-Israeli soil. This type refers to cases such as the assassination of the Israeli consul in Istanbul, Turkey (May 22, 1971).

Type VI refers to acts of terrorism against non-Israelis on non-Israeli soil from which the terrorist organizations try to disassociate themselves. This type includes cases like the hijacking and bombing the Japanese airliner in Dubi (July 20, 1973), or the shooting attack of Athens Airport (August 5, 1973). There is something unique in these cases since it is the first time that Arab terrorists are standing trial for hijacking in an Arab country—Libia—that has openly supported the various terror groups. Even more surprising is the attempt made by the various terrorist groups to deny any connection to the act, and not showing any protest for the treatment of the terrorists as common criminals. Although it is too early to say conclusively, it may be an indication of a new trend adopted by the Palestine liberation organizations. If this is actually the case, one hypothesis may suggest that institutionalization and routinization are taking place in the Palestinian camp, and as a result less extreme activities are persued. However one must be cautious in drawing this conclusion based only on these two most recent cases.

This classification scheme is based upon the actual occurrences of violent acts and is in part simply a logical taxonomy based on possible combinations of variables.

The Offender

Over the years recruitment and membership in the terror organizations has been subject to change and modification. When the Fatah movement emerged in the middle of 1960's and even earlier, as with the Fedayeen, when sabotage activities were carried out as unorganized, highly individualized operations (mostly supported by Egyptian intelligence), the recruits were drawn from the Palestinians who had lost their homes and properties in Israel, and were living in misery in refugee camps. However, despite the hate and vengenance nurtured in the camps, it was very difficult to get volunteers for sabotage missions across the border. Those who were finally recruited were most often criminals whose punishment ended with their participation in their terrorist activities in Israel. In addition, they received some monetary reward for participation. However, a totally different population has been attracted into the Palestine Liberation Movement since 1967. More highly educated persons joined the movement (Ph.D.'s, M.D.'s, lawyers, journalists, writers and poets).

These intellectually elite persons, it should be noted, have become the planners and ideologues of the movement rather than its foot soldiers.

The reason for this new pattern of recruitment and expansion of membership is rooted in the disenchantment of the Palestinians with their dream that the Arab countries would solve their problems by defeating Israel. Another contributing factor was increasing national awareness, combined with political ideology—ideology that is alien, to a large extent, to the traditional Arab society. The national awareness grew concurrently with the decrease in the belief in the power of Arab military might to bring about a solution to the Palestinian problem. There is no doubt that this national awareness, fueled by the Egyptian, Jordanian and Syrian defeat, presented the Palestinians with an incentive to rely on themselves alone to redress their grievances.

Another contribution to this national self consciousness resulting in terrorism was the socialist-communist ideology. Among the various factions in the Palestine Liberation Movement one can find varieties of socialist ideologies from the most moderate to the most radical and extreme. This ideological input was very significant since it enabled the members to perceive themselves not only as national liberationists and freedom fighters, but also as soldiers and pioneers in the "international revolution." Given this international socialist ideology the Palestinians involved in the guerrilla movement, view their Arab hosts as targets for revolution and confrontation. Hence the caution, suspicion and rejection that is manifested by most of the Arab leadership of the host countries to the guerrillas on their soil.

There are also indications that the Palestinians in the Liberation Movement are more socially advanced than the rest of the Arab society. One interesting manifestation of this is the status of women as partners in the movement, and occasionally even as heroic symbols (such as in the case of Lila Khaled, the hijacker). Female participation in some terrorist missions adds a critical element to the understanding of the terror itself. We hypothesize that the participation of women on the team generates non-normative behavior—even for terrorists. This occurs because Arabs have traditionally avoided sexually mixed company. For generations women were perceived as inferior and treated as objects to be desired and owned like property. The sudden change, the instant partnership, represents a total disruption of the Arab male pattern of intersexual relations, and thus, in part an anomic situation. This anomie, defined herein as a departure from previous expectations for conduct, even in terrorism, is manifested in the bizarre behavior involved in the hijacking of a Sabena airliner by a mixed team of terrorists. The incident occurred on May 6, 1972. The plane was directed to land at its initial destination, Lod Airport in Israel. Holding all the passengers hostage, the guerrillas demanded the release of some 300 Arab terrorists held in Israeli prisons. This demand was made despite the well established policy of the Israelis not to accede to extortion attempts.

In addition to the enlistment of women as participators, the movement has also sought to recruit non-Arabs who, for various reasons, want to cooperate with the Palestinians, by smuggling explosives, supplying information, and even by murder. Some of these sympathizers join the Palestinians for ideological reasons and identify with the cause. Others do it for romantic reasons, and are not even always aware of the consequences of their activities. Some non-Palestinians may not even be aware of the fact that they are involved in illegal acts. The latter, in fact, was the case of two British girls who were given a record player by two Arab male acquaintances to deliver to Israel, not knowing that the record player was loaded with explosives and designed to detonate while the jet, carrying the two girls, was airborne.

As international police agencies became more concerned with preventing acts of terror, the Palestinian organizations began to experience an increasing need for cooperation from non-Arabs who are sympathizers and sometimes even innocent perpetrators.

Neutralization of the Violent Act

The commission of a criminal or deviant act requires some justification, rationalization, and self-accounting. This process of justification is subsumed under the term neutralization (Sykes and Matza, 1957). The Palestinian commandos are not exceptional in their need to neutralize their acts. Regardless of dedication to one's cause, goal, or ideology, there is the continuing need for self-reassurance and justification. Neutralization eliminates the negative connotation that the violent act usually produces.

Of the five most common techniques of neutralization suggested by Sykes and Matza, four seem to be utilized by the Arab commandos (one can identify the neutralization statements from the official reasons, demands or explanations of the acts by PLO spokesmen). These are:

1. Denial of the Victim. Attacks on Israel's jetliners are explained by the Palestinians as attacks, not on innocent civil aircraft, but as attacks on "military installations." Thus perceived, the aircraft and its passengers and crew become legitimate targets for attack.

110

2. Denial of Responsibility. The Palestinians tend to rationalize their generally violent operations by holding the Israelis responsible for frustrating their national aspirations. Thus, bereft of other alternatives for redressing their grievances, terrorism and the resort to violence are justified as acts of desperation.

Another line of rejecting responsibility for their acts is found in the case of the Munich massacre during the Olympic games. In that case, the Palestinians argued that they were not after the lives of the Israeli athletes, and were forced to kill only after the W. German police failed to live up to their promises of safe conduct and attacked them.

3. Condemnation of the Condemner. Some terrorist actions have been justified as retaliation for the allegedly brutal and inhumane treatment of Arabs in the occupied territories. To charges of brutality in their operations, Palestinians often refer to the way that the Israelis act in retaliation, thereby reducing their own perceived blame.

4. Appeal to Higher Loyalties. Violent acts like bombing and murder are justified by several supreme values to which the Palestinians claim fidelity. These include nationalism and revolutionary Marxism, brotherhood, and justice. In the name of these values, as well as loyalty to their fellow conspirators they embrace violence as an appropriate means to fulfill these loyalties.

The fifth type of neutralization, denial of the injury itself, clearly is inapplicable in this case. Quite the contrary! Various groups have at times credited themselves with actions, usually accidental, in which they absolutely had no part.

Ideological indoctrination makes this neutralization quite effective. However, there are also other elements that prevent stigmatization. While neutralization is important in maintaining self composure, and positive self-perceptions in the commandos, the latter are also much influenced by "significant others." We hypothesize that had the Palestinians commandos been universally labeled as criminals, they would have been unable to maintain their heroic self-identities and willingness to act as guerrillas.

The reality however is different. The terrorists gain support from their colleagues in the organization, from governments who support the Palestinian cause (although not necessarily enthusiastic about the means used), and from a variety of left wing groups in Europe and elsewhere. This support reinforces their claim as foot soldiers in a righteous cause.

Another element that conditions this muted world reaction is the status of the Palestinians as underdogs. Although their violent acts are not approved by many, the fact that the Palestinians are the major losers in the Middle East conflict generates considerable sympathy.

In every national state violence, in whatever form it may take, is considered intolerable and is repressed in every possible way. The entire criminal justice apparatus, and a formidable one it usually is, is enlisted to end the violence, to arrest, prosecute and punish the perpetrators and to deter any and all others with similar appetites for such expressive conduct. Perpetrators are duly labeled, stigmatized and removed from society. To do all this, the public has created the conditions for effective labeling. It has designed criminal justice agencies, endowed them with legitimacy and empowered them to exercise power and to act in the name of ultimate social values. Further, even the perpetrators of violent events, individual or collective, are likely to accept the legitimacy of the social control agencies and agents. Hence, when a label is applied by these agencies, the stigma "takes."

All of this is lacking in international attempts to control terrorism. There is no universal labeling agency to sanction violators and impose penalties across national and cultural borders. Nor can any international agency transcend political and national ideologies in generating social and personal isolation, degradation, condemnation and stigmatization of terrorists and guerrillas. In other words, and in Garfinkel's phrase (1956), all of the conditions for successful degradation ceremonies (and consequently for imposing a negative self concept) are lacking. In the absence of such countervailing pressure, and in the presence of social, psychological and material support from large numbers of "significant others", the major types of terrorism described above are likely to continue in the near future.

How then is it possible to contain this terrorism especially on foreign soil with victims wholly innocent of any partisanship or partiality to Israel? In the absence of international agencies comparable to national criminal justice systems, Arab terrorism has evoked a mechanical law enforcement response including heavier policing and better intelligence at least in European cities. Unprecedented searches, seizures, spying, surveillance and related activities indicate that most European nations are determined to eliminate terrorist activities on their soil. Effective as such measures may be, no methods yet exist for discouraging violence among sympathizers of the terrorist cause such as the Japanese nationals who perpetrated the Lod Airport Massacre. Until the public rejects international violence to the same degree that is rejects internal violence, the repudiation of terrorism cannot be translated into legal and moral statutes conferring stigma rather than a label as hero.

112

Notes

1. Original data is available from author.
2. Acts against Israelis are defined as any act directed against any identifiable Israeli target such as an airplane, even if as a result of the violent act these are also non-Israeli victims or potential victims.

References

Aichhorn, A.
   1936   Wayward Youth. New York: Viking.

Alexander, F., and W. Healy.
   1955   Roots of Crime. New York: Knof.

Cleckley, H.
   1950   The Mask of Sanity. St. Louis: C. V. Mosley.

Feierabend, I. K., B. L. Feierabend, and B. A. Nesvold
   1969   "social change and political violence: cross-national
           patterns" Vol. 2, Pp. 497-542 in Violence in America:
           Historical and Comparative Perspectives. Washington:
           U.S. Government Printing Office.

Garfinkel, H.
   1956   "Conditions of Successful Degredation Ceremonies." Ameri-
           can Journal of Sociology 61 (March):420-424.

Redl, F., and D. Wineman.
   1951   Children Who Hate. New York: Free Press.

Sykes, G. M., and D. Matza.
   1957   "Techniques of Neutralization: A Theory of Delinquency."
           American Sociological Review 22 (December):664-670.

Wolfgang, M. E., and F. Ferracutti.
   1967   The Subculture of Violence: Toward an Integrated Theory
           in Criminology. London: Tavistock.

10

FIREARMS AND INTERPERSONAL RELATIONSHIPS IN HOMICIDE: SOME CROSS-NATIONAL COMPARISONS

J. Homero E. Yearwood

Any comparative study of criminal homicide must be attempted with great trepidation; for as Bohannan (1960) has observed, homicide is a cultural trait, which, like any other cultural trait, must be studied within its social and cultural setting. The present effort represents an attempt to examine a number of similarities and differences in the use of firearms and interpersonal relationships among victims and offenders as reported in selected studies. The Brazilian data presented in this analysis include all known homicides that occurred in Belo Horizonte between January 1, 1961 and December 31, 1965. (For detailed information of this research, see Yearwood 1972.)

Method and Weapon of Offense

One of the more interesting controversies in homicide literature centers on the effect the availability of weapons has on the incidence of homicide. Many seem to suggest that most murderers are not concerned with the nuances of technique. As Morris (1955:156) writes:

> Murders are chiefly viscereogenic or 'gut-type' responses of the uncontrolled id. Of my 2700 cases, only thirty-seven were clearly planned or intended to gain economic, political, or other considered ends such as relief from suffering (as in so-called mercy killings) or even a planned vengeance. The large number of cases of stabbing, beating with and without weapons, strangling and pushing is associated with quarrels in which the killer simply makes use of a bottle, a poker, a tire iron, or whatever happens to be handy and who resorts to feet and fists if there is nothing more serviceable at his disposal.

Earlier, Harlan (1950) had written: "Murder is . . . brutal, direct, and simple: a slash or stab with a knife, a shot from pistol or shotgun; a crushing blow from a billiard cue or rock." Wolfgang, on the other hand, recognizes the importance of the availability of weapons but rejects the hypothesis of a causal relationship between the homicide rate and proportionate use of firearms in killings. He writes:

> It is probably safe to contend that many homicides occur only because there is sufficient motivation or provocation, and that the type of method used to kill is merely an accident of availability; that a gun is used because it is in the offender's possession at the time of the incident, but that if it were not present, he would use a knife to stab, or fists to beat his victim to death. (Wolfgang, 1966a: 79)

He (1966a: 83) later suggests that "probably only in those cases where a felon kills a police officer or vice versa would homicide be avoided in the absence of a firearm."

Generally, studies in the United States have found firearms to be the commonest weapon used by most assailants.[1] Studies by Harlan (1950), Bensing and Schroder (1960), Gillin (1934a), Hepburn and Voss (1970), and Brearly (1932), all found firearms to be the most widely used weapon. Wolfgang's finding in Philadelphia is contrary to the general trend.[2] In that city, "39 percent of all 588 criminal homicides were due to stabbings, 33 percent to shootings, 22 percent to beatings, and 6 percent to other and miscellaneous methods." (Wolfgang, 1966a: 320) With regard to any overall correlation between the availability of firearms and murder, it is Wolfgang's (1966: 83) contention that "few homicides due to shootings could be avoided merely if firearms were not immediately present, and that the offender would select some other weapons to achieve the same destructive goal."

We agree with Wolfgang's (1966: 83) position that

> to measure quantitatively the effect of the presence of firearms on the homicide rate would require knowing the number of types of homicides that would not have occurred had not the offender, or in some cases the victim, possessed a gun. Research would require determination of the number of shootings that would have been stabbings, beatings, or some other method of inflicting death had no gun been available.

However, it should be clarified that the availability of a gun or other weapon capable of removing the physical inferiority of some women and some older offenders is likely to make a significant difference in the incidence of homicides as committed by such groups. An important factor not generally considered is that guns are in fact more lethal than knives. And, that whereas the individual may be assaulted "with intent to kill," his survival often depends on the weapon used in the assault. Schrag uses the findings of a recent Chicago study to demonstrate the superior killing power of guns over knives. He summarizes: "While knife attacks outnumbered shootings by nearly 3 to 1, they resulted in only half as many fatalities. Although a greater proportion of knife wounds involved vital organs, the ratio of deaths per 100 attacks was five times as great for guns as for knives." (Schrag 1969: 1245) In this view, the absence of a gun would not lessen the frequency of assaults, but it might tend to reduce the number of attacks that result in homicides. Certainly, unplanned attacks (in which guns are unavailable) would be less likely to result in homicides. In support of this view, one could cite as additional evidence the numerous studies that have found murderers to be first offenders;[3] the implication being that law-abiding persons not physically capable of murder without a lethal weapon might "cool off."

Violent killings in Mexico ranked fourth as a cause of death. And, according to Bustamante and Bravo (1957), the majority of those were committed by shooting. The most frequently used method of killing in England (Gibson and Klein, 1961: 41) was an attack either with a blunt instrument or by hitting or kicking. Shooting was the least common method of killing. The overall pattern in the Belo Horizonte study was 50.9 percent shootings, 21.8 percent stabbings and 24.9 percent beatings.

Interpersonal Relationships

Most researchers agree that the extent to which victims and offenders are known to each other distinguishes homicide from other crimes. Contrary to what propagandists say, the offender seldom goes in search of a victim. As Morris (1955: 16) puts it: "The victim is generally at hand, is, in fact, often the immediate stimulus to the aggression that ends in murder."

Wolfgang (1966a:203) has suggested that "criminal homicide is probably the most personalized crime in our society." As this chapter will verify, homicide is as much a crime among intimates in our society as it is in others.

A number of studies go a step further and classify the victim/ offender relationship according to the proximity of residence. Mac-Donald (1968: 13), among others, found that

116

Although distance between them ranged from less than one block to eight miles, the average was less than one mile. In fact, more than 70% of the assailants and their victims lived less than two miles apart. The fact that 32.8% of them lived at the same address or within the same block makes us know how extremely the distribution on the basis of distance is skewed in favor of spatial proximity.

In Philadelphia, Wolfgang (1966a: 206) found that only 12 percent of all homicides were committed by strangers, whereas 65 percent were committed by relatives or close friends of the offender. Further refining his data he discovered the following relationships:

Relatively close friends (28 percent) and family associations or relatives (25 percent) are the two relationships with highest frequency, and account for over half the 550 known associations. Acquaintances (14 percent), strangers (12 percent), and paramours (10 percent) account for a third of all relationships. (Wolfgang 1966a: 206)

Researchers in Baltimore (Maryland, Criminal Justice Commission, 1967:60) found that strangers accounted for only 21.7 percent of all homicides in that city.[4] In Houston, Bullock (1955) discovered that in 87 percent of the cases the victims and offenders had previously associated on a basis of personal intimacy. Similar results were obtained by a number of other researchers (Hepburn and Voss, 1970; Frankel, 1939; Hogan, 1969). For the United States in general, Schrag (1969: 1249) found that

In nearly one-third of the murders reported in 1967, for example, the offender and the victim were of the same family. Romantic triangles and lovers' quarrels account for another 9 percent, and other arguments presumably involving persons who were at least casually acquainted, 42 percent.

Victim Offender Relationships in Other Societies

As alluded to earlier, in other regions of the world murder remains a crime among intimates. In Denmark, Svalastoga (1956) found that in nine cases out of every ten, murderers chose their victims within a circle of relatives or friends. However, Danes differ significantly from North Americans and Belo Horizontinos[5] in that six out of every ten Danes selected their victims from among members of their own family. Only one in ten selected a stranger. In a later study of Denmark, Siciliano (1966: 45) found that

> 59% of homicides were family tragedies, that is, killing of spouse or children, and that 44% of all victims were under twelve years of age (practically all of these children being murdered by their own parents), and that 85% of those who killed their children subsequently committed suicide. . . . The commonest type of homicide in Denmark was a woman in the 25-40 age group, with one or two children under twelve, who gasses them and herself out of despair or depression.

In England, murder was very much a domestic affair, but there were differences in the patterns of relationships with victims. In Gibson and Klein's analysis of all homicides in the six-year period from 1955-60, it was found that

> female victims outnumber males in the ratio of 6 to 4 . . . over 40% of adult women were killed by their husbands, and most of the remainder by relatives or associates. Adult male victims were less likely to be killed by relatives and were seldom killed by their wives. About half of them were killed by strangers. (Gibson and Klein, 1961: 41)

In India, Driver (1961: 157) found that

> In general, irrespective of the sex of the criminal, victims are seldom strangers but rather kinsmen or close associates, i.e., neighbors, friends, sweethearts, or co-workers. Of the total victims, 70 were kinsmen, 61 were close associates, and only 13 were strangers. Of the strangers, 10 were killed while attempting to thwart the commission of a crime and they constitute over one-half the persons thus killed.

An important difference among Indian murderers appears to be their patience in actually attempting to secure other avenues to resolve disputes. The act of murder was, for them, a culmination of growing enmity between the offenders and the victims. Thus, Driver (1961: 157) concludes: "When the customary devices employed to resolve disputes fail, enmity increases and finally culminates in homicide."

The Belo Horizonte data on the victim/offender relationship is, in many ways, remarkably similar to that of studies conducted in the

United States. It was found that homicides occurred among relatives and friends in 78 percent of the cases. These relationships are distributed as follows: friends 53.3 percent (155); strangers 21.6 percent (63); spouses 13.4 percent (39) (wives killed by husbands, 8.2 percent (24), husbands killed by wives 5.2 percent (15)); family or in-law relationship 9.3 percent (27).

These classifications require some explanation. As indicated in Table 10.1 the category "stranger" or, as listed in police and court files, desconocido (unknown) is slightly higher than found in most studies conducted in the United States. However, the number of desconocidos in this study in inflated by a number of unusual circumstances. For example, two strangers who intervened in a domestic quarrel were killed. At least another three were killed by a hired gunman.[6] Six desconocidos were killed by offenders who were defending a third party, nine more desconocidos were killed by insane individuals. Thus, almost one-third of the 63 offenders listed as strangers in this study are somewhat unusually classified.[7]

The category "family"[8] includes in-laws generally living in the same house. Since we were unable to secure data that would enable us to properly distinguish degrees of friendship, the category "friend" does not differentiate between a somewhat casual relationship and a close friendship. This category does indicate that the individuals were known to each other on amicable terms.

In Belo Horizonte there were 43 female victims. Of these, 37 were slain by men. Significantly, 24 of the 37 were slain by their husbands; of these, 18 (wives) were killed after a domestic quarrel. Thus, as has been observed in other studies, in Belo Horizonte a higher proportion of primary group relationships were involved when females were the victims than when men were the victims.

Of the 26 female offenders, 20 killed men; 15 of the men slain were their husbands, 13 of the 15 were killed after a domestic quarrel. Clearly, in Belo Horizonte men generally killed other men, but when they killed women, they killed their wives. On the other hand, when women committed homicide they killed men, usually their husbands. When the husband/wife relationship is examined by color (Table 10.2), it was found that of the 24 wives killed, 6 were slain by blacks, 11 by browns, and 7 by whites. Of the 11 husbands slain, 1 was killed by a black woman, 6 by brown women, and 7 by white women. There are otherwise no significant differences when color and the relationship to the victim is considered.

119

TABLE 10.1

Motive in Criminal Homicide by Relationship to the Victim
(Criminal Homicide, Belo Horizonte 1961-65)

			Relationship to Victim			
Motive	Spouse	Friend	Family/ In-law	Stranger	D.K.*	Total
Domestic quarrel						
number	31	17	12	2	—	62
percent	50.0	27.4	19.4	3.2	—	
Altercation/Trivial						
number	3	79	3	27	4	116
percent	2.6	68.1	2.6	23.3	3.4	
Altercation/Money						
number	—	22	—	3	—	25
percent	—	88.0	—	12.0	—	
Vengeance						
number	—	18	6	—	1	25
percent	—	72.0	24.0	—	4.0	
Exer. legal duty						
number	—	2	—	3	—	5
percent	—	40.0	—	60.0	—	
Felony						
number	1	1	—	9	—	11
percent	9.1	9.1	—	81.8	—	
Defense of 3rd person						
number	—	10	2	6	—	18
percent	—	55.6	11.1	33.3	—	
Accidental						
number	3	3	1	3	—	10
percent	30.0	30.0	10.0	30.0	—	
Denied complicity						
number	1	2	1	1	2	7
percent	14.3	28.6	14.3	14.3	28.6	
Insanity						
number	—	1	2	9	—	12
percent	—	8.3	16.7	75.9	—	
Total						
number	39	155	27	63	7	291
percent	13.4	53.3	9.3	21.6	2.4	100

*D.K. = Don't Know

TABLE 10.2

Color of Offender by Relation to Victim
(Criminal Homicide, Belo Horizonte, 1961-65)

Color		Spouse	Friend	Blood Relative In Law	Stranger	D. K.*	Total
Black							
	number	7	27	3	9	2	48
	percent	14.6	56.2	6.3	18.7	4.2	
Brown							
	number	17	80	13	27	4	141
	percent	12.1	56.7	9.2	19.1	2.8	
White							
	number	14	42	11	18	1	86
	percent	16.3	48.8	12.8	20.9	1.2	
D.K.*							
	number	1	6	—	9	—	16
	percent	6.3	37.5	—	56.2	—	
Total							
	number	39	155	27	63	7	291
	percent	13.4	53.3	9.3	21.6	2.4	100

*D.K. = Don't Know

Conclusion

Unfortunately, the question concerning the importance of the availability of firearms on the incidence of homicide remains unsolved. For, with the exception of Wolfgang's carefully documented Philadelphia study, wherever easily available, firearms were the weapon of choice. On the other hand, wherever firearms are not easily accessible particularly in England, their use is infrequent. Therefore, we take the position that Philadelphia during the 1948-52 quinquenium remains an exception, although we agree with Marvin Wolfgang's basic position that a causal relationship has not been demonstrated in any of the other studies. Otherwise, we have observed that there are probably a greater number of similarities than differences in the nature of human conduct that ultimately result in one human being taking the life of another.

One of the important considerations emerging from this type of crossnational comparison is the clearer picture of the need for a deeper look into the situations out of which homicides occur, rather than continuing the previous emphasis of research on the murderer, differences in age, race, spacial and temporal patterns, and so forth. Although the areas of similarities and differences presented in this study are not intended to be exhaustive, it is felt they do represent areas that deserve serious consideration. It is possible, for example, to suggest that in the cities considered in this study, there are distinct social conditions and cultural expectations that serve to induce certain individuals to respond by selecting the alternative of taking the life of an adversary.

Criminal homicide was observed to be a crime that takes place principally among primary social relationships. It follows, therefore, that it takes place most frequently among members of the same social class and background. For the United States, this homogeniety between victims and offenders includes race, social class, and sex. In Brazil it includes social class, and sex, but not color (race). In India it involves homogeniety of religion, caste, and sex. In England, it includes social class, but not sex.

In all the countries considered it was found that heterosexual relationships, whether within or outside marriage, are a definite source of friction and potential for violence. Homicide was also found to occur more frequently in the loosely structured areas of society and among its lowest ranks.

Among the most striking differences found in England and Denmark was that homicide was overwhelmingly a domestic affair that was followed by remorse and suicide. In the United States and Brazil the incidence of murder followed by suicide was quite low. On the other hand, in Belo Horizonte, the compulsion to murder in defense of home and honor was frequently followed with a feeling of elation for having done an "honorable deed." Homicide in India was more closely associated with rationality than in any other country.

What we may learn from these similarities and differences ultimately depends on our willingness to attempt the structural alterations necessary to create changes in the patterns of human behavior and social conditions that lead to homicide. Clearly, each culture and each society wittingly or unwittingly creates homicidogenic conditions that definitely lie outside the scope of legal control, but within the possibility of being reduced through the alteration of certain social values.

Notes

1. In 1965 a gun was used to inflict death in 57 percent of the homicides in the United States, while a knife was utilized in 23 percent of the cases, and 16 percent of the victims were beaten to death (see Hepburn and Voss 1970).

2. For the United States there appear to be racial and cultural preferences in the choice of method and weapon used in killings. Most U.S. studies indicate that blacks show a preference for stabbings; however, it should be noted that at least in the mid 1920s this was not the case. Brearley (1932) found that black victims were slain with firearms in 72.7 percent of the cases, while whites were slain with firearms in only 68.3 percent of the cases. It is likely that for Belo Horizonte one would need to add middle class persons as a group of offenders for whom the availability of an offensive weapon would make a significant difference; for in Brazil, physical aggression is viewed with disdain (more so than in the U.S.) and considered a sign of lower-class status.

3. In Belo Horizonte (see Yearwood 1972), 75 percent of the murderers were first offenders.

4. It is interesting to note that the percentage of strangers in Baltimore is identical to that in Belo Horizonte.

5. A resident of Belo Horizonte.

6. It is suggested that the employers of these gunmen knew their victims and that such killings were, therefore, not without selectivity.

7. For a more complete explanation of these differences, see Yearwood (1972). We reiterate that throughout this study the attempt has been made to retain Brazilian classifications and descriptions. We made the choice to "explain" the data rather than make arbitrary changes.

8. For the sake of accuracy, in some instances these relationships have been analyzed separately.

References

Bensing, Robert C., and O. Schroeder, Jr.
1960   Homicide in an Urban Community. Springfield, Illinois:
Charles C. Thomas.

Berg, I. August, and V. Fox.
1947   "Factors in homicides committed by 200 males." Journal
of Social Psychology 26 (August):109-119.

Bohannan, Paul (ed.)
1960   African Homicide and Suicide. New Jersey: Princeton
University Press.

Brearley, H.C.
1932   Homicide in the United States. Chapel Hill:University of
North Carolina Press.

Bullock, H. Allen.
1955   "Urban homicide in theory and fact." Journal of Criminal
Law, Criminology and Police Science 45 (January-February):
565-575.

Bustamante, M. E., and M. A. Bravo.
1957   "Epidemiologia del homicidio en Mexico." Higiene 9:21-
33.

Christiansen, J. (ed.)
1954   Scandinavian Studies in Criminology. Vol. 1. London:
Tavistock Publications.

Cuaron, A. Q.
1962   La Pena de Muerte en Mexico, Mexico, D.F.: Ediciones
Botas.

Delgado, M. D.
1956   De la Autoria Intelectual en el Delito de Homicidio. Bogota:
Pontificia Universidad Catolica Javeriana.

De Porte, J. V., and E. Parkhurt.
1935   "Homicide in New York State. A statistical study of the
victims and criminals in thirty-seven counties in 1921-30."
Human Biology 7 (February):47-73.

Driver, E. D.
    1961   "Interaction and criminal homicide in India." Social Forces
             40 (December):153-158.

Gibson, E., and S. Klein.
    1961   Murder. Reading Berkshire: Charles Elsbury and Sons,

Gillin, S.L.
    1943a "Winconsin murder." Social Forces 12 (May):550-556.

    1935b "Social backgrounds of sex offenders and murderers."
             Social Forces 14 (December):232-239.

Guitierrez-Anzola, and E. Jorge.
    1962   Violencia y Justicia. Bogota: Ediciones Tercer Mundo.

Harlan, H.
    1950   "Five hundred homicides." Journal of Criminal Law and
             Criminology 40 (March-April):737-752.

Hepburn, John, and H. L. Voss.
    1970   "Patterns of criminal homicide, a comparison of Chicago
             and Philadelphia." Criminology (May).

Hogan, H. W.
    1969   "Homicide patterns in New Orleans." Human Mosaic 4
             (Fall):69-77.

Hungria, N.
    1958   Comentarios Ao Codigo Penal. Vol. 5. Rio de Janeiro:
             Forense.

MacDonald, J. C.
    1968a Homicidal Threats. Springfield, Illinois: Thomas Publishers.

    1961b The Murderer and His Victim, Springfield, Illinois: Thomas.

Maryland Criminal Justice Commission.
    1967   Criminal Homicides in Baltimore, Maryland. Baltimore.

McClintock, F.H.
    1963   Crimes Against the Person. Manchester: Norbury Lock-
             wood and Company, Ltd.

Moran, R.
1971   "Criminal homicide: external restraint and subculture of violence." Criminology 8 (February):357-374.

Morris, A.
1955   Homicide: An Approach to the Problem of Crime. Boston: Boston University Press.

Mulvihill, D. J., and M. M. Tumin.
1969   Crimes of Violence. Vols. 11-13. Washington, D.C.: U.S. Government Printing Office. A staff report submitted to the National Commission on the Causes and Prevention of Violence.

Pena-Guzman, G.
1969   El Delito De Homicidio Emocional. Buenos Aires: Abeledo Perrot.

Schrag, C. C.
1969   "Critical analysis of sociological theory." P. 1245 in Donald J. Mulvihill and Melvin Tumin (eds.), Crimes of Violence. Washington, D.C.: U.S. Government Printing Office.

Siciliano, S.
1966   "Resultati preliminari di un 'indagine-sull 'omicido in dinimarca." P. 45 quoted in D.J. West, Murder Followed by Suicide. Massachusetts: Harvard University Press.

Straus, J. H., and A. Murray.
1953   "Suicide, homicide and social structure in Ceylon." American Journal of Sociology 58, 4 (January):461-469.

Svalastoga, K.
1956   "Homicide and social contact in Denmark." American Journal of Sociology 62 (July):37-41.

Verkko, V.
1951   Homicides and Suicides in Finland and Their Dependence on National Character. Copenhagen: G. E. C. Gads Forlag.

Von Hentig, H.
1948   The Criminal and His Victim. New Haven: Yale University Press.

Voss, H. L., and J. R. Hepburn.
  1968   "Patterns in criminal homicide in Chicago." The Journal
          of Criminal Law, Criminology and Police Science 59:499-508.

West, D.J.
  1966   Murder Followed by Suicide. Massachusetts: Harvard
          University Press.

Wolfgang, M. E.
  1966a   Patterns in Criminal Homicide. New York: Wiley.

  1967b   Studies in Homicide. New York: Harper and Row.

Wolfgang, M. E., and Ferracuti.
  1967   The subculture of Violence. London: Tavistock Publications.

Wood, A. L.
  1961   "A sociostructural analyses of murder, suicide and economic
          crime in Ceylon." American Sociological Review 26 (Octo-
          ber):744-753.

Yearwood, H.
  1972   "Court adjuducation of criminal homicide in Belo Horizonte,
          Minas Gerais, Brazil." Unpublished doctoral dissertation,
          University of California, Berkeley.

11

LEGAL STIGMA
AND HOMOSEXUAL
CAREER DEVIANCE

Ronald A. Farrell
and Clay W. Hardin

In recent years the labeling approach to deviance has begun to compile a substantial body of literature. While this perspective is current among many students of deviance, it is noteworthy that there is a paucity of empirical research bearing on its major assumptions. One of the few systematic studies carried out in this area was done by Williams and Weinberg (1971). In Homosexuals and the Military, they sought to clarify many of the assumptions of the labeling perspective by studying the objective and subjective effects of "less than honorable discharge" for homosexuals who had been in military service. Their sample consisted of 64 homosexuals, equal numbers of which had been dishonorably and honorably discharged, the latter being randomly selected from a larger sample. The results of their analyses indicated that there were only minimal differences between the two groups on both the objective and subjective dimensions. Thus their findings give very little support to labeling theory.

In concluding Williams and Weinberg suggest that work in this area must take into account the nature of the label. The label "less than honorable discharge" may have been limited in its consequences due to its low level of publicity and the fact that such information is not circulated to other agencies of social control. As such, it may have been a weak label to employ in a study of formal public labeling. In addressing ourselves to this issue, we attempted to partially replicate their study by utilizing arrest for homosexual behavior as the formal label. It was felt that such labeling would operate as a stigma that is widespread in its consequences, publicly available, and that is circulated to other agencies of social control. Thus the basic

---

We wish to acknowledge the very helpful comments and suggestions of Martin S. Weinberg.

assumption was that, relative to unlabeled homosexuals, those who had been arrested would be more likely to hold self attitudes and engage in behavior that are indicative of career deviance.

Labeling Theory

The labeling approach to deviance draws heavily from symbolic interactionism as exemplified in the writings of Cooley (1902), Mead (1934), and Thomas (1923). The emphasis is on the effects of the interaction process on the formation of the self and subsequent behavior. The basic theme is that the individual defines himself based on his interpretation of others' definitions of him and then acts in accordance with these definitions.

The first direct application of these processes to deviance was offered by Tannenbaum (1938). In his work on crime and delinquency, he explained that as delinquent acts produce increased conflict between the individual and his community, there is a gradual shift from the definition of these specific acts as evil to a definition of the individual as evil, so that all his acts come to be looked upon with suspicion. The person's recognition of this ascription leads to the development of a criminal self definition, isolation from the larger community, and to an identification and integration with a group that shares his activities.

Developing these ideas into a systematic explanation of deviance, Lemert (1951) likewise maintains that if deviant acts are severely sanctioned, they may be incorporated as part of the Me of the individual and the integration of existing roles may be disrupted and reorganization based on a deviant role may occur. He refers to these latter roles as "secondary deviation" and suggests that they develop as means of adjustment to the problems created by the societal reaction to the original or specific (primary) deviation. According to Cohen (1955), these adjustments often involve breaking relations with the larger society and developing an intense social involvement with others who share the same stigma and who have collectively established a normative system within which they are capable of conformity and the attainment of a more positive status.

Developing similar points of view, Garfinkel (1956) and Erikson (1962) add that the community's action toward the deviant is like a sharp rite of transition, at once removing him from his normal position and into the deviant role. Garfinkel suggests that more formalized reactions in particular are likely to have this effect. Discussing these "status degradation ceremonies," he states that "the denunciation effects the recasting of the objective character of the preceived other: The other person becomes in the eyes of his condemners literally a different and new person" (Garfinkel, 1956: 421). An important part of this process, according to Kitsuse (1962) and Schur (1971), is for persons to retrospectively interpret other aspects of the individual's behavior in terms of his deviance, thus invalidating his prior identity and giving increased meaning to the deviation. Becker (1963) suggests that this status often remains his master status, since in the future he will be identified deviant before other identifications are made. He and Goffman (1963) point out that the deviation also may have a generalized symbolic value, so that people may assume that the individual possesses undesirable traits thought to be associated with it. According to Scheff (1966) and Scott (1969), these stereotypic definitions and reactions cause those who are labeled eventually to organize their identity and behavior around the stereotype of their deviance.

While a number of theorists have focused on the effects of organizational responses in the development of career deviance, Lemert (1967) has suggested that stigmatization involves more than just formal action of the community; we must also consider what happens afterwards. He points out that while formal action may dramatize deviance, it may be limited in its consequences for the individual. This point has been substantiated by Williams and Weinber in the case of less than honorable discharge for homosexuals and is the major issue to be explored in this work in the case of arrest for the same group.

Propositions

Williams and Weinberg viewed the consequences of formal labeling as having two dimensions: the subjective and the objective. The latter deals mainly with the behavioral characteristics of the individual, while the former is related to the way in which the individual interprets himself and his situation in light of a new status. Their study dealt with a large number of propositions related to these dimensions. Due to the limitations of our data, however, we were unable to test all of these propositions. Furthermore, only the first of those which we tested deals with the subjective consequences of labeling. The focus of our work, therefore, is on the behavioral aspects of career deviance. The propositions which were tested are summarized as follows. Relative to unlabeled homosexuals, those who are officially labeled will be more likely:

1. to have a stereotypic self definition;
2. to be frequent, overt, and exclusive in their homosexuality;
3. to be involved in the homosexual "way of life" or subculture;
4. to be influenced by homosexual friends;

5. to be known as a homosexual;
6. to have lost a job due to their homosexuality;
7. to be a member of a homophile organization;
8. to be less religious; and
9. to have sought professional help for their homosexuality.[1]

As was indicated by Williams and Weinberg, these propositions do not comprise a test of labeling theory, but rather focus on major assumptions contained in this still unorganized perspective. In re-testing some of their assumptions by employing legal processing as a form of official labeling, this research will hopefully contribute to a further clarification of the approach.

The Sample

The propositions were tested by using data from a matched sample of 32 homosexuals. These cases were drawn from a larger sample of 148 male homosexuals taken in and around a large mid-western city. The data were obtained as part of a broader social psychological study and by the use of a questionnaire distributed through four homosexual bars and social clubs, two different organizations for homosexuals, and through individual contact with persons from various social class backgrounds (Farrell, 1972). From this sample, 16 persons indicated that they had been arrested for homosexual behavior. Rather than comparing these persons with the remainder of the sample, 16 respondents who had never been formally labeled in any way were matched with them case by case on the basis of factors that have been shown to be related to type of homosexual adaptation; thus allowing for a more controlled analysis of the effects of the formal label. The variables on which the sample was matched are age, social class, and level of initial homosexual activity. For observations of the relation of these variables to homosexual adaptation, see Simon and Gagnon (1969) Farrell and Morrione (1974), Leznoff and Westley (1955), Williams and Weinberg (1971), and Farrell (1972).

In the absence of probability sampling, nothing can be said of the representativeness of the sample. A comparison with the urban male population, however, showed them to be younger, disproportionately white, more educated, and consisting of more persons from the higher level occupations.

Methodology

The composite scales to tap various concepts were first developed from information obtained from the existing literature and from a period of field study. The items were then revised after pretesting the questionnaire. Following the return of the questionnaires, each scale's items were tested for their internal consistency and those with low reliability levels were omitted.[2] Scale scores were then computed for each person based on his combined response to a given scale's items. For each of these scales, the median has been established as the cutting point between the high and low scores.

The method of testing the propositions was to determine the extent of differences between the formally labeled homosexuals and the control group on the various indicators of career deviance. All the computations were done by using four cell ordinal-ordinal tables and gamma was used as a measure of association (Mueller, 1970).

Findings

Table 11.1 shows the relationship between formal labeling and the various indicators of homosexual career deviance. For the purpos of simplicity in listing the proposed related variables, only the numbers and percentages for the predicted direction of each relationship are presented; one "residual" row has been omitted in each case. Of the eleven variables considered in this table, Williams and Weinber found only "knownaboutness" (by father and employer) to be related to less than honorable discharge. The figures from our analyses, however, show that five of the indicators of career deviance were related to formal labeling by legal authorities. The related variables are: (1) a high frequency of homosexual activity; (2) a high stereotypic image; (3) high knownaboutness; (4) loss of a job; and (5) membership in a homophile organization. Contrary to assumptions contained in the literature, persons who were labeled were not more likely to have incorporated conceptions of themselves as deviant, neither in terms of the societal stereotype nor by defining themselves as exclusively homosexual. They also did not show significantly more involvement with the homosexual subculture nor influence from homosexual friends, and likewise were not more isolated from interaction in the more conventional area of religion. The fact that those who were arrested did not seek professional help significantly more than those who were not labeled, might suggest that such labeling also did not contribute significantly to problems of psychological adjustment.

If one follows William and Weinberg's method of treating the eleven variables in Table 11.1 as being dependent on formal labeling, our findings would seem to indicate that legal processing is a more powerful lable than less than honorable discharge. However, the relationships may be more intricate than is suggested by this approac The problem is one of asserting cause and effect relationships in the

TABLE 11.1

Indicators of Homosexual Career Deviance by
Formal Labeling

Indicator of Career Deviance	Formally Labelled				
	Yes(n=16)		No(n=16)		
	number	percent	number	percent	Gamma
High in stereotypic self definition	(8)	50	(8)	50	.000
High in frequency of homosexual activity	(14)	87	(9)	56	.690
High in stereotypic image (overtness)	(13)	81	(5)	31	.810
Considers oneself to be exclusively homosexual	(9)	56	(7)	44	.246
High in subcultural involvement	(9)	56	(7)	44	.246
High in influence by homosexual friends	(7)	44	(9)	56	-.246
High in knownabout- ness	(12)	75	(5)	31	.737
Lost a job due to homosexuality	(5)	31	(1)	6	.744
Member of a homophile organ- ization	(9)	56	(2)	13	.800
Low in religiosity	(10)	62	(7)	44	.364
Sought professional help	(9)	56	(7)	44	.190

absence of temporal control. As Williams and Weinberg (1971: 63) themselves point out, "findings attributed to the effects of discharge could in fact be predisposing elements in getting caught in the first place - for example, 'swishy' behavior and other aspects cited as secondary deviance."[3]

Thus, it was thought that at least some of the related variables may be antecendent and contributory, rather than subsequent and dependent in relation to formal labeling. It didn't seem likely that arrest would result from the loss of a job, membership in a homophile organization, or a high frequency of homosexual activity.[4] While uncertain of the possible effects of knownaboutness of such labeling, it was thought however (as Williams and Weinberg have suggested), that a possible factor influencing the likelihood of arrest might be the public image that the individual presented. This possibility has been discussed by one of the authors who has pointed out that those who possess additional qualities concurring with the stereotypic image of the homosexual are more likely to be legally processed (Farrell, (1971). Such highly visible behavior may invite the intervention of police who tend to operate on "normal" (stereotypic) cases and convince them of guilt once they have apprehended the individual. The fact that one does not display overt and effeminate behavior will, on the other hand, give his deviation low visibility and may raise the more basic question in the minds of some as to whether he is in fact homosexual.

If a stereotypic image is a cause rather than an effect of arrest, it is also possible that some of the other variables found to be related to legal processing may be more directly a result of a high stereotypic image and, therefore, spurious in their relationship to formal labeling. In an attempt to explore this possibility, the other related variables were analyzed in relation to homosexual image. The findings of these analyses are shown in Table 11.2. The figures show that of the four variables under consideration, only knownaboutness was related to the individual's public image. As might be expected, those who presented a highly stereotypic image also were very likely to be known as a homosexual. The fact that a high frequency of homosexual activity, loss of a job, and membership in a homophile organization were not related would seem to support (in a very limited way) our impression that these factors are more likely results of formal labeling.

The data also show that the relationship between a stereotypic image and knownaboutness (see Table 11.2) is stronger than that between formal labeling and knownaboutness (see Table 11.1). This suggested that the latter relationship may be operating through the kind of public image that the individual presented. In order to determine if this was the case, the relationship between formal labeling

TABLE 11.2

Other Variables Related to Formal Labeling by Homosexual Image

| Other Variables Related to Formal Labeling | Homosexual Image | | | | |
| | High Stereotypic(n=18) | | Low Stereotypic(n=14) | | |
	number	percent	number	percent	Gamma
High in frequency of homosexual activity	(14)	78	(9)	64	.321
High in known-aboutness	(15)	83	(2)	14	.935
Lost a job due to homosexuality	(4)	22	(2)	14	.263
Member of a homophile organization	(8)	44	(3)	21	.492

and knownaboutness was reexamined after stratifying the sample on the basis of homosexual image and a partial coefficient for Goodman and Kruskal's gamma was obtained. In the original relationship (as shown in Table 11.1), the gamma value was .737, while the partial coefficient (as indicated in Table 11.3) is .355. Thus, the strength of the relationship between formal labeling and knownaboutness is reduced by more than half when the public image is controlled, therefore lending support to the argument that the original relationship is not as strong as it appeared. A high stereotypic image, then, seems to contribute to both formal labeling and knownaboutness, with the relationship between these two latter variables being considerably weakened when the public image is held constant. Thus, it would appear that the crucial factor influencing legal processing is not whether individuals are known to be engaging in homosexual activity, but rather if they appear to be homosexual in a stereotypic sense.

Conclusion

To conclude, the literature has pointed to formal labeling as an important influence in the development of deviant careers. In sum,

TABLE 11.3

Partial Coefficient for Knownaboutness by Formal
Labeling, Controlling for Homosexual Image

Overtness	S Multiplications	D Multiplications
High	11x1 = 11	2x4 = 8
Low	1x10 = 10	2x1 = 2
Total	21	10
Gamma		

Note: Knownaboutness, Formal Labeling/Overtness = + .355

it is suggested that the individual who has been labeled will develop
a deviant identity, become known publicly as deviant, subsequently
be socially isolated, and eventually come to organize his life around
his deviance. While a lack of temporal control makes it difficult to
assert cause and effect relationships, it would appear from the preceding analyses that our data may support (at least in part) three of
nine propositions that Williams and Weinberg derived from these
more general assumptions. Relative to unlabeled homosexuals, those
who were arrested were more likely: (1) to have lost a job due to
their homosexuality; (2) to be a member of a homophile organization;
and (3) to be frequent in their homosexual activity.

The fact that those who were arrested were more likely to have
lost a job suggests that such labeling may bring about the individual's
isolation from the larger society, at least from the very important
area of work. It is not surprising that arrest and subsequent knowledge
of the homosexuality might be communicated to an employer, since
employers may have access to otherwise confidential information.
While the dismissal may occur because knowledge of the individual's
homosexuality has been disclosed as a result of the arrest, the fact
that the person was arrested for such activity may be the more important cause of this action. One who is known to be homosexual
might be retained in employment as long as he is viewed as being
discrete in his sexual practices and not jeopardizing the reputation
or economic status of the organization employing him. The fact that
he is arrested, however, may discredit this impression and transform
his image to that of an individual who is perceived as a serious threat
to the status of the organization. As Garfinkel (1956) has suggested,
formal labeling serves to socially redefine the individual so that
others come to view him in a new light.

The data also seem to suggest that those who were labeled tended to organize their life around the fact of their deviance, to the extent that they more frequently engaged in homosexual activity and were more likely to hold membership in a homophile organization. Both of these outcomes would appear to represent forms of secondary deviation as it has been discussed by Lemert (1951, 1967). This latter involvement with the homophile movement may (as Lemert suggests about secondary deviance in general) serve as a mode of adjustment to the problems posed by arrest. In the homophile organization the individual can find acceptance and collective support for his deviance as well as be provided with an opportunity for the expression of his political beliefs regarding homosexuality. Experiencing bitterness and a sense of injustice for having been selected out for legal processing, he may feel an urgent need to change the laws that he sees as responsible for his problems. Through his participation in the political activities of an organization whose primary objective is to abolish sanctions for homosexual acts he may be able to satisfy this need.

We can only speculate as to the social psychological dynamics which give rise to an increase in the individual's frequency of homosexual activity. Our guess is that what may be occurring here is a reevaluation and reinterpretation of the significance of his sexual orientation in light of the formal label, the net effect of which is for him to devote more of his energy to the satisfaction of what he comes to perceive as a more important need. While further discussion of this process is beyond the scope of this paper, a more thorough understanding of what is involved here would seem essential to an explanation of the development and maintenance of homosexual careers.

Although our data do not support many of the propositions derived from labeling theory, one could hardly conclude that arrest is limited in its consequences for the homosexual. Unlike the label "less than honorable discharge," arrest may effect some very important aspects of the individual's life. If our findings and their interpretations are correct, such labeling may disrupt his integration in society and influence the extent of his social as well as psychosexual involvement with his deviation.

Notes

1. These propositions correspond roughly to the following statements from Williams and Weinberg (1971: 19 and 22). They proposed that, "compared to those homosexuals who received honorable discharges, those homosexuals who received less than honorable discharges from the military should be more likely — . . . (1) to

see themselves as 'abnormal'; (2) to engage in frequent, overt, and exclusive homosexuality; (3) to be involved in the homosexual 'way of life' or subculture; (4) to value the opinions of homosexuals more than heterosexuals; (5) to be known as homosexual to persons or groups; (6) to have experienced problems in the world of work; (7) to be politically active (especially in the homophile movement) and politically radical; (8) to be less involved with religion; (9) to be less psychologically adjusted—for example, show more symptoms reflective of anxiety."

2. Coefficient alpha was used to obtain the exact coefficient of equivalence for each composite scale. This statistical procedure provides a measure of internal consistency, taking into account the number of items, by giving the average split-half correlation for all possible ways of dividing the test into two parts (see Cronbach, 1951). The rationale for operationalizing each concept and the scale items and their alpha coefficient can be obtained by writing the senior author.

3. To put it another way, formal labeling may have resulted from certain stable behaviors characteristic of some persons as early as childhood. Although our groups were matched on the basis of their level of "initial homosexual activity," we cannot be certain that this is an adequate control, since the items used in operationalizing this phenomenon are not entirely consistent with the "dependent variables" under consideration in our analyses.

4. While the frequency of homosexual activity might at first appear to play a part in the labeling process, it should be noted that the item used to tap this variable says nothing to the public nature of the behavior; and there is no reason to assume that such activity would become public information. Furthermore, the public aspect of the sex was dealt with in the index of subcultural involvement which was found to be unrelated to formal labeling.

References

Becker, H. S.
   1963   Outsiders. New York: Free Press.

Cohen, A. K.
   1955   Delinquent Boys. New York: Free Press.

Cooley, C. H.
   1902   Human Nature and the Social Order. New York: Charles
          Scribner's Sons.

Cronbach, L. J.
1951　"Coefficient alpha and the internal structure of tests."
Psychometrika 16:297-334.

Erikson, K. T.
1962　"Notes on the sociology of deviance." Social Problems 9
(Spring):307-323.

Farrell, R. A.
1971　"Class linkages of legal treatment of homosexuals." Criminology 9 (May):49-67.

1972　"Societal Reaction to Homosexuals: Toward a Generalized
Theory of Deviance." University of Cincinnati. Ph.D.
dissertation.

Farrell, R. A. and T. J. Morrione.
1974　"Social interaction and stereotypic responses to homosexuals." Archives of Sexual Behavior. 3 (Sept).

Garfinkel, H.
1956　"Conditions of successful degradation ceremonies."
American Journal of Sociology 61 (March):420-424.

Goffman, E.
1963　Stigma: Notes on the Management of Spoiled Identity.
Englewood Cliffs, N.J.: Prentice-Hall, Inc.

Kitsuse, J.
1962　"Societal reaction to deviant behavior: probelms of theory
and method." Social Problems 9 (Winter):247-256.

Lemert, E. M.
1951　Social Pathology: A Systematic Approach to the Theory
of Sociopathic Behavior. New York: McGraw-Hill.

1967　Human Deviance, Social Problems and Social Control.
Englewood Cliffs, N.J.: Prentice-Hall, Inc.

Leznoff, M. and W. Westley.
1955　"The homosexual community." Social Problems 3 (April):
257-263.

Mead, G. H.
1934　Mind, Self & Society. Chicago: The University of Chicago
Press.

Mueller, J. K. Schuessler and H. Costner.
1970 Statistical Reasoning in Sociology. Boston: Houghton Mifflin Company.

Scheff, T. J.
1966 Being Mentally Ill. Chicago: Aldine Publishing Company.

Schur, E. M.
1971 Labeling Deviant Behavior: Its Sociological Implications. New York: Harper & Row.

Scott, R. A.
1969 The Making of Blind Men. New York: Russell Sage.

Simon, W. and J. H. Gagnon.
1969 "Homosexuality: The formulation of a sociological perspective." In Ralph N. Weltge (editor), The Same Sex. Philadelphia: Pilgrim Press, 14-24.

Tannenbaum, F.
1938 Crime and the Community. Boston: Ginn and Company.

Thomas, W. I.
1923 The Unadjusted Girl. Boston: Little, Brown and Company.

Williams, C. J. and M. S. Weinberg.
1971 Homosexuals and the Military. New York: Harper & Row.

12

BLACK MAN, WHITE WOMAN—
THE MAINTENANCE OF
A MYTH: RAPE AND THE
PRESS IN NEW ORLEANS

Daniel J. Abbott
and James M. Calonico

Rape and the fear of rape create deep emotional responses varying from sheer rage to an overwhelming sense of disgust and hatred. When the act takes on an interracial dimension, particularly between black men and white women, it triggers ingrained fears and hostilities with a long history of cultural development. The reactions reflect and, to a certain extent, typify the culmination of several hundred years of exploitive domination and subordination. Within the context of the present precipitous change in interracial relations in the U.S. the topic of rape holds an especially sensitive position in the broad range of conflicts which punctuate the black-white confrontation. The news media may play a significant role in molding the public's perception of rape in general and of the prevalence of interracial occurences in particular. This paper represents an initial report of a more extensive analysis of the relation between the media and public attitudes with regard to rape.

Although the paradigm has been questioned in more recent works, (Blauner, 1969), Dollard's analysis of caste remains one of the more basic statements about the place of rape within the white mythology about black men. Dollard states:

> The Negro man is held to be perpetually desirous of such contacts (raping a white woman) and Southerntown seems set to credit the slightest suspicion that they have occurred. Undoubtedly rapes do occur with sufficient frequency, at least to give color to the unconscious conviction of whites that this is one of the main desires of every Negro man. (Dollard, 1937:62)

The white woman was supposedly idealized as the paragon of virtue and delicateness. Although this stereotype may have been a

141

production of the upper class, the caste position demanded a vigilant negation of all black access to white women. More than the basic protection of white women, the white male abhorence of rape by a black man may be founded in multiple suppressed fears of retaliation, greater black virility, and erosion of status position; and it often releases some of the more violent white responses to black infringement upon racial boundaries. An overt or latent hostility engendered by a belief in the myth and reinforced by the media could be a strong component of the continued rejection of black by white.

In contrast to this rejection, one might consider the emotional reaction of black men toward white women. Eldridge Cleaver in his book, Soul on Ice, provided an updated personal expression of his conflicting feelings toward white women which reflects the earlier analysis by Dollard. In his allegory, the Black Eunich states:

> I love white women and hate black women. It's just in me, so deep that I don't even try to get it out of me any- more. I'd jump over ten nigger bitches just to get to one white woman . . . It's not just the fact that she's a woman that I love, I love her skin, her soft, smooth white skin. I like to just lick her white skin as if sweet, fresh honey flows from her pores, and just to touch her long, soft silky hair. (Cleaver, 1968:159)

To Cleaver who eventually was imprisoned for raping a white woman, rape became not a pure act of lust as envisioned in the earlier white version of the black man's desires:

> Rape (of white women) was an insurrectionary act. It delighted me that I was defying and trampling upon white man's law, upon his system of values, and that I was defiling his women - and this point, I believe, was the most satisfying to me because I was very resentful over the historical fact of how the white man has used the black woman. (Cleaver, 1968:159)

To the extent that Cleaver represents the thinking of a portion of blacks, it would seem that the white community has cause for real concern. Careful studies of rape in urban areas, however, suggest that the crime is an interracial act where a black man rapes a white woman in only a small proportion of the total cases, (Amir, 1971) but other work has suggested the existence of the belief that rape tends to be an interracial act with blacks predominating as offenders.

A biased reading of Cleaver's work without attention to the systematic studies in the field could have several harmful effects, especially if the media reinforced rather than ameliorated the myth of black-white rape. First, in this period of rapid change in civil rights, especially with the advent of black power, white paranoia may be expanded beyond all reasonable proportions, leading to an exaggerated fear on the streets and insecurity in the home.[1] Secondly, authorities could be pressured to institute forceful methods of control which inflict more harm than the preventive capabilities of the measure warrant. The threat or use of force might seriously retard whatever processes of accomodation are occurring between the two races; thus the ultimate resolution of racial differences could be postponed and the likelihood of violence markedly increased.

Media and Public Perceptions of Criminality

From the above discussion it appears that in considering such a highly sensitive subject as interracial rape, it is important to address the role of the mass media, in this case the press, as represented by a newspaper,[2] in the formation and support of public images of rape. Joseph T. Klapper (1960) in his definitive work, The Effects of Mass Communication, indicates three general functions of the media with regard to public opinion: reinforcement of pre-existing opinions, minor change of opinions, and conversion from one opinion to another. According to Klapper, as well as other authors, (Hennessy, 1965; Lane, 1959) the reinforcement effect of the media is greatest, followed by minor change and then conversion. In addition to such conceptualizations, Quinney, in discussing the public versus social reality of crime, indicates that "public conceptions of crime are created in part by the images of crime in the mass media" (Quinney, 1970:284) and that "a specific kind of crime coverage in the media provides the source for building criminal conceptions." (Quinney, 1970:285) Finally, in her fairly recent work, "Media Myths on Violence," Knopf directly addresses the question of race and crime and concludes that "We have all grown so used to viewing blacks as stereotyped criminals that it is difficult to picture them in any other role. She continues by indicating that the media tends to "pander the public's prejudice, reinforcing stereotypes, myths and other outmoded beliefs. The media not only frightens the public but confuses it as well." (Knopf, 1970:23)

The above evidence seems to indicate that the media, and primarily newspapers, do have some effect on the support and formation of public opinion. Furthermore, it is believed that this effect can, indeed, be of a biased nature and has, in fact, contributed to the stereotyping of blacks as criminals. A recent case in the city of New Orleans indicates that whether the racial bias is exhibited in the media can depend upon the type of criminal case. This particular case, occurring in mid-April, 1973, found a white girl raped and murdered while performing her duties as a student nurse in a black housing project. A young black male was arrested and charged with the crimes (eventually the rape charge was dropped and then reinstituted in mid-May) and a local daily newspaper followed the case with nearly a week of headlines and with virtually the entire front page on two separate issues devoted to the incident. In contrast, in early February of 1973, the same black male was arrested for the murder of a black man in the same housing project but the newspaper in question gave this incident comparatively little attention.

In a city such as New Orleans where the potential for racial mixture is quite high—the non-white population is approximately 46 percent and the overwhelming majority of these are blacks-but where the actual mixture of the races, if measured in terms of neighborhood integration, is quite low, and where racial tension seems to be increasing, it is important to know the potential role of the newspaper regarding public opinion. Especially regarding an issue such as rape, what kinds of images of interracial and intraracial rape are portrayed compared to the images which might be indicated through police statistics? Is a racially biased picture being painted thus reinforcing racial prejudices? And, if so, what consequences might follow? It is these kinds of questions which this paper intends to raise and attempts to answer.

Methodology

The study was conducted in New Orleans, an urban area enveloped in the traditions and culture of the South. In many ways New Orleans is a unique city with a more cosmopolitan approach to many controversial issues, but various community decisions suggest a basic growing white fear of blacks with a concomitant escalation of surveillance and possiblity of violence. When the impact of federal desegregation orders filtered into the New Orleans metropolitan area, a suburb adjacent to the city, Jefferson Parish, segregated its entire secondary public school system on the basis of sex. The presumed but unstated intent was to separate black boys from white girls. Unless, as Dollard suggested earlier, there was an unconscious fear of white girls attraction to black males, the ostensible motivation was to protect the white girls from the perceived danger of being molested by black youths. In a more recent incident the New Orleans police force introduced the Felony Action Squad (FAS) as a response to the murders and rapings in the city. The FAS consists of a special force of plain-clothed policemen sent into high crime areas in an attempt to intercept acts of violent crime. The police chief hearalded the beginnings of the special team with a much publicized "Shoot-to-Kill" order. The angry reaction of the black community was predictable, and the response of some white officials was to dismiss the protest as black political opportunism. Although it would be highly inaccurate to describe the introduction of this particular squad as a pure racist act, it indicates the pressure directed toward the police force to curtail what is perceived as an alarming increase in crime undoubtedly attributed to the black population in the city.

The analysis focused upon the largest daily newspaper in New Orleans, the Times-Picayune. In both readership and size it surpassed the evening paper, The States-Item. Both past experience and an initial perusal of the two newspapers over a several month period clearly suggested that the Times-Picayune had a more extensive coverage of crime news; in addition, it had been accused of a racial bias in its policies. In a recent meeting between the editor and representatives of the NAACP, the newspaper was asked to alter various policies which emphasized racial differences. In a front page article, the Times-Picayune boldly presented the FBI data which set the rate of rape in New Orleans as double that of New York City for 1972. Although there is a move to change the laws now, in 1972 prosecutors needed the evidence of a witness to secure a conviction for forcible rape. This requirement undoubtedly seriously discouraged a victim's willingness to report rape in New York City and its implications were not presented to the public.

A form of content analysis was employed to assess in a systematic manner the paper's policy on reporting rape to the community. All 1972 editions of the paper were searched for articles on rape and several factors were noted-whether the account mentions the race of the victim and offender, the degree of violence, the relationship between the victim and offender, and the place of occurrence. Along with this a questionnaire regarding individuals' perception of rape rates was administered to a sample of students who would be expected to have a similar, or more accurate conception of the actual nature of rape than their parents.

Data and Analysis

Studies of rape indicate that its true nature conforms very little to the myth frequently held by the white population. Amir's (1971) study of forcible rape in Philadelphia for 1958 and 1960 found that only 3.3 percent of reported rape involved a black offender and a white victim. This percent was the lowest for any of the four possible offender-victim racial combinations in a case of rape. The overwhelming majority of the cases were intraracial - 76.9 percent and 16.3

percent white. The comparable statistics for New Orleans during 1971 were 73.4 percent black and 7.8 percent white. A black man raped a white woman in 17.7 percent of the reported incidents, a figure considerably higher than that found by Amir, but still only a minor part of the total reported cases. Blacks dominate the data on rape, but in Amir's study most incidents occurred within two or three blocks of the victim's home and in almost half the cases the two parties knew each other on a primary basis. Assuming a consistency in the pattern, rape in New Orleans generally takes place within the black community between persons who are acquainted with each other, and it is much more restricted outside of this context.

It should be noted here that rape is one of the most underreported crimes. The President's Crime Commission (1968) conducted an extensive survey among the general population to obtain an estimate of the difference between actual and reported crime. The study found that there were at least three and one half times more rapes in the U.S. than official data indicate. Several of the explanations are readily understandable. The trauma of the experience may reduce the willing-ness of the woman to relive and recall the entire episode in front of a jury filled with strangers. Reports have suggested that sometimes the complaining victim may be mistreated by police at the station. (Ramparts, 1971) Victims may want to protect themselves from the possible notoriety and disgrace incumbent upon a publicized court case. Additionally, laws for acceptable evidence to prove rape often demand added humiliation and victims may simply perceive the further stress involved in pursuing the event as not commensurate with the probability of an arrest and conviction.

A further complicating factor particularly for the present study, is the nature of race relations in the U.S. and its effect on the propen-sity of blacks to report crime to white dominated police agencies. It is generally acknowledged that blacks in the ghettos and slums of urban areas distrust and dislike the police whom they tend to view as a force designed to maintain the status quo in the ghettos. (Presi-dents Crime Commission, 1968). The strain is reflected in an unwill-ingness to cooperate and report incidents of crime to the authorities. Since rape is one of the most underreported crimes, the amount of "unknown" rape occurring in black neighborhoods may be quite exten-sive. On the other hand, the indignation generated by a case of black raping white plus the greater affinity of the white victim for white police could increase the likelihood of official recognition in this instance. The end result of each factor would be a tendency to over-represent in the official statistics the actual small proportion of instances where black-white rape occurs; thus, the already low per-centages presented in the crime statistics could be assumed to be much lower in reality.

For the New Orleans study, in 1971, 155 cases of rape or attempted rape were reported in the Times-Picayune.[3] However, police records showed a total of 278 victims and 364 perpertrators of rape in their annual summaries, for that same year. It is relatively rare when there are multiple victims in a single instance of rape so that the number of victims would be a reasonable approximation of the number of cases known to the police. The daily newspaper therefore reported approximately 55 percent of the total number of instances of rape which had come to police attention during 1971. Such a large sample could accurately provide valid representation of the reality of rape in New Orleans if there were no biases operating in the decisions on matters for publication. On the other hand any significant departures from the distribution noted in police figures would suggest the presence of a conscious or unconscious bias in the selection or reporting of cases for print.

Prior to the analysis of the possible effects of news coverage, it is necessary to explore the possible meanings the ordinary citizen might give to different types of articles. When an event has a bi-racial component, newspapers will sometimes note in the article that a particular person or persons were black but not that the remainder were white. It is assumed, that, when a report states "John Doe, a black man, raped a nurse," the readership believes that a black man has raped a white woman.

Table 12.1 indicates that there are nine possible combinations when reporting racial composition in cases of rape and each category has at least one case. In 33.6 percent of the cases the race of both the victim and the offender were given in the newspaper account and there was no information on race in 34.2 percent of the cases. In 32.3 percent of the articles the race of either the victim or the offender, but not both, was mentioned in the report.

If the public interprets newspaper reports according to the rules described above, serious distortions of reality arise in the coverage of rape by the Times-Picayune. Categories three and seven in Table 12.1 account for 53.6 percent of the cases and imply that a black man has raped a white woman. In the first instance, in 41 cases (27%) the newspaper reported the race of the victim and the offender where a black man had raped a white woman. This figure alone is well above the 17.7 percent found in police records. In another 40 cases (26.3%) only the race of the offender, black, was cited in the article thus suggesting a white victim. The total impression contrasts sharply with the available police data on known rapes for 1972. The 81 accounts which suggested black raping white mean that on the average the general readership encountered such a story one day out of every four. At the other extreme, the population could receive the impression from category two that only five percent of the

147

TABLE 12.1

Racial Characteristics of Offenders and Victims in
Rape Cases Reported in Times-Picayune,
New Orleans, 1971a

Race of Victim	Offenderb	Number	Percent	Percent with Category #1 Omitted
1 N G^c	N G	52	34.2	
2 Black	Black	7	4.6	7.0
3 White	Black	41	27.0	41.0
4 Black	White	1	0.7	1.0
5 White	White	2	1.3	2.0
6 Black	N G	5	3.3	5.0
7 N G	Black	40	26.3	40.0
8 White	N G	1	.7	1.0
9 N G	White	3	2.0	3.0
Totals		152	100.1	100.0

aThis includes 19 cases of attempted rape

bThere were 27 cases of group rape reported but the offenders were from both races in only one case which was omitted from the analysis

cN G means that race was not given

rapes, or at least a very small number, consist of a black attacking a black. The overall belief among whites and white legislators who read the newspaper could indeed be that black males preponderantly cross racial lines when they commit an act of rape. It could reinforce, through a gross misrepresentation of reality, the belief that the black man is drawn toward and even prefers the white woman sexually.

In an initial attempt to assess conceptions about the racial composition of those involved in rape events, a questionnaire was given to students in an introductory course in social problems. Since it was the general course for non-majors in sociology, it contained a broad cross-section of the different colleges on the campus. The proportion of blacks in the sample was 12.7 percent which is consistent with the total black representation at the university. It was assumed that the student's perceptions would be at least as correct as, and possibly less biased than their parents. The respondents were asked to estimate the proportion of the total number of rapes in New Orleans for each possible racial combination and to round their figures to the nearest ten percent. The goal was merely to gain an estimate on how the four possibilities were ranked. The percent estimates were then averaged for each combination and the average percent was used as a measure of the perceived frequency of the different racial combinations.

Table 12.2 indicates that this cross-section of students at LSUNO ranks black raping white as the most frequent type of racial composition in this form of criminal behavior. In the method used, black raping black is a close second but the enormous distortion of reality remains. When sex of the respondent is controlled, women perceived a predominance of black raping white, but the men ranked black raping black first although the difference in average percent from black raping white was extremely small. (Table 12.3) Since the largest group in class was white women, the responses may reflect an ingrained fear of such occurrences, especially when the relatively few incidents of this nature receive an extraordinary amount of publicity.

Table 12.4 suggests that blacks in the sample ranked the various types of racial composition in their proper order and reported the largest difference between black raping black and black raping white. On the average, the black student at LSUNO probably has more direct contact with the reality of the situation than the whites. The school is not generally patronized by the middle and upper elites of the town; most parents of students have a working class background. Since rape is concentrated in the lower class culture, which is predominantly black in most large urban centers, the blacks are more likely to know of such events in their own neighborhood experience. They, too, undoubtedly experience communications which declare the predominance of black raping white but do not seem to perceive or accept the messages. There may be black rejection of white myths reflected in the responses, but these factors were not explored. The fact remains that this particular sample of whites quite erroneously perceived a preponderance of black raping white, and there are reasons to suggest that the distortion is even greater among the general population.

Conclusion

A newspaper's editorial page is supposedly limited to a clearly designated section; the remainder comprises a factual reporting of world events. The decision to include an article, however, may reflect a conscious or unconscious editorial policy which may have greater influence on readers than the editorial statements. Such a bias appears to be operating in New Orleans to the detriment of blacks

TABLE 12.2

Average Percentage Estimates on the Racial Composition of Rape in New Orleans

Race of Offender	Victim	Average Percent	Rank
Black	Black	29.7	2
White	Black	14.2	4
Black	White	31.6	1
White	White	24.1	3

Note: N = 157

TABLE 12.3

Average Percentage Estimates on the Racial Composition of Rape in New Orleans by Sex

Race of Offender	Victim	Male Average Percent	Rank	Female Average Percent	Rank	Total Average Percent
Black	Black	32.5	1	27.6	2	29.7
White	Black	12.2	4	15.8	4	14.2
Black	White	31.0	2	32.4	1	31.6
White	White	24.1	3	24.0	3	24.1

Note: N = Male = 68; N = Female = 89

150

TABLE 12.4

Average Percentage Estimates on the Racial Composition
of Rape in New Orleans by Race

Race of Offender	Victim	Black Average Percent	Rank	White Average Percent	Rank	Total Average Percent
Black	Black	32.5	1	29.3	2	29.7
White	Black	17.0	4	13.9	4	14.2
Black	White	26.5	2	32.5	1	31.6
White	White	24.0	3	24.2	3	24.1

Note: N - Black = 20; N - White = 137

and race relations in general. On the explosive issue of rape, the nature of black involvement is distorted in the transition from the police blotter to the news article. The proportionate amount of incidents in which a black man rapes a white woman is overreported and articles which describe an intraracial rape are written in such a manner that they suggest an interracial event.

Although newspapers are influenced by their perceptions of the public's appetite, it is incumbent upon them to accurately reflect reality on inflammatory issues. The tendency of the Times-Picayune to misrepresent the truth in 1971 could only further the separation between races and increase levels of hostility. It is reasonable to question the influence such reporting had on hardening white opinion and unleashing bigoted paranoia. The escalating cycle of action and response is undoubtedly affected by perceptions gained through the media (even if they only represent a reinforcement of prior sentiments). Ignorance of what may be considered the most heinous racial affront may have led to acts by whites which furthered the willingness of a few blacks to resort to terroristic acts against police and other symbols of white oppression.

Notes

1. At least one third of the American population feel unsafe when they are out alone at night in their own neighborhoods. The Challenge of Crime in a Free Society, a report by the President's Commission on Law Enforcement and Administration of Justice (1968).

2. Hennessy indicates that "the mass media, in order of importance for public opinion, are: the press, television, radio, and movies. By the press I mean, first, newspapers, and, second, news and opinion journals." (Hennessy, 1965:271) This indicates newspapers to be the most important medium with regard to the effect of media upon the public opinion. Furthermore, a Bureau of Advertising research project (as reported April 29, 1972 in the New Orleans Times-Picayune) recently found that on the average weekday 77 percent of all adults read a daily newspaper. The report also indicated crime news as one of the most widely read kinds of content.

3. The following table shows the distribution of students in the sample by college at the University.

References

Amir, M.
1971   Patterns of Forcible Rape. Chicago: University of Chicago Press.

Blauner, R.
1969   "Internal colonialism and ghetto revolt." Social Problems 16 (Spring):393-408.

Cleaver, E.
1968   Soul On Ice. New York: Delta Publishing Company.

Dollard, J.
1937   Caste and Class in a Southern Town. Gordon City, New York: Doubleday Anchor.

Griffin, S.
1971   "The Politics of Rape: An Inquiry." Ramparts (Sept.)

Hennessy, B. C.
1965   Public Opinion. Belmont, California: Wadsworth Publishing Company.

Klapper, J. T.
1960   The Effects of Mass Communication. Glencoe, Illinois: The Free Press of Glencoe.

Knopf, T. A.
1970   "Media myths on violence." Columbia Journalism Review 9 (Spring):17-23.

Lane, R. E.
   1959   Political Life: Why People Get Involved in Politics. New
            York: The Free Press of Glencoe.

President's Commission on Law Enforcement and Administration of
   1968   Justice
            The Challenge of Crime in a Free Society, New York:
            Avon Books

Quinney, R.
   1970   The Social Reality of Crime. Boston: Little, Brown.

13

THE DECISION TO REFER
TO JUVENILE COURT FOR
A JUDICIAL HEARING

Lawrence Rosen
and Arlene Carl

As in the case of adults, a formal arrest of a juvenile does not necessarily result in a formal court hearing. In most jurisdictions juvenile arrests are "screened" and only a portion receive a formal court hearing. The remainder of the cases are placed on informal probation referred to a social agency, or simply released with nothing more severe than a rebuke and warning. This critical decision is usually made in the smaller jurisdictions by probation officers. In the larger jurisdictions, however, they are usually "intake officers" whose primary task is to screen cases for the juvenile court.

This juncture in the juvenile justice system is an important one from the perspective of both youths in the system and the state. For youths it represents the last "exit" before being enmeshed within the formal court process with the substantially increased likelihood of severe restrictions subsequently being placed on his freedom such as institutionalization or probation. For the state, a case continued for a formal court hearing involves the expenditure of considerable resources (appointing defense counsel pre-trial investigations, assignment of prosecutors, etc.),

Although there has been a fair amount of speculation about the factors that influence the decision to release before a court appearance there is very little systematic evidence on this issue. The research that is available is primarily concerned with race and socio-economic class. Robert Terry (1967) in his study of 9,023 cases in a "midwest community" (population about 100,000) concluded that race and S.E.S. were weakly related to the decision to release; when controlled for "seriousness of the offense" (the measure of seriousness is not given) these relationships were reduced to almost zero. In addition he found males more likely than females to be referred to court, but this relationship was also appreciably diminished when controlled for seriousness of the offense. Thornberry (1973) claimed to be studying the "intake hearing" in his study of almost 10,000 cases in Philadelphia. However, included as "released" cases were boys discharged by a juvenile court judge, as well as those released by the intake officer. Thus, a portion of the "released" cases were in reality referred for a formal court hearing. Consequently, Thornberry's conclusions about the intake decision should be viewed with some skepticism. (He concludes that race and socio-economic status were associated with the "intake" decision even when controlled for by the Sellin-Wolfgang seriousness score of the offense and previous arrest record.)

A major difficulty with both studies is their limited data analysis. For the most part neither study was able to systematically handle more than three independent variables at one time. Considering the lack of systematic knowledge on this important decision in the juvenile justice system, what is required is a technique that can handle many independent variables simultaneously while being able to detect unsuspected statistical interactions. One such technique is Automatic Interaction Detection (to be described below). The purpose of this paper is to apply this technique in an analysis of a sample of males being screened for a juvenile court hearing in Phildelphia.

Before discussing the technique and the sample, it will be helpful to briefly describe the intake process in Philadelphia.

Intake Procedures

After a youth is formally arrested by the police he or she is taken to a screening and detention facility (Youth Study Center) to begin an intake process that in most cases lasts a minimum of two days. A youth may be "petitioned" to court by other individuals such as parents, school authorities, etc. However, in Philadelphia more than 90% of the males received at intake are police arrests.:

> The intake process consists of two separate interviews.
> Children under arrest have a "first" intake interview
> soon after they arrive at the center to determine
> whether they should be detained. At this interview the
> intake interviewer examines the arrest report and
> any previous court record on the child. The parents
> of the child are required to attend this interview. A
> "second" interview takes place on the following day.
> At this time the case is either adjusted or referred
> to court for hearing. (Court of Common Pleas, 1971:
> 24)

Present at the second interview are the youth, his parents or guardians and a stenographer in addition to the intake officer. In some instances the victim, a police officer and a defense lawyer (although very rare) may also attend. In addition to questions about the offense the interviewer may inquire about the youth's home and school situation. This information is sought because of the explicit juvenile court philosophy that non-legal factors should be considered in choosing the appropriate courses of action. Supposedly, the youth's innocence or guilt is not the only consideration in juvenile court decisions. There are both black and white intake officers, all of whom are former probation officers. There is no attempt to match the race of interviewer with that of the youth, however, there is matching for sex.

The Sample

For the present study a random sample of 295 males was selected from a list of all boys referred to the intake facility during the period of May 1, 1971 to January 31, 1973. Approximately 44 percent of these cases were released (adjusted) and the remaining 56 percent referred to court. This is almost identical to the court referral rate of 57 percent reported for all male cases processed through intake for 1971 (Court of Common Pleas, 1971) consequently, there is confidence that the sample was representative.

Because of some difficulties, primarily in locating records, 35 cases had to be dropped from the sample. A large portion of these dropped cases (approximately 82 percent) had been released. Apparently the major reason for the relatively high release rate is that for all practical purposes an adjusted case is one which is terminated and the paperwork of the case is handled in a more casual manner, especially for youths who have no previous court appearance. Therefore there is a greater likelihood that adjusted cases will become "lost" within the record system. Most of the dropped cases were black (consistent with the proportion of total intake) and involved relatively minor offenses (disorderly conduct, vandalism etc.). Although these 35 cases are in some areas somewhat different from the remaining 260 cases, it is our considered opinion that their exclusion involved no serious distortions in the general findings.

All the data was obtained from official court records, and as expected, the quality of the data was variable. For some items the information is reasonably valid and reliable (age, race, legal charge) while for others there is much less confidence (income, welfare status). A few items were dropped from the analysis because of a large number of unknowns. Unfortunately, they were, for the most part, related to the socio-economic status of the youth (family income, welfare status, occupation of main wage earner). Consequently, we were unable to consider the potentially important variable of socio-economic status. (See Table 13.1 for the complete list of independent variables.)

Data Analysis

The analytical technique employed in this study is Automatic Interaction Detection (AID) (Sonquist, 1970; Sonquist et al, 1971). It is a multivariate procedure which detects patterns of unsuspected statistical interaction and is designed to specify a set of independent variables that best "predict" or specify the value of a criterion variable. In the present case the criterion variable is whether or not the youth is referred to court for a hearing. The technique procedes in the following way:

1. It first determines the degree of association between each of the independent variables and the criterion variable.
2. It next selects that variable with the highest degree of statistical association and splits the sample into two parts defined in terms of the independent variable. For example in the present study the variable with the highest association was the Sellin-Wolfgang seriousness score of the current offense with the sample being divided into those cases with a score of zero and those with a score of one or more. The percent of the cases referred to court for each group was 40.8 percent and 80.2 percent respectively.
3. For each of the two groups steps 1 and 2 are repeated and each group is further subdivided.
4. The process continues until the group size is too small (in this analysis no group was considered for a further split if either of the prospective groups had 20 or less cases); or there is no variance left to explain; or all the remaining variables are too weakly related to the dependent variable In this study that limit was reached when the independent variable accounted for less than 0.6 percent of the original variance of the dependent variable.
5. The final result is a "tree" consisting of a series of terminal sets which can be viewed as a typology that "best" predicts the likelihood of being referred to court (see Figure 13.1 and Table 13.2)

If the dependent variable were continuous, AID can be viewed as a series of one way analysis of variance tests which produce final sets that maximize the between groups variance and minimizes the within cell variance. (For dichotomous dependent variables the analysis of variance model is valid if the dependent variable is treated

157

TABLE 13.1

Independent Variables Used in AID and
Percent Referred to Court for Hearing

Variable Name	Number	Percent Referred
1. Race		
White	67	43.3
Black (Includes 8 Puerto Ricans)	193	66.3
2. Age		
Below 11	27	63.0
12	27	51.8
13	27	66.7
14	47	48.9
15	60	60.0
16+ (Includes 1 unknown)	72	68.1
3. Family Status		
Intact	118	57.6
Broken (Includes 3 unknowns)	142	62.7
4. Number of Brothers with a Record		
0	131	60.3
1+	129	60.5
5. Current Court Status		
No record	86	50.0
Inactive	63	57.1
Active	111	70.3
6. Current Charge		
Person offense	66	78.8
Property offense	96	70.8
Drug offense	19	36.8
Miscellaneous adult offense	69	36.2
Juvenile status offense	10	50.0
7. Weapon		
None (Includes 1 unknown)	216	55.6
Yes	44	84.1
8. Amount of Property Damage		
None (Includes 2 unknowns)	175	53.7
Under $10	20	60.0
Above $10	65	78.5
9. Number of Boys Involved in Offense		
0 (Includes 3 unknowns)	111	54.9
1	67	65.7
2	37	59.5
3+	45	66.7
10. Sellin-Wolfgang Score (SW Score)		
0 (Including 1 unknown)	98	34.7
1	31	58.1

Variable Name	Number	Percent Referred
2	58	75.9
3	28	67.9
4+	45	93.3
11. Number of Past Arrests		
0	84	51.2
1	40	65.0
2	28	57.1
3	26	80.8
4+	82	62.2
12. Number of Past Adjudications		
0	154	57.8
1	43	55.8
2	31	71.0
3+	32	68.8
13. Number Past Arrests for Juvenile Status Offenses		
0	229	58.5
1+	31	74.2
14. Number Past Arrests for Person Crimes		
0	191	57.1
1	49	67.4
2+	20	75.0
15. Number Past Arrests for Robberies		
0	208	59.6
1	33	57.6
2+	19	73.7
16. Number Past Arrests for Property Crimes		
0	138	55.1
1	40	72.5
2+	82	63.4
17. Number Past Arrests for Miscellaneous Adult Offenses		
0	172	61.0
1	47	57.4
2+	41	61.9
18. Time Spent in an Institution		
None	219	58.9
Yes	41	68.3
19. Time Spent on Probation		
None	156	55.8
1 month	24	58.3
2 months	28	67.9
3+ months	52	71.2

as a dummy variable.) In this paper variance is defined as the number of "mistakes" made in predicting the dependent variable (or total sums of squares). At each split in the tree the number of mistakes reduced (or between sums of squares) divided by the original number of mistakes is the same as the "proportion of variance accounted for" (or r^2) by the splitting variable. Thus, the larger the number of mistakes reduced, the more important the variable. Usually the variables become less important as the splitting progresses. The total amount of variance accounted for by the final typology (or R^2) is simply the ratio of the total between sums of squares (i.e., for all splits) to the original total sums of squares.

It should be stressed that AID selects the "best" variables. Because a variable is not included in the final tree does not necessarily mean that the particular variable is unimportant. It is possible that a variable may evidence some relationship to the criterion variable, but was not selected because other variables were more strongly associated with the criterion variable.

Findings

The referral rates for the values of each variable are presented in Table 13.1. The variables exhibiting a moderately strong zero-order relationship with the dependent variable are race, current court status, current charge, presence of weapon in the current offense, and Sellin-Wolfgang seriousness score of the current offense.

The pattern that emerges from these findings suggests that the characteristics of the current offense are of primary importance. One variable related to past record (current court status) and one reflected a characteristic of the youth (race) were also of some importance. For the most part these findings are consistent with the findings of Terry (1967) and Thornberry (1973). However many of the independent variables are highly intercorrelated, reaching conclusions based upon the zero-order findings is extremely hazardous.

The "tree" from the AID analysis is given in Figure 13.1. The variable exhibiting the highest degree of association (r^2 = .167) with the decision to refer is the seriousness of the current offense as measured by the Sellin-Wolfgang Seriousness Index (Sellin and Wolfgang 1964). Of those involved in an offense with a score of one or more, 76 percent were referred to court compared to 35 percent of those with a score of zero.[1] The only competitor to that variable was the legal charge of the event (r^2 = 130). This is to be expected because of the interdependence of these two independent variables.

Seriousness score also proves important for group three in that it split that group further, and in the same direction (i.e., the more serious the offense, the higher the referral rate).

160

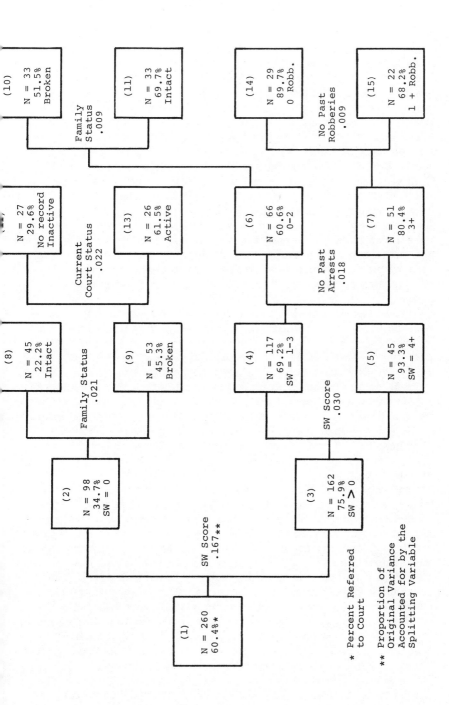

(10)
N = 33
51.5%
Broken

(11)
N = 33
69.7%
Intact

Family
Status
.009

(14)
N = 29
89.7%
0 Robb.

(15)
N = 22
68.2%
1 + Robb.

No Past
Robberies
.009

N = 27
29.6%
No record
Inactive

(13)
N = 26
61.5%
Active

Current
Court Status
.022

(6)
N = 66
60.6%
0-2

(7)
N = 51
80.4%
3+

No Past
Arrests
.018

(8)
N = 45
22.2%
Intact

(9)
N = 53
45.3%
Broken

Family Status
.021

(4)
N = 117
69.2%
SW = 1-3

(5)
N = 45
93.3%
SW = 4+

SW Score
.030

(2)
N = 98
34.7%
SW = 0

(3)
N = 162
75.9%
SW > 0

SW Score
.167**

(1)
N = 260
60.4%*

*   Percent Referred
    to Court

** Proportion of
    Original Variance
    Accounted for by the
    Splitting Variable

161

For those committing the least serious offenses (group 2) family structure emerged as the most important variable (r^2 = 058). Those coming from broken homes were more likely to be referred (45 percent) than the boys having both parents present (22 percent). The variable of race was almost as strongly related to the referral decision with this group (r^2 = .054), and it is quite possible that sampling error was responsible for it not appearing at this point in the "tree." Interestingly, the only other demographic characteristic of the youth involved in this analysis, age, was also a "competitor" (r^2 = 041). This suggests that in minor or trivial offenses, the characteristics of the youth influence the decision of the intake officer.

Variables related to past record appear at groups nine and four. In the former, 62 percent of those who have an active status with the court (e.g. on probation, awaiting a hearing on another charge, etc.) were referred to court while 29 percent of the inactive cases or those with no previous record were referred. The number of past arrests splits group four, with the more serious past record being more likely to be referred.

Groups six and seven were split, but in a direction inconsistent with the zero-order relationships, as well as what might be expected on theoretical grounds. Since there is a fair amount of instability at the outer limits of the tree, where the groups are relatively small, it is possible that these results are a consequence of sampling error.

In summary, the AID analysis indicates that the variables of seriousness of the current offense and the past court record of the youth are of primary importance. The only place where characteristics of the youth (family structure, race and age) seem to have some significant effect are in cases where the youth was charged with a "trival" or minor offense (i.e., no physical injury or property damage or loss).

Clearly race does not emerge as a significant variable. Although it did have a moderate zero-order association with the dependent variable, as well as in group two, its effect on the remainder of the tree was very weak. This suggests that race was not important in this decision process or, at least, other factors were significantly more important.

The terminal groups of the tree are listed in Table 13.2 in descending value of their referral rates. The group with the highest referral rate (93 percent) included youths who were charged with an offense with a Sellin-Wolfgang seriousness score of four or more.[2] The group with the lowest referral rate (22 percent) were those charged with minor offeses (seriousness score of 0) and coming from intact homes. In general, any combination of "unfavorable" factors (serious offense, current court involvement, serious past court record) results in a high likelihood of being referred. Conversely any

TABLE 13.2

Terminal Groups for AID Figure 13.1

Group No.	Characteristics	Number	Percent Referred
5	SW = 4+	45	93.3
14	SW = 1-3; 3 or more past arrests; 0 past robberies	29	89.7
11	SW = 1-3; 0-2 past arrests; intact family	33	69.7
15	SW - 1-3; 3+ past arrests; 1 + robberies	22	68.3
13	SW = 0; broken home; active court status	26	61.5
10	SW = 1-3; 0-2 past arrests; broken home	33	51.5
12	SW = 0; broken home; inactive or no record	27	29.6
8	SW = 0; intact home	45	22.2
Total		260	60.4

Note: R^2 = 0.2759.

combination of "favorable" factors produces a low referral rate. Intermediate referral rates are the consequence of a combination of both "favorable" and "unfavorable" factors. The variance accounted for by this typology was 27.6 percent.

If the two anomalous splits at the end of the tree are dropped (this includes groups ten, eleven, fourteen and fifteen) then the pattern found in Table 13.2 is even more pronounced. This can be seen in the typology presented in Table 13.3. Disregarding these two splits yields a more interpretable typology at the cost of a small decrease in the explained variance (the R^2 drops from 0.276 to 0.258).

Conclusion

The single most important variable associated with the decision to refer an arrested juvenile to court is the seriousness of the current offense. Very serious offenses (S.W. score of four or more) almost guarantee that the youth will receive a formal court hearing regardless of any other factors (race, age, etc.).[3]

TABLE 13.3

Terminal Groups for AID Figure 13.1 with
Groups Ten, Eleven, Fourteen and Fifteen Deleted

Group No.	Characteristics	Number	Percent Referred
5	SW = 4+	45	93.3
7	SW = 1-3; 3+ past arrests	51	80.4
13	SW = 0; broken home; active court status	26	61.5
6	SW = 1-3; 0-2 past arrests	66	60.6
12	SW = 0; broken home; in- active or no record	27	29.6
8	SW = 0; intact home	45	22.2
Total		260	60.4

Note: $R^2 = 0.2579$.

When the offense was less serious other factors achieved some importance. For the moderately serious offenses (S.W. scores of one to three) the past court record has the most influence, whereas family structure (broken vs. intact) was the most important for the minor offenses (S.W. score of zero).

This analysis did explain 27.5 percent of the variance but a major part remains "unexplained" (approximately 72 percent). In addition to error variance (due primarily to measurement error) probably the major reason for the unexplained variance is that important variables have not been included in this analysis. Potentially important variables, for which we had either bad data (e.g., S.E.S.) or no data (e.g., attitude or demeanor of the youth, the demands of the complainant towards prosecution and the quality of evidence in the case) might have reduced further the unexplained variance.

We should also indicate that this study was clearly not a direct and explicit investigation of the decision making process. Such an analysis was not possible because:

1. No data was available on characteristics of the decision maker;
2. Not all possibly relevant factors were included (see the previous paragraph);
3. One could not be certain that the intake officer had all the information at the time of the decision that we subsequently abstracted from the court records for this study.

Nevertheless, this research does provide evidence for what factors, among those considered, are associated with the decision to refer and should be a guide for any future investigation of this issue. In addition the findings suggest that racial discrimination is not of major significance in this decision, at least for Philadelphia.

Notes

1. This indicates no personal injury, or threats to do personal harm, or forcible entry of premises or loss or damage to property.
2. A score of four is equivalent to one person being sufficiently injured to require medical treatment (but not hospitalized) or $2,000-$9,000 worth of property stolen, damaged or destroyed.
3. Although it was not sufficiently strong to produce a split in the tree, all youths having two or more past arrests (N = 22) in this group were referred to a formal court hearing.

References

Court of Common Pleas of Philadelphia
1971   Annual Report of the Family Court Division, Philadelphia.

Sellin T. and M. E. Wolfgang
1964   The Measurement of Delinquency. New York: J. Wiley.

Sonquist, J. A.
1970   Multivariate Model Building: The Validation of a Search
        Strategy Ann Arbor, Michigan: Institute for Survey Research,
        University of Michigan.

Sonquist, John A., E.L. Baker and J.N. Morgan
1971   Searching for Structure: An Approach to Analysis of
        Substantial Bodies of Micro Data and Documentation for a
        Computer Program. Ann Arbor, Michigan: Institute for
        Survey Research, University of Michigan.

Terry, Robert M.
1967   "Discrimination in the handling of juvenile offenders by
        social control agencies." Journal of Research in Crime
        and Delinquency 4 (July):218-230.

Thornberry, Terence P.
1973   "Race, socio-economic status and sentencing in the juvenile
        justice system," The Journal of Criminal Law and Crimi-
        nology 64 (March):90-98.

14

CHANGING PRACTICES OF
PROSECUTING ATTORNEYS
Peter G. Garabedian

The prosecuting attorney is generally acknowledged to be the most powerful person in the system of criminal justice. He stands mid-way between arrest and criminal proceedings. The decisions he makes can dramatically alter the course of an individual's life. Filing a criminal complaint, and the initiation of criminal proceedings resulting in a conviction, can stigmatize the individual to the point of isolating him from the main-stream of community life, whereas a refusal to prosecute means a second chance for the subject. In other words, as Newman (1956), Sudnow (1965), Blumberg (1967), and others have shown, the district attorney has extremely broad discretionary powers, and the great majority of his decisions are not visible either by the judiciary or the public-at-large. Even when his decisions are visible, they are almost never subject to judicial review. Perhaps the only other group of officials given a comparable degree of discretionary power are the paroling authorities of state and federal correctional systems. Yet, despite the enormous importance of district attorneys, relatively little is known about the conditions under which they will refuse to prosecute. Even less is known about their charging practices when criminal proceedings are initiated against defendants.

The aim of this paper is to present systematic empirical evidence that bear on a number of prosecutorial decisions which are almost never visible to the general public or to the judiciary. These decisions have to do with the prosecutor's refusal to file a criminal complaint, and the various types of charging strategies that are adopted against criminal defendants.

Research Setting and Methods

The data to be reported in this paper were collected in San Mateo County, California, in 1970. San Mateo County is divided into three judicial districts, the Northern, Central, and Southern. Several departments of the county's municipal court are located in each of the judicial districts. Four deputy district attorneys are located in each area office, and have the task of screening and prosecuting cases at the municipal court level. There are approximately five municipal police departments located within each of the judicial districts.

The data were collected by means of a one-page schedule designed specifically for this study. Each of the twelve deputy district attorneys in the three branch offices completed this schedule every time he reviewed a police report alleging a criminal violation against a suspect. The study period lasted for six weeks (June 1, 1970 to July 15, 1970). It is estimated that 99 percent of all the police reports submitted to the deputy district attorneys in the county during this period were included in the study. This methodology yielded the following types of information: (1) the total number of police reports submitted to each of the three judicial districts during the six week period; (2) the identity of the police department submitting the report; (3) the number and types of charges requested by the police in each of the reports; (4) the decisions of the prosecuting attorneys indicating whether or not a criminal complaint was filed; and (5) the number and types of charges contained in the complaint.

Results

At the end of the six week study period, the police had referred 1,878 separate cases with a total of 2,819 charges. Eight out of ten of these cases were prosecuted while in only 20 percent of the cases did the deputy district attorneys refuse to issue a criminal complaint. The decision to prosecute varied for the three judicial districts: 90 percent of the cases were prosecuted in the Southern Judicial District; 70 percent in the Central; and 75 percent in the Northern Judicial District.

Referral of Suspects and Refusal to Prosecute. At this point the question arises as to whether or not the refusal of the district attorney to prosecute is associated with the rate at which cases are referred to him by the police. Police departments contributing a disproportionately large number of cases may also be the same ones having the highest attrition rate. To gain some indication of the activity-level of the various police departments, a suspect-referral rate was computed by dividing the number of cases referred by the number of police officers in the department. While this measure is not an entirely satisfactory measure of police activity, it does provide some indication of the relative contribution of input into the criminal justice system. The referral rates varied from 12.6 suspects per ten officers for the Menlo Park Police Department to 43.3 suspects for every ten police in the Brisbane Police Department. The attrition of cases varied from no cases lost to over 37 percent. Ranking police departments according to the suspect-referral rate and also their attrition rate indicated that police departments with high referral rates were about as likely to have either high or low rates of attrition. The same was true for police departments having relatively low referral rates. In short, there was almost no relationship between the relative frequency of input of cases and the refusal to prosecute.

Charging Rates of Police Departments and Refusal to Prosecute. Skolnick (1966), and others have noted that the police will frequently charge a suspect with more than one crime so as to build as "strong" or "convincing" a case as possible in the eyes of the deputy district attorney. This practice is called multiple charging or "stacking", and is done with the aim of enhancing the likelihood that the prosecutor will initiate criminal proceedings against the suspect. Multiple charging is a common phenomenon when the commission of a crime logically includes committing other lesser crimes. Thus, for example, a person charged with armed robbery, may also be charged with assault with a deadly weapon, and carrying a loaded firearm in a public place, and so on. Multiple charging is also common in traffic violations where a person could be charged with drunk driving, faulty tail light, bald tires, defective equipment, no license in possession, and so on. It is also a common practice when the police have illegally arrested a person, or illegally searched and seized evidence. As Chevigny (1969) has illustrated, in these cases the police will attempt to provoke the person into making a hostile or aggressive move against them, so that "cover" charges of resisting arrest and/or assaulting a police officer can be made.

That the police engage in multiple charging practices cannot be disputed. And whether these practices are justified or not, they are generally done with the belief that the case will have a better chance of being accepted for prosecution by the deputy district attorney. Hence, at this point the question arises as to whether the acceptance or rejection of a case by the prosecuting attorney is in any way associated with multiple charging practices of the various police departments.

In the present study it was possible to determine which police departments made it a practice of charging suspects with several crimes by obtaining the total number of charges requested by each police department and dividing the total by the number of suspects each department referred to the D.A. Converting this proportion into a rate provided a measure of the number of charges requested per every ten suspects referred.

The picture which emerged, is certainly not consistent with commonly held beliefs about this police practice. The deputy district attorneys were least likely to prosecute those cases that had been referred by police departments having the highest rates of multiple charging. They were most likely to prosecute those cases that were referred by police departments having the lowest charging rates. While on the surface this finding may appear to be anomalous, it should be kept in mind that we are dealing with rates which reflect department practices, and not with individual cases. Hence, this relationship does not necessarily suggest that individual cases involving several different recommended charges are not likely to be prosecuted. Rather, the finding suggests that the police department which generally engages in this practice is going to lose a relatively large proportion of its cases when they are reviewed and evaluated by the deputy district attorney.

It is not unreasonable to assume that those departments making it a common practice to charge suspects with as many crimes as possible may be the same ones that deviate too noticeably from acceptable legal procedures. Most police deviate from the procedural rules laid down for them, and generally it is possible for a deputy D.A. to "reconstruct" police behavior so as to be consistent with these procedural rules, and thus be acceptable in a court of law. But when the deputy prosecutor cannot obscure or "reconstruct" police deviance so that it will be acceptable in the eyes of the court, then he must refuse the case. The data suggest the inference that a number of the police departments are not particularly concerned with procedural rules, and hence have adopted the attitude that the prosecuting attorney can use his expertise to smooth over the legal kinks in their cases. They reason further that the chances of a case being accepted by the deputy D.A. are increased if they charge suspects with as many crimes as possible. The data quite clearly suggest, however, that this reasoning does not stand the test of the decision to file a criminal complaint. For the practice of multiple charging, on a departmental level, is associated with the prosecutor refusing to file on any of the charges requested.

Parenthetically, it might be noted that the cases which the police are most likely to multiple charge are also the ones most likely to be "sticky" in terms of legal problems such as arrest, search, and seizure.

The Norm of Multiple Charging by Prosecutors. The finding that prosectuors were more likely to refuse cases from police departments which commonly engaged in the practice of multiple charging, does not mean that they were opposed to the idea of multiple charging. Indeed, the charging rate for prosecutors was substantially higher than it was for the police as a whole.

The police charging rate in the county was 12.9 charges per every ten suspects, while for the prosecutors it was 14.8 for every ten defendants. However, it cannot be assumed that once a case was accepted by the deputy district attorney, he would automatically charge the defendant with more crimes than were requested or recommended by the police. Rather, data from this study suggest the existence of a norm that defines a "fair" or "reasonable" number of charges. Thus, for example, the average charging rate for police departments in the Northern Judicial District was 16.5. Apparently this was considered to be excessive, and the prosecutors made an appropriate adjustment downward to 15.3. On the other hand, they considered the charging rate for police departments in the Southern Judicial District to be inadequate and made an appropriate adjustment upward. In short, the data suggest that the prosecutors did have a fairly clear idea of what constitutes a "fair" or "effective" (in terms of winning a conviction) number of charges. Indeed, according to my observations, there was a great deal of interaction and communication, both formal and informal, among the prosecuting attorneys, when information was exchanged on questions of charging.

The Practice of Stacking Charges. The finding that the charging rate among prosecutors was higher than it was among the police clearly leads to the conclusion that they were not opposed to multiple charging, but rather made it a common practice themselves. Indeed one of the most widely held beliefs among those interested in understanding the decision-making behavior of prosecuting attorneys is that they "stack" charges in the criminal complaint. "Stacking" refers to the practice of charging the defendant not only with those recommended by the police, but also charges above and beyond those requested. The psychology of "stacking" is to place the greatest possible amount of pressure on the defense during the pre-trial proceedings so as to force a plea of guilty to one charge (ideally the most serious charge), rather than go to trial and risk being convicted on several charges. The principle is to "charge high and work down".

One test of the extent to which the deputy district attorneys "stacked" charges is to determine whether they increased or decreased the number of charges that were recommended by the police. Considering each case separately, the number of charges requested by the police was compared with the number of charges that were filed by the prosecutors. Several trends emerged from this part of the analysis which is presented in Table 14.1.

First, the likelihood of a case being completely "kicked out" by the deputy district attorneys decreases as the number of charges requested by the police increases. Second, the likelihood of the prosecutors filing the same number of charges as were requested by the police also decreases. Thus in 75 percent of the cases, where

171

TABLE 14.1

Relationship Between the Number of
Charges Requested by Police and the Number of
Charges Filed by Prosecutors
(Percents)

Number of Charges Requested	No Charges Filed	At Least One Charge Filed, but Fewer than Requested	Same Number Filed as Requested	More Charges Filed than Requested	Number
1	20	—	73	7	1,269
2	21	20	52	6	504
3	17	25	48	10	107
4	14	26	48	12	42
5+	10	57	33	—	40

only one charge was requested, one charge was also filed. But in only
33 percent of the cases, where five or more charges were requested,
did the prosecutors file the same number. The third trend involves
the prosecutors' decision to reduce the number of charges short of
kicking out the case completely. The data indicate a progressive
increase, so that the likelihood of charge reduction (in terms of number of charges) goes up as the number of requested charges increases.
Another way of viewing this is that the chances of at least one charge
being filed by the D.A. is quite high when there are many charges
made by the police against the suspect. The final trend has to do
with the practice of "stacking" as defined in this paper. Table 14.1
shows that while the practice is not pronounced, it nevertheless does
exist. As the number of requested charges increases, the practice
of "stacking" also increases, that is, the number of charges filed by
the D.A.'s exceeds the number of charges requested by the police.
Compared to stacking, the D.A.'s are more likely to reduce the number of charges. However, the differential between these two types
of decisions tends to become less, and the phenomenon of "stacking"
becomes somewhat more pronounced as the number of requested
charges increases.

One would have expected "stacking" to be more pronounced in
those cases where the police had requested only one or two charges.
But just the reverse is true. It is possible that cases with many

charges tend, on the average, to be the weaker ones, and the prosecutors compensate for it by adding to the list of those recommended by the police. This interpretation does in fact receive support from data presented in a subsequent section. Another possibility is that in multiple-charge cases the police are not likely to request all of the charges possible, either because of an oversight or because of lack of familiarity with the various sections of the penal code. In this event, the D.A. would catch these additional charges and include them in the criminal complaint.

Convictability and Multiple Charging. Generally speaking, the charging practices of prosecuting attorneys are linked to their perception of the chances of winning a conviction. Charging of defendants, therefore, is a crucial decision; it can mean the difference between a dismissal and a conviction. While the deputy district attorney is constrained in deciding whether or not to file a criminal complaint or in the types of charges to file, by whether he believes a suspect to be guilty of a crime as charged by the police, by far the most important constraint is the likelihood of his winning a conviction. His effectiveness as a prosecutor is measured almost exclusively in terms of the number of convictions he wins. Thus, as a general rule, if a case stands a good chance of resulting in a conviction, the deputy D.A. is very likely to proceed with the complaint. But if the case is a "dog", he might refuse the case. However, because many cases that are referred by the police are technically weak and do not stand a good chance of conviction, the deputy feels constrained to "go" on the case anyway; refusing to prosecute too many cases, no matter how weak, can result in a reputation of being too "soft". Hence the deputy must use all of his experience and skill to make the case as strong and convincing as possible, not only to the court, but also to the defense attorney. One way of "making a strong case out of a weak one" is to multiple charge or "stack" charges against the defendant, thereby improving the "convictability" of the case. Given a relatively weak case, a defendant charged with several crimes is more likely to plead guilty than one who is charged with only one crime. Using this perspective, then, we should observe the practice of multiple charging to be more frequent in those cases which the deputy district attorneys believe to be difficult to win. Conversely, we should not observe as high a charging rate in those cases that have a high probability of conviction.

To test this argument, two measures were constructed. The first is the defendant rate and is defined as the number of defendants prosecuted per ten suspects referred by the police. This rate provides an indirect measure of the "willingness" of the D.A.'s to prosecute defendants. If the defendant rate is high, then it may be assumed that the deputy district attorneys believe they have a good chance of winning a conviction for the particular category of defendant. If the defendant rate is low, then this would suggest a more conservative attitude, indicating that the deputies believe the chances of conviction are not good.

The second measure is the gross charging rate, and refers to the total number of charges filed against the defendants under consideration. In a strong case, as reflected in a high defendant rate, there should be a low gross charging rate. A weak case, as defined by a low defendant rate, should be associated with a high gross charging rate.

The defendant rates for persons charged with different types of crimes were computed, and then ranked. The gross charging rates for defendants in each of the different offense categories were also computed and ranked. The resulting data are presented in Table 14.2. The first column in Table 14.2 shows the rank order of the defendant rate for different types of offenses.

As can be seen, the defendant rate for violence against police is lowest, while the same rate for drugs is the highest. The gross charging rate for each offense category is shown in the last column on the right. Comparison of the first and last columns indicates a fairly clear inverse relationship.

The picture depicted in Table 14.2 is one that suggests considerable rationality on the part of the prosecuting attorneys. Based on their socialization and experience in prosecuting different types of cases, they become sensitized to the various legal and technical problems associated with different types of cases. They learn what the parameters are for each type of case and charge accordingly. They learn that certain types of cases will result in a conviction no matter what; other types of cases have inherent problems built in them. The data strongly suggest that those cases which involve the greatest number of technical and legal problems, as reflected by the defendant rate, are the same ones that have the most charges filed against them. From the rank order of the defendant rates, it is apparent that the deputies demonstrated a clear reluctance to prosecute cases involving violence and weapons because of the problems they present in winning a conviction. Hence when the D.A. decided to proceed with this type of case, they filed as many charges which they believed the "facts" of the case warranted. Thus, for example, there were 16 persons suspected of committing an act of violence against the police. Only 11 of these persons were prosecuted, but they had a total of 44 charges filed against them by the deputy district attorneys. On the other hand, the rank order of the defendant rates for minor theft, major theft, and offenses against public order indicates that the D.A.'s were clearly more willing to prosecute these types of cases. Their confidence in the ultimate outcome of these cases is

TABLE 14.2

Rank Order of Defendant-Suspect Rate and
Gross Charging Rate

	Defendants per Ten Suspects	Total Number Charges Filed	Number of Defendants	Gross Charges per Ten Defendants
Violence against police	6.9	44	11	40.0
Violence against civilians	7.0	203	74	27.4
Illegal driving	7.7	580	384	15.1
Weapons	8.3	79	29	27.2
Major theft	8.6	277	133	20.8
Public disorder	8.7	279	182	15.3
Minor theft	9.5	221	147	15.0
Drugs	9.7	262	110	23.8

reflected in the fact that they filed fewer charges against these defendants.

Table 14.2 indicates that there were only two instances where
the deputies were not, at least on the surface, entirely "rational".
The first of these involves the category of illegal driving offenses,
such as speeding, reckless driving, and drunk driving. The rate of
prosecuting defendants charged with this type of offense is low, and
at the same time the charging rate is low as well. From my observations, the conviction for drunk driving is almost a certainty; these
is also true for other speeding offenses. Hence, it is understandable
as to why the D.A.'s charged at a low rate. What is not clearly understood, however, is why the deputies were reluctant to prosecute this
type of case in the first place? Perhaps the police are more likely
to make "charging errors" in the category of illegal driving. This
might be especially true with the categories of reckless driving,
speed contest, basic speed law, etc., where the municipal police,
especially, do not have a sufficient opportunity to "clock" a driver
believed to be speeding.

The second instance where the deputy district attorneys are
not seemingly rational is in the area of drug-related offenses. Here
the defendant rate is the highest of all. The data show that the D.A.'s
were most willing to prosecute these cases, and yet they also had a

very high charging rate as well. The contradiction is more apparent than real, however, because the head administrator of the agency - the district attorney - had set a policy instructing his deputies to prosecute all drug-related cases that came to their attention. Hence, the defendant rate in this instance was high, not necessarily because of easy or sure convictions, but rather because of a policy-decision made by the administration.

Summary and Conclusions

This paper has dealt with the discretionary dispositions of deputy district attorneys at the municipal court level. After reviewing the data collected, it is clear that these decisions, at least on the municipal court level, cannot be understood apart from the activities of law enforcement agencies. First, it is clear that if a case referred by the police contains several charges it has a considerably better chance of being accepted for prosecution than if the case contains only one or two charges. Second, while it may be of interest to learn that the prosecutors refused to file complaints in about 20 percent of the cases, of much greater significance is the finding that refusal to prosecute is bound closely with police deviance as implied in department practices of multiple charging of suspects. Refusal to prosecute may be viewed as a form of sanction used by the deputies against the police. It is invoked not so much to keep police from deviating from procedural norms as it is for their failure to refer cases in an "acceptable" form, that is, in a way that would make it possible for the deputy to build a convincing enough case to result in a conviction. Police deviance from the perspective of the D.A., is not failure to conform to legal procedural rules; it is failure to do those things that must be done in order to successfully prosecute a case. An acceptable case need not be technically and legally perfect. Indeed, police cases are almost never free of problems, and it is the D.A.'s task to iron them out. Some problems, of course, can never be ironed out no matter how diligent and zealous the prosecutor might be. If it is not possible for the D.A. to somehow link the suspect in time and place to the commission of the crime, the case is not prosecutable. Hence, an acceptable case must be one that the D.A. can "work with"; there must be something that he can "salvage" from it in order to have a reasonable chance of winning a conviction.

But not all cases have an equal chance of being "acceptable". Certain categories of cases have more "build-in" problems than others. As a result, the police vary in the rates at which they refer different types of cases, and prosecutors vary in the rates at which they prosecute different types of cases. In general, cases involving drugs and violence are plagued with more problems than cases involving theft. To compensate for these built-in inadequacies, both the police and prosecutors use the strategy of multiple charging.

These general rules are tempered by the policies set down by the administration in the district attorney's office. Political considerations frequently enter into the decisions of whether or not to prosecute; drug-related offenses are the best examples of this in the county studied. According to the perspective developed here, drug-related offenses have many built-in problems, and therefore should not be processed either by the police or prosecutors, at a very high rate. This is certainly true for the police, but it is not true for the prosecutors. The latter group prosecuted almost 10 defendants for every 10 suspects referred to them for this type of offense. The policies of the bureaucracy took precedence in this particular instance.

References

Blumberg, A.
  1967   "The practice of law as a confidence game: organizational
          cooptation of a profession." Law and Society Review 1
          (March):15-39.

Chevigney, P.
  1969   Police Power: Police Abuses in New York City. New York:
          Pantheon.

Newman, D. J.
  1956   "Pleading guilty for considerations: a study of bargain
          justice." Journal of Criminal Law, Criminology, and Police
          Science 46 (March-April):780-790.

Skolnick, J. H.
  1966   Justice Without Trial. New York: Wiley.

Sudnow, D.
  1965   "Normal crimes: sociological features of the penal code
          in a public defenders office". Social Problems 12 (Winter):
          255-276.

15

INCOMPETENCY TO
STAND TRIAL:
THE EASY WAY IN?
Henry J. Steadman
and Jeraldine Braff

The issues surrounding the area of competency to stand trial have probably become more visible in the United States during the past decade than at any time since the advent of special security hospitals for the criminally insane in the late 19th and early 20th century.[1] This visibility has resulted from a number of forces. There have been the activities of Legal Aide Societies and the ACLU that have resulted in court decisions giving criminally committed patients the right to treatment (Nason v. Superintendent Bridgewater S.H. 233 NE 2d 908 (Mass, 1968)), granting them equal protection with civil committment procedural safeguards (Baxstrom v. Herold 383 U.S. 107 (1966)), and requiring the release or civil committment of defendants who will not regain competency within a "reasonable period of time" (Jackson v. Indiana 92 Ct. 1945 (1972)). Another major force increasing this visibility has been the ferment in U.S. prisons leading to proposals for more humanitarian treatment and rehabilitation partly by expanding psychiatric services. Such suggestions raise serious, broad questions of what types of psychiatric services should be incorporated and their appropriateness in the criminal justice system. There even has been some public interest in many of these issues generated by such works as Titicut Follies.

The plethora of issues surrounding incompetency statutes, procedures, and uses are important, among other reasons, because they may be raised at any point in criminal justice processing from arrest through sentencing. It is the first possible diversion from the criminal justice system into the mental health system. This question of competency may be raised by just about anyone involved in the case, the arresting officer, the defendants' family, defense counsel, the arraigning judge, or the trial judge. The literature suggests, with little empirical justification, that the trial judge and the defense counsel are the two most frequent referers. The roles of the police and other agents in raising the question of competency are completely open to question and may be considerably more significant than the literature currently indicates.

There are many suggestions in the research literature (Cooke et al., 1973; Laczko, et al., 1971; Brackel and Rock, 1971; McGarry, 1969 and 1965; Matthews, 1967; and Hess and Thomas, 1963) that competency proceedings serve a multitude of purposes other than a genuine concern for the defendant's mental state and ability to stand trial; that it becomes secondary to other functions served by the diversionary process. Hess and Thomas (1963) concluded that the question of competency was raised not on the basis of a defendant's mental status, but rather was employed as a means of handling situations for which there seemed to be no other recourse under the law. Eizenstat (1968) similarly suggested that incompetency was simply an easier method than civil committment to handle minor offenses which could have been unprosecuted, but had high nuisances value. Matthews (1967):1574)concluded that there was "a tendency on the part of officials to transform by conscious manipulation the competency procedures into a sophisticated vehicle for dispositional decisions."

McGarry has contended that through the use of the incompetency diversion the defendants, ". . . right to a trial on the merits tends to be obscured out of concern for the protection of society" (McGarry, 1965:626). This societal protection rationale is especially ironic in light of the three studies which compare the recidivism rates of incompetent defendants (and other "criminally insane patients) with convicted offenders (Zeidler, 1955; Morrow and Peterson, 1966; and McGarry, 1971). In every case they found rates lower for the criminally insane than for comparable criminal populations. This system has traditionally functioned with few checks for patient civil liberties permitting instead, very long detention in mental facilities with minimal review for return to trial or involuntary civil, rather than criminal hospitalization (Hess and Thomas, 1963; McGarry, 1965; Morrow and Peterson, 1966; Tuteur, 1969; Lewin, 1968; and Steadman and Halfon, 1971). In the balance between individual rights and the protection of society, the latter has consistently been dominant. This is especially questionable in light of the data indicating this perceived need for special protection is illusory. The research on competency indicates that a primary reason that the right to trial is denied to these individuals is that this might be the most organizationally convenient way to process them through a complicated system.

One major difficulty in integrating previous work to reach some closure on how incompetency is actually used is the incomparability between and within these studies of the charges of defendants evaluated for competency and of those found incompetent. The research concerning the charges of defendants referred for competency evaluation are quite inconsistent, ranging from serious property crimes being the most frequently reported in Massachusetts (Balcanoff and McGarry, 1969) and Florida (Drummond, 1970) to serious assault crimes in Pennsylvania (Jablon et al., 1970 and Sadoff, et al., 1967) to non-serious crimes being most frequent in Kansas (Maxon and Neuringer, 1970). The most recently reported data, which are from Michigan, (Cooke et al., 1973) suggest that the previous data on the offense frequencies are inadequate and they attribute the inconsistencies to one confounding variable - the difference among state crime rates. By analyzing the charges of defendants referred for competency evaluations as a function of the rate for each crime within the state, Cooke et al. imply that some means will exist for interstate comparisons.

This problem of developing comparable base rate statistics for incompetent defendants anchored in state crime rates is very critical. Only with such statistics is it possible to address many of the questions about the uses of incompetency as a diversionary process from the criminal justice system. To find that the highest frequency of crimes among a group of defendants evaluated or found incompetent is for violent crimes says little of substantial value. If, for example, violent crimes are also the most frequent offenses in that state, there would be nothing remarkable about this distribution among incompetency cases. The same would be true of any offense category. Thus, most of the previous studies, excepting the most recent one of Cooke et al., do not provide these base rates and are not really able to address the serious question that they nevertheless have discussed. It is our intent here to develop such rates for New York and then to proceed with a brief discussion of some implications of the obtained rates.

Methods and Sample

The larger research project from which this material was developed was undertaken to focus on the problems of those defendants who were actually found incompetent. We began our work when New York's revised Criminal Procedure Law (CPL) became effective on September 1, 1971. A significant section of this revision dealt with some major changes in the handling of incompetent defendants. Central to the intents of these revisions was the confinement of fewer incompetent defendants in maximum security hospitals and their more rapid return to trial. To effect this, criminal charges were dropped in misdemeanant cases with a finding of incompetency and a 90 day commitment to a civil mental hospital was ordered. The only incompetent felony defendants who were eligible for maximum security institutionalization in a correctional mental hospital were those indicted and found dangerous by the court. All other incompetent felony defendants were to be detained in civil mental facilities. A number of facets of these changes and their effects are currently under study by us such as: how dangerousness is actually being determined; who these incompetent people actually are; and how the Department of Mental Hygiene is adapting to the care and custody of a large number of incompetent felony defendants who formerly would have been in correctional facilities.

The material we are reporting here deals with all 541 male felony defendants who were found incompetent to stand trial in the CPL's first year of operation. The portion of our data which we are discussing centers on the offense distributions of these individuals. It seems reasonable to generalize whatever findings we may reach from these defendants found incompetent to all those defendants evaluated, since the two research reports which examine the relationship between charges and determinations of competency (Laczko et al., 1970 and Cook, 1969) found no significant relationship.

The two data sources we employed were the NYS Department of Correctional Services arrest statistics for 1971, the most recent available at the time of the research, and institutional and district attorney records for the defendants in our research population.

Findings

Comparing the rankings of the frequency of arrest charges of our 541 incompetent defendants with all felony arrests in New York presents some striking similarities. In our population Robbery, Burglary, and Assault charges rank one, two, and three, while in state arrest statistics they rank, respectively third, second, and fourth.

However, further analysis of this table does indicate that the most frequent statewide charge, Dangerous Drugs, representing 20.7 percent of all felony arrests, is not among the top eight charges in the incompetent population. On the other side, Murder, the charge of 14.4 percent of the incompetent defendants, is not among the top eight state offenses.

The significant differences that are initially suggested by the drug and murder offense rankings come clearly into focus when these arrest figures are converted into base rates. In New York in 1971, there were 941 arrests for murder, .8 percent of the 114,948 felony arrests. Thus, of every 1,000 arrests, 8 were for murder. However, of every 1,000 incompetent felony defendants, 144 were accused

TABLE 15.1

Comparison of New York State Felony Arrest Charges
Statewide and for Incompetent Defendants

| NYS 1971 Felony Arrests | | NYS Incompetent Defendants 9/'71-8/'72 | |
Offense	Percent	Offense	Percent
Dangerous Drugs	20.7	Robbery	21.2
Burglary	18.6	Burglary	18.9
Robbery	13.4	Assault	15.8
Assault	10.4	Murder	14.4
Grand Larceny-Auto	6.4	Arson	6.6
Crim. Poss. Stolen Prpty.	5.9	Misc. Felonies	4.1
Dangerous Weapons	5.4	Rape	3.4
Forgery	4.4	Grand Larceny-except Auto	3.2
All Others	14.8	All Others	12.4
Total	100.0	Total	100.0

of murder, making murder charges 18 times overrepresented among defendants found incompetent than would be expected based on the frequency of this charge among all felony arrests.

A greater grasp of some of the vast discrepancies that are evident among the charges of incompetent defendants can be seen in Table 15.2.

Here it is apparent that violent crimes against persons are consistently and highly overrepresented among incompetent defendants. Contrarily, drug and property offenses are drastically underrepresented. For example, dangerous drug offenses represent 20.7 percent of all state felony arrests, but only 2.6 percent of the charges of our incompetent population. Of every 1,000 drug arrests, .6 are found incompetent, which compares with 82 murder defendants per 1,000 murder arrests.

Murder defendants are being declared incompetent at a substantially higher rate than any other offense category. Following closely are arsonists (67 incompetent determinations per 1,000 arson arrests). Arsonists are also considerably overrepresented in our research population compared to arson arrests statewide (.5 percent total arrest statewide as compared to 6.6 percent of all incompetency determinations). The high rate of incompetency determinations per statewide arrests in that category coincide with Cooke et al.'s (1973) finding where arson had the highest rate of referal for competency evaluations. In their work Cooke and colleagues attributed this high rate to the fact that arson is thought by persons who evaluate mentally ill offenders to be related to psychopathology and they suggest that judges and attorneys have also become aware of this. Also, in keeping with the Cooke study, is our finding that rape and other sex offenses, particularly inflamatory offenses of public concern, have the fourth highest incompetency rate with 11 incompetent cases per 1,000 such arrests compared to one of every 1,000 felony arrests being for sex offenses. The violent or potentially violent offenses are ranked first, Robbery and assault follow, while the property offenses of Burglary and Larceny were at the lower end of offenses associated with incompetency determinations, although the latter are among the most frequent arrest charges.

Discussion

There are two dominant, but opposing explanations that are suggested as most probable for the significant discrepancies in the offense distribution rates we have found. The first is that such discrepancies between violent crime arrest rates and offenses among incompetent defendants are to be expected since mental illness is

TABLE 15.2

Base-Rates of New York State Felony Arrest
Charges Statewide and for Incompetent Defendants

Offense	1971 NYS Arrests		Incompetent Defendants		N/1,000 Arrests per offense
	Number	Percent	Number	Percent	
Murder	941	.8	77	14.4	81.8
Arson	525	.5	35	6.6	66.7
Nelg. Homicide	95	.1	2	.4	21.1
Rape	1,598	1.4	18	3.4	11.3
Other sex off.	811	.7	9	1.7	11.1
Malic. Misch.	596	.5	5	.9	8.4
Manslaughter	268	.2	2	.4	7.5
Robbery	15,355	13.4	113	21.2	7.4
Assault	12,012	10.5	84	15.8	7.0
Burglary	21,346	18.6	101	18.9	4.7
G.L.-ec. auto	4,965	4.3	17	3.2	3.4
Dang.Weap.off.	6,182	5.4	14	2.6	2.3
Driving w. into.	508	.4	1	.2	2.0
G.L.-Auto	7,382	6.4	11	2.1	1.5
Crim.Poss.St.Prop.	6,740	5.9	5	.9	.7
Forgery	5,084	4.4	3	.6	.6
Dang.Drug Off.	23,803	20.7	14	2.6	.6
Gambling	2,314	2.0	0	.0	.0
All other fel.	4,423	3.8	22	4.1	5.0
Total	114,948	100.0	533*	100.0	

*There were eight individuals for whom arrest charges were not available.

linked to such behavior. The second explanation is that such discrepancies are the result of dispositional ploys on the part of both
prosecution and defense. This latter argument is the one which appears the most viable to us on the basis of existing research and our
own data.

The idea of isomorphism between violent crime and mental
illness has been associated with the mentally ill label since this label
evolved. It now appears to be an idea whose time has gone. There
is striking consistency among recent discussions of the relationships
between violent crime and mental illness that "the terms sociopath,
latent homosexual schizophrenic and others have been carelessly
used, with a resulting impression that everyone, especially the criminal, is mentally ill. . . . Is every irresponsible, ill conceived or
criminal act evidence of underlying mental illness? Few would say
so" (Mueller, 1968:189). Support for this statement comes from
numerous sources. There are research studies such as Guze et al:
(1969:590) whose nine year follow-up of convicted felons concluded,
"Schizophrenia, manic-depressive disease, organic brain syndromes,
the neuroses, and homosexuality are apparently not seen more frequently in criminals than in the general population." Rollins' (1972)
and Rubin's (1972) literature reviews similarly determined that
"epidemilogical data indicate that (1) major mental illness rates are
not comparable to violence rates and (2) the distribution of major
mental illness is not the same as the distribution of violence" (Rubin,
1972:400). Finally, Schwartz defining dangerousness as aggressiveness,
hatred, and psychopathy (1971:22) concluded that "it is usually the
less mentally ill person who is more dangerous."

Explaining the overrepresentation of violent crimes among the
incompetent defendants studied here by linking mental illness to the
commission of such crimes appears untenable. Rather, it would
seem to be what has been suggested in a number of previous studies -
the use of incompetency as a diversion from the criminal justice
system greatly depends on non-medical, dispositional, and procedural
machinations. In this latter frame of reference there are some very
serious questions surrounding determinations of incompetency that
arise. What is it about the referral sources that makes them more
inclined to refer for evaluation persons with particular charges
(murder, arson, sex offenses)? Do police officers consider the crimes
of murder, arson, etc. as those offenses most indicative of mental
illness? Does referral at the prosecution stage perhaps indicate
that prosecutors are glad to rid themselves of immediate or, in some
cases, eventual prosecution of certain crimes, knowing that the accused
will be detained in a secure facility for a considerable amount of time?
Precisely for what reasons are people being diverted into these mental
health systems? Is incompetency the easy way into detention and

the easy way out of proseuction? For these critical questions no
data presently exist.

The overrepresentation of violent crimes in our population is
further significant when we consider that those accused of serious
crimes are more likely to spend more time being detained in the
mental health system without the protections afforded by the criminal
justice system. Since this time may be "dead time," it often means
a longer total institutionalization than if conviction had ensued before
the incompetency diversion. Furthermore, from the rationale of
protecting society, these are the people who have lower recidivism
rates once returned to the community.

These are some of the very serious questions our data and
previous research raise about the use of incompetency determinations
as diversions from the criminal justice system. There is much in
our work to suggest that incompetency may be the procedurally easy
way of getting a defendant into a custodial situation while serving as
the prosecution's easy way out of immediate or eventual trial. Vann
(1965:30) reflects on such practices:

> In practice this means that as long as an alleged offender
> is not at large the actual disposition of a case will not
> tend to arouse the populace. The removal of accused
> persons to hospitals for the criminally insane at the
> pretrial stage effectively disposes of most of these
> cases unless the mass media should arouse the com-
> munity to the danger of an accused's possible return to
> the community. A rather odd, but fascinating, situation
> can thus arise where an accused person who has been
> committed to a hospital for the criminally insane asks
> a court for release from the institution. The granting
> of this request permits not freedom, but the ability to
> return to the jurisdiction of the court for the purpose
> of standing trial. In these situations the nature of the
> adversary system, community strategy, and in some
> cases lack of a presentable case at trial (due to time
> intervals) find the prosecutor opposing the petition of
> the accused person to be released from the mental
> institution and thus continuing the individual's "hospi-
> talization" in many instances as a substitute for prison.
> While the practical result may be to prevent community
> concern, there is also an additional obfuscation of the
> judicial administrative process when prosecutors at-
> tempt to keep untried persons away from the judicial
> resolution of the charges against them.

Certainly, the other possible explanation for our findings, that mental illness goes hand in hand with the commission of violent crimes against persons, is easily and comfortably accepted by the public, but it is a link which empirically has been rejected by psychiatry. The differential crime distributions in our data, appear related to questionable uses of incompetency. Unfortunately, data on the dynamics and impacts of the process of evaluation and determination of incompetency are characterized by vast gaps. However, the attention which has been paid to these burgeoning sources of criminal justice diversion indicate questionable practices and inappropriate diversions.

Note

1. The incisive comments of Joseph Cocozza on earlier drafts of the manuscript contributed greatly to the final product. This research was partially supported by PHS Grant MH 20367 from the Center for Studies of Crime and Delinquency.

References

Balcanoff, E.J. and A. L. McGarry
  1969   "Amicus Curiae: the role of the psychiatrist in pre-trial examination," American Journal of Psychiatry 126 (September):342-347.

Brackel, S. J. and R. S. Rock
  1971   The Mentally Disabled and the Law. Chicago: University of Chicago Press.

Cooke, G.
  1969   "The court study unit: patient characteristics and differences between patients judged competent and incompetent." Journal of Clinical Psychology 25 (April):140-143.

Cooke, G. N. Johnston, and E. Pogany
  1973   "Factors affecting referral to determine competency to stand trial." American Journal of Psychiatry 130 (August): 870-875.

Drummond, G.
  1970   "Characteristics of 273 offenders referred for evaluation to the Department of Forensic Psychiatry, Jackson Memorial Hospital, August 1966 through December, 1967." Southern Conference on Corrections Proceedings 15:23-31.

Eizenstat, S.
  1968   "Mental competency to stand trial," Harvard Civil Rights-
          Civil Liberties Law Review 4:379-413.

Guze, S. B., D. W. Goodwin, and J. B. Crane
  1969   "Criminality and psychiatric disorders," Archieves of
          General Psychiatry 20 (May):583-591.

Hess, J. H., Jr. and H. E. Thomas
  1963   "Incompetency to stand trial: procedures, results, and
          problems," American Journal of Psychiatry 119 (February):
          713-720.

Jablon, N.C., R. Sadoff, and M.S. Heller
  1970   "A unique forensic diagnostic hospital." American Journal
          of Psychiatry 126 (May):1663-1667.

Laczko, A.L., J.F. James, and L.B. Alltop
  1970   "A study of four hundred and thirty five courtreferred
          cases." Journal of Forensic Sciences 15 (July):311-323.

Lewin, T H.
  1968   "Disposition of the irresponsible: protection following
          committment." Michigan Law Review 66 (February):
          721-736.

Matthews, A. R.
  1967   "Mental illness and the criminal law: is community mental
          health the answer?" American Journal of Public Health
          57 (September):1571-1579.

Maxon, L.S. and C. Neuringer
  1970   "Evaluating legal competency." Journal of Genetic Psy-
          chology 117 (December):267-273.

McGarry, A. L.
  1965   "Competency for trial and due process via the state hospi-
          tal." American Journal of Psychiatry 122 (December):
          623-631.
  1969   "Demonstration and research in competency to stand trial
          and mental illness: review and preview." Boston University
          Law Review 49 (Winter):46-61.
  1971   "The fate of psychotic offenders returned to trial," American
          Journal of Psychiatry 127 (March):101-104.

Morrow, W. R. and D. Peterson
    1968   "Follow-up of discharged psychiatric offenders -'not guilty
              by reason of insanity' and 'criminal sexual psychopath'."
              The Journal of Criminal Law, Criminology and Police
              Sciences 57 (March):31-34.

Muller, D. J.
    1968   "Involuntary mental hospitalization." Comprehensive
              Psychiatry 9 (May):187-193.

Rollins, R.
    1972   "Crime and mental illness viewed as deviant behavior."
              North Carolina Journal of Mental Health 6 (Winter):18-25.

Rosenberg, A.H. and A.L. McGarry
    1972   "Competency for trial: the making of an expert," American
              Journal of Psychiatry 128 (March):82-86.

Rubin, B.
    1972   "The prediction of dangerousness in mentally ill criminals,"
              Archives of General Psychiatry 77 (September):397-407.

Sadoff, R.L., S. Polsky, and M.S. Heller
    1967   "The forensic psychiatric clinic: model for a new approach,"
              American Journal of Psychiatry 123 (May):1402-1407.

Schwartz, D. W.
    1971   "Psychiatry and the new Criminal Procedure Law: III
              the problem of the malingering defendant," Mimeo. Depart-
              ment of Psychiatry, SUNY, Downstate Medical Center.

Steadman, H. J. and A. Halfon
    1971   "The Baxstrom patients: backgrounds and outcomes,"
              Seminars in Psychiatry 3 (August):376-385.

Tuteur, W.
    1969   "Incompetent to stand trial: a survey." Corrective Psychi-
              atry and Journal of Social Therapy 15 (July):73-79.

Vann, C. R.
    1965   "Pre-trial determination and decision making: an analysis
              of the use of psychiatric information in the administration
              of criminal justice," University of Detroit Law Review 43
              (1):13-33.

Zeidler, J.C., W.H. Haines, V. Tikuisis, and E.J. Uffelman
1955 "A follow-up study of patients discharged from a hospital for the criminally insane," Journal of Social Therapy 1 (January):21-24.

16

THE USE OF DISCRETION
IN PUNISHING CONVICTED
ADULT OFFENDERS

Joseph Elmo Scott
and Richard D. Vandiver

Over the years, sentencing theories have fluctuated between two extremes: identical disposition of all persons convicted of the same offense, and individualized disposition based on the character of the offender. The rigidity and subsequent harshness of uniform sentencing without consideration of mitigating factors led to the development of the indeterminate sentence and the utilization of parole boards to determine when offenders had undergone sufficient punishment (or treatment). Individualized disposition as it operates today, however, presents the possibility that parole boards will abuse their discretion by requiring different periods of incarceration for the same offense without justification.

The extent of the parole boards' discretion varies greatly from one jurisdiction to another. The use of discretion by parole boards has been a topic generally neglected by students of criminology (Dawson, 1966). Few studies have investigated the processes which determine when, how, and why legal norm violators, who have been found guilty and incarcerated, should be released from penal institutions (Vasoli, 1965; Editorial Note, 1960). In part, this situation emerges from the maxim in American correctional ideology, that release from prison before the maximum portion of the sentence has been served "is a privilege rather than a right". However, the increasing concern for "due process" and for curtailment and control of arbitrary use of power in administering justice makes the

The Authors wish to thank Curt Griffiths and Ed Hall who gathered the data for the Western sample and Dr. Gordon Browder who made it available. For a more extensive description of the Western data see Edwin Holt, "The Indian Offender in Montana," unpublished M.A. thesis, University of Montana, 1973.

correctional process and particularly, the paroling process likely candidates for scrutiny at this time (Dressler, 1967; Editorial Comment, 1972).

This study focuses specifically on the criteria utilized by parole boards in determining the proper amount of punishment a convicted adult felony offender should receive. Specific attention is focused on three principle factors: (1) legal, (2) institutional and (3) socio-biographical, which are similar to those used in Green (1966). These three factors were selected because of their relationship to correctional ideology and criminological theory. The legal factor is the primary consideration in determining the punishment according to the retributive perspective. The severity of punishment is to be determined by the seriousness of the crime. The institutional approach (factor) is closely associated with the reformative approach to corrections, which advocates the incarceration of individuals only until they are rehabilitated. An indicator of an individual's rehabilitation is his institutional behavior. Finally, the personal biographical factor is closely associated with the conflict or power theory of criminology. This theory maintains that those individuals with more power in society will receive more consideration and more favorable treatment by representatives of the legal institutions.

Method

The data for this study was gathered from the prison records of one Midwestern state's adult penal institutions for felony offenders and the records of the Board of Pardons of one Western state. The prison records consist primarily of information compiled and submitted to the parole boards before each inmate's parole hearing. The Board of Pardons' records contain similar information collected by an institutional parole officer. In all cases these records provide the respective parole boards with the documentary information they have to act upon in deciding whether the inmate is to be released.[1]

The research sample consists of the records of all female inmates released from two prisons for women in 1968 (Midwestern Women's Prison N = 34, Western Women's Prison N = 5); a twenty-five percent random sample of the records of all male inmates released from two Midwestern Adult felony penal institutions during 1968 (N = 325); and the records of all male inmates released from one Western Prison also in 1968 (N = 152). In addition to the prison records, field observations were conducted at each of the three Midwestern institutions over a six month period.[2] The data will be analyzed and discussed as Midwestern or Western data.

Correlation and multiple regression analysis is used to analyze the data. Pearson correlation coefficients provide an indication of the linearity of the relationship of each independent variable to the dependent variable. By using multiple regression analysis, the effect of variations within each independent variable upon the dependent variable is provided (unstandardized b) as is the importance of the ability of various independent variables to explain variation in the dependent variable (standardized β). In addition, using this type of analysis allows examination of variables categorized as legal, institutional or social-biographical sets and thereby allows determination of the relationship of each set to the dependent variable.

The variables examined for their possible effect upon variations in the severity of punishment comprise three factors:

Legal Factor. The seriousness of the crime (the legal minimum sentence, in months, imposed by the courts),[3] and the prior criminal involvement of each inmate (prior criminal involvement was quantified by weighting prior prison incarcerations, felony and misdemeanor arrests and convictions).[4]

Institutional Factor. Disciplinary reports (the number received while incarcerated) and institutional adjustment (for the Midwest prisons composed of eight separate indicators from which a scale was constructed by item analysis, Cronback's Alpha = .621). The eight indicators are:

Inmate's Overall Progress
Inmate's Overall Cooperation
Inmate's Overall Attitude
Inmate's Participation in Institutional Programs and/or
    Clubs (Number)
Inmate's Work Reports
Inmate's Housing Reports
Inmate's Participation in Vocational Training
Inmate's Participation in School Program

Because of limitations in the data, institutional adjustment for the Western sample consists solely of having enrolled in school at some time during an inmate's incarceration or not having so participated.

Personal-Biographical Factor. Age (at time of release), education (number of years of school completed), I.Q. (as determined by the Revised Beta Examination administered shortly after an inmate's admittance to prison), information on I.Q. was available on only eight of the 157 Western inmates and therefore not included in the analysis of the Western data, marital status (single; separated, widowed, or divorced; or married at the time of inmate's appearance before the

193

parole board), race (white and nonwhite), residence (resident of state in which incarcerated or not), sex, and socio-economic status (for the Midwestern offenders, as measured by Hollingshead's Occupational Status Scale on the basis of each inmate's self-reported occupation). In the Western state, an inmate's occupation was recorded only by whether he was employed full time, part time, or unemployed, at the time of his arrest.

The dependent variable, severity of punishment, is simply the number of months an inmate was incarcerated.

Findings on Legal Factors

Seriousness of Crime. The seriousness of crime for which inmates were convicted was the best predictor of the severity of punishment for both the Midwestern and the Western inmates ($\beta = .64$, $\beta = .86$). The correlation coefficients ($r = .84$ and $r = .87$) indicate a very strong relationship between the seriousness of crime and the severity of punishment. The data imply that parole boards operate on the assumption that an inmate is not ready for parole until he has suffered commensurately for the crime he committed.

Prior Criminal Involvement. The data from the Midwestern and the Western prisons differ as to the importance of prior criminal involvement. Data from the Midwestern prisons indicate an inverse relationship between prior criminal involvement and severity of punishment ($r = -.02$, $\beta = -.06$), while data from the Western prisons indicate a direct relationship between these two variables ($r = .15$, $\beta = .13$).

One possible explanation for these differences is that the Midwest parole boards often hear as many as 100 to 150 parole hearings during a typical day (five or six hours of parole board hearing time). Much of the information available for the parole boards is simply not used due to the speed with which decisions are made. The Western parole board on the other hand, has a much lighter work load and could conceivably spend more time taking such variables as prior criminal involvement into consideration. This explanation is somewhat supported by field observations in the Midwestern state. These observations revealed that if one of the parole board members indicates that the inmate whose case is being considered has a lengthy record, this inmate may be denied parole on that basis. Because decisions are made so quickly, however, reference is seldom made to anything other than the seriousness of the crime.

Findings on Institutional Factors

Disciplinary Reports. Information on disciplinary action taken against inmates was available only for the Midwest parole boards. There, the number of disciplinary reports an inmate received while incarcerated was directly related to the severity of punishment ($r = .24$). Those inmates receiving the most disciplinary reports were incarcerated the longest even when the legal seriousness of the crime and all other independent variables were controlled ($\beta = .18$). Disciplinary reports had a much stronger relationship with the severity of punishment than did an inmate's institutional adjustment. The number of disciplinary reports an individual received is already quantified for the parole board members' use, so that the condensed and readily comprehensible information on disciplinary reports is more often relied upon for information concerning an inmate's "rehabilitation" than is his institutional adjustment. Parole board members also appear to assume that inmates who receive disciplinary reports in prison are much more likely to get into trouble on the outside and thus need more time to prepare for release. The partial regression coefficient ($b = 3.37$) indicates that where two inmates are similar in all relevant characteristics (legal, institutional, and social biographical) except that one more disciplinary report the latter would be held nearly three and one-half months longer.

Institutional Adjustment. The data from neither the Midwestern sample nor the Western sample indicate that institutional adjustment is significantly related to the severity of punishment. The laws in both states however, stipulate that an inmate's institutional behavior is one of the major factors to be considered by the parole boards in determining whether to grant parole or not.

Even more surprising was the observation made by one of the authors in the Midwestern prisons, that parole board members often encouraged inmates denied parole to join institutional programs to attempt to better themselves. In fact, of one Midwestern parole board's five members interviewed, three indicated that after the seriousness of the crime, an inmate's institutional adjustment was the next most important factor in determining whether parole should be granted. The behavior to the boards, however, belies such attitudes. The manner in which decisions are made may explain why the Midwestern parole board members accept an inmate's ability to avoid disciplinary reports as the best indicator of his institutional behavior.

The extensive workload of the Midwestern parole boards probably accounts for the speed with which they make decisions. As indicated above, one of the Midwestern parole boards often hears from 100 to 150 cases per day. In an effort to adequately gauge the decision time spent per case, one of the authors recorded the time the board spent

195

one day discussing or examining material before reaching a decision on each case. The median time per case was eight seconds.[5] The time allocated to decision making gives some indication, perhaps, why variables such as an inmate's institutional adjustment and prior criminal record, neither of which are quantified and which therefore require some time and effort to assess, have little effect on the predicted severity of punishment.

Findings on Social-Biographical Factors

Age. Both the Midwestern and the Western parole boards punish older offenders more severely than younger offenders ($r = .59$, $r = .17$). The Beta coefficients indicate that of all the social-biographical variables, an inmate's age is the best predictor of the punishment to be imposed when all other variables are taken into account. The partial regression coefficient indicates that where two inmates are alike in all characteristics considered except that one is ten years older than the other, the punishment of the older inmate will be approximately sixteen months longer (10 X 1.58) in the Midwestern state and two months longer (10 X .23) in the Western state. Parole board members appear to view young offenders as being immature and simply having made a mistake. Older offenders are apparently assumed to have more control over their behavior and consequently to require more extensive treatment (punishment) before being released. This is somewhat surprising in light of numerous studies which have found younger offenders more likely to recidivate than older offenders.

Education. There was no significant relationship between severity of punishment and education. We had assumed that the better educated would receive more consideration. The correlation coefficients ($r = -.27$ and $r = -.09$) supported our assumptions as did the average time served for those with six or less grades of school completed ($\overline{X} = 79$ months and $\overline{X} = 23$) while the average time for those with thirteen or more years of school was considerably less ($\overline{X} = 16$ months and $\overline{X} = 13$). However, when the seriousness of the crime, the offenders prior criminal involvement, and all other variables were controlled, the negative relationship completely disappeared ($\beta = .00$ and $\beta = .03$) and variation in education had an insignificant effect on predicted severity of punishment.

Intelligence Quotient. Inmates with higher I.Q.'s were granted parole sooner than those with lower I.Q.'s ($r = -.16$). Offenders with I.Q.'s between 53-89 received, on the average, 59 months punishment, those with I.Q.'s above 110 averaged only 33 months punishment. Again the parole board indicated many times that an inmate with an

I.Q. "that high" should be able to stay out of trouble. However, when other variables are once again controlled, the relationship between I.Q. and punishment is statistically insignificant ($\beta = -.02$).

Marital Status. Inmates who were married were granted parole sooner than those with broken marital ties, who in turn were paroled sooner than single inmates (r = .03, b = 7.15 and r = .06, b = 2.18). This relationship was statistically significant even after controlling for the seriousness of the crime and all other independent variables.[6] Field observation once again revealed that the Midwestern parole boards often indicated to inmates that marital ties could be considered a stabilizing factor in helping a man stay out of prison, because marital ties could provide added support to the released offender.

Race. The initial analysis of the data gathered from the summary reports indicated that nonwhites were punished more severely than whites in the Midwestern state while whites received more severe punishment than nonwhites in the Western state. In the Midwestern state, the average time of incarceration for whites was 43 months compared to 60 months for nonwhites. The average time of incarceration for whites in the Western state was 21 months compared to 14 months for the nonwhite. However, the nonwhite group in the Western state was composed primarily of Indians (21 of the 25 offenders). Indians were incarcerated on the average approximately 10.5 months compared to 27 months for the nonwhite nonIndians (included in this group were two Mexicans, one Black and one individual coded simply other). Those in the Western state who are not Indians but nevertheless classified as nonwhite receive more punishment than whites—a pattern similar to that observed in the Midwestern state.

When the seriousness of the crime and other independent variables are controlled, whites receive slightly more severe punishment than nonwhites in both states, although the difference is not statistically significant. The partial regression coefficients indicate whites are punished approximately one-half month more on the average than are nonwhites in the Midwestern state (b = -.54) and approximately one month in the Western state (b = -.1.03).

There are a number of possible explanations for this most unexpected finding concerning punishment and race. First, the presence of a black on each of the parole boards in the Midwestern state and of an Indian on the parole board in the Western state may have inhibited the white members from discriminating against nonwhites in granting paroles. A second possible explanation is that members of the majority group tolerate nonconformity by members of a minority as long as such nonconformity is primarily limited to the victimization of other minority group members (Bullock, 1961). A third plausible explanation is that race is simply not a consideration in the parole board's decision-making (Green, 1966; Reiss, 1968). Still another possible explanation is that nonwhite inmates derive power from the growth of powerful civil rights groups, as well as receiving other organized political support unavailable to the majority of poor white inmates.

Residence. Although nonresidents were punished more severely than residents of the Midwestern state ($r = .02$) the opposite relationship existed in the Western state ($r = -.01$) and neither of the relationships were statistically significant. These relationships may have been significant and much stronger if comparisons had been made exclusively for residents and nonresidents not being paroled to detainers. Inmates who have detainers filed against them are generally paroled and discharged to the detainer, which absolves the paroling state from any parole supervision responsibility. Inmates who have detainers filed against them are most often nonresidents. Nonresidents who do not have a detainer filed against them are not released as early as residents in the Midwestern state. The parole board members of the Midwestern state expressed the opinion that nonresidents, if paroled to another state, are more expensive to return to prison if they do violate parole, and if paroled within the state (in which they are incarcerated) are more likely to abscond from parole. Thus, their policy is to hold nonresidents in prison longer, until they are "better prepared" for release, than is generally required for resident inmates. However, if a detainer is filed against an inmate, special consideration is often given as the following case demonstrates.

> The inmate, a former resident of New York, had been sentenced to serve ten to twenty-five years in prison for armed robbery. This thirty-seven year old inmate had recently been granted clemency (by the clemency commission—the parole board simply acting as the clemency commission) and had his minimum reduced to three years which was the exact amount of time he had served. He had a long criminal record, thirty-two previous arrests (eighteen for felonies), and this was his third time in prison. He admitted committing forty-three armed robberies in a three month period prior to this arrest, conviction, and incarceration. Two states had filed detainers against him for armed robberies he had admitted committing prior to his arrest. He had received seven disciplinary reports in the three years he had been incarcerated and had twice attempted to escape from prison. The board voted to parole and discharge him to either one of the detainers.

In the case illustrated above, the researcher inquired as to the possibility of the inmate "beating" the armed robbery charges, now three or four years old, for which the inmate had not yet been tried. A member of the board responded: "Oh, well, he'll be their problem then and not ours. There's no need for us to keep paying his room and board if New York or Wisconsin will."

Sex. Women in both the Western and Midwestern states were incarcerated for shorter periods of time than were men. Women on the average were punished 18 months in the Midwestern states and eight months in the Western states compared to 51 months and 20 months for men respectively. When all other variables are taken into account, women are incarcerated for a much shorter period of time in both states. The regression coefficients (b = -33.9 and b = -3.3) indicate that when all other independent variables are controlled, the predicted severity of punishment for women would be 34 months less in the Midwestern state and three months less in the Western state.

Prior research has already substantiated the contention that women receive more consideration than men by the police and the courts in applying formal sanctions. This research supports the same pattern, namely, that parole boards also give women more consideration than men in releasing them from prison. It appears to be a basic tenet of the American ideology that females should be treated differently than men at every stage of the criminal justice system.

Socioeconomic Status. Inmates in both states with higher socioeconomic status (SES) received more lenient treatment (punishment) than those with lower SES (r = -.01 and r = -.15). Parole board members often expressed concern with inmates ability to stay out of trouble when paroled, and apparently assumed that those who had better jobs would encounter fewer problems. Therefore, those who indicated prior experience with more prestigeful occupations were granted parole earlier even when all other independent variables were controlled (β = -.10 and β = -.07). The partial regression coefficient indicates that when all other variables are considered, a unit change in SES will decrease the predicted severity of punishment in the Midwestern state six months (b = -5.85), and in the Western state one month (b = -1.12).

Analyzing Data Categorized as Sets

When the variables categorized as legal, social-biographical, and institutional are treated as sets and examined with regards to their relationship to the severity of punishment, the legal set is by far the most significant. The legal set in the Midwestern state accounts for 70 percent of the variation in punishment ($R = .84$, $R^2 = .70$) and over 78 percent of the variation for the Western state ($R = .88$, $R^2 = .78$). The social-biographical variables, treated as a set, account for approximately 45 percent of the variation in punishment in the Midwestern state ($R = .67$, $R^2 = .45$) and for ten percent of that variation in the Western state ($R = .32$, $R^2 = .10$). The institutional data, treated as a set, accounts for only eight percent of the punishment variation in the Midwestern state ($R = .28$, $R^2 = .08$) and for a mere one percent of that variation in the Western state ($R = .11$, $R^2 = .01$).

In the Midwestern state, only an additional nine percent of the variation in the severity of punishment can be accounted for when using all eight social-biographical variables and both institutional variables after the two legal variables have explained all the variation they can. In the Western state, only an additional one percent of the variation in punishment can be accounted for when using all the social-biographical and institution variables after the two legal variables have been used.

Discussion

The positivists' ideology that an inmate should be sentenced to prison until he is rehabilitated or "ready" to return to society would appear still far removed from realization. Particularly is this the case in light of the fact that an inmate's personal social-biographical characteristics are substantially better predictors of the punishment he will receive than is his entire institutional adjustment, cooperation and participation and the prison's evaluation of his rehabilitation. Perhaps what should be seriously questioned at this point is the present usefulness of either indefinite sentences and/or of parole boards.

As indicated earlier, the extent of the parole boards' discretion varies greatly from one jurisdiction to another (O'Leary and Nuffield, 1972). However, the discretionary power of parole boards have apparently increased concommitantly with the apparent shift in the ideology of the criminal justice system from an almost exclusively "retributive" basis to a more "retributive-reformative" approach. This change in ideology has resulted in more frequent use of the indefinite or indeterminate sentence. The increased usage of the indefinite or indeterminate type of sentences by the various states has transferred the primary responsibility of determining the proper length of incarceration for each defendent from the judiciary to the parole board. By simply imposing the statutory sentence passed by the legislature for the specific offense for which the defendent was found guilty, the judiciary, in many states, has left any reconciliation of the seriousness of the crime with severity of the sentence entirely at the discretion of the parole board. Not only does the parole board have the responsibility of determining the proper length of incarceration for each offender given an indefinite sentence, but in addition many parole boards also function as the state clemency commission. In this capacity, they have the prerogative to overrule legislatively enacted minimum sentences or judicially imposed minimum or definite sentences and to release inmates when they, the clemency commission, feel that release is appropriate. This board power was conferred on the parole board in order to implement the "reformative" approach to corrections. The idea was for an agency or board to periodically review each inmates case and release him at the optimum time for him to adjust and function adequately in society. The thinking was that the judge, schooled in law and not human behavior, would not be as well qualified to determine how much treatment (punishment) specific inmates needed. Similarly, it would be difficult to predict in advance how offenders would respond to the various treatment programs provided. A solution to both of these problems was to create parole boards, composed of citizens trained in understanding human behavior, which would determine on the basis of the offenders response to institutional treatment his degree of readiness when he was ready to return to society.

The data analyzed from two states certainly do not demonstrate that parole boards function in the manner expected. The data suggest that parole boards base their decisions on legal criteria (the very ones the judge used in determining whether or not to send the offender to prison). The variables which parole boards might use in determining an offenders adjustment and improvement while incarcerated either are not provided for their use, of if provided, are relied upon very little in determining when an inmate should be released.

To make matters worse, parole board decisions have generally lacked judicial safeguards, and in addition, have not been subject to public scrutiny. Inasmuch as one of the reasons often given for prison riots is the poor and unjust parole policies, the entire parole concept should perhaps be re-examined at this time. Some have recently concluded that the entire parole concept should be abandoned (Report on New York Parole, 1974; Schwartz, 1973).

The National Council on Crime and Delinquency (1973), in a recent policy statement focused on parole. Their major concern was that:

> ... the prisoner, comparing his case to that of others who were granted parole, may see the denial as a capricious decision. He is often at a loss to understand what he has gone wrong or how he can improve his performance.

Parole board silence compounds his cynicism and his hostility to authority.

At the very least, unexplained parole denials obstruct rehabilitation yet they are quite common in many state and local jurisdictions.

Given the manner in which parole boards operate, other alternatives should perhaps be considered for deciding when offenders should be released. Several have been suggested including strict administrative guidelines for parole decision-making (Palmer, 1973). This would require parole boards to follow strict rules and regulations in making decisions, justifying denials of parole, and possibly granting certain rights to inmates previously unavailable (e.g., the right to examine records upon which decisions are based for their accuracy, or the right to appeal or have the parole decision reviewed).[7] Others have suggested the utilization of an independent ombudsman to intervene when parole and other penal injustices are observed (Fitzharris, 1973; Badillo, 1972). Still another alternative would be to simply return the punishing power strictly to the courts (Mueller, 1966). The courts could then determine the punishment a particular offender should receive either by returning to the utilization of more definite type sentences or by utilizing indefinite type sentences with specific rules and regulations concerning eligibility for release from prison. This approach would at least provide "due process" to the releasing procedure and would eliminate much of the uncertainty prevalent in prisons today.

If an inmate's institutional adjustment and development are not being used to determine the amount of punishment (or treatment) he needs, there seems to be little justification for the continued use of parole boards and for that matter the continued utilization of indefinite or indeterminate type sentences. As Norval Morris (1966) recently demanded of various segments of the criminal justice system: "... practices must cease to rest on surmise and good intentions; they must be based on facts." This is certainly applicable for parole boards. If they are not operating as expected and not fulfilling some other unsurmised purpose, then their usefulness must be reconsidered. There is little justification for a social control agency to simply increase the apprehension and uncertainty of offenders unless they are providing some legitimate social function.

Research has already indicated that there is little if any relationship between institutional adjustment and recidivism (Miller, 1971). Therefore, the continued use of parole boards and indefinite type sentences on the assumption that parole boards can better determine than a judge when an inmate is "ready" for release appears to be possibly based on a false assumption at the outset.

TABLE 16.1

Regression Analysis for Twelve Variables in Relation to Severity of Punishment

| | DEPENDENT VARIABLE | | | | | | | |
| | MIDWESTERN PRISONS[s] | | | | WESTERN PRISONS[t] | | | |
Independent Variable	Pearson's r	Regression Coefficient b	Beta Coefficient β	N	Pearson's r	Regression Coefficient b	Beta Coefficient β	N
Legal Factor[u]								
Seriousness of Crime	.84*	.31*	.64*	359	.87*	.28*	.86*	157
Prior Criminal Involvement	-.02	-.02*	-.06*	359	.15*	.02*	.13*	157
Institutional Factor[w]								
Disciplinary Reports	.24*	3.37*	.18*	338	—	—	—	
Institutional Adjustment	-.10	.33	.05	175	d-.12	-1.52	-.03	157
Socio-Biographical Factor[y]								
Age	.59*	1.58*	.31*	354	.17*	.23*	.09*	157
Education	-.27*	-.04	.00	357	-.09	.41	.03	157
I.Q.	-.16*	-.10	-.02	321	—	—	—	8
Marital Status	d.03	7.15*	.08*	357	d.06	2.18*	.06*	157
Race	d.13	-.54	.00	359	d-.10	-1.03	-.01	155
Residence	d.02	.24	.00	359	d-.01	-2.88	-.05	157
Sex	d-.16*	-33.91*	-.17*	359	d-.08	-3.32	-.02	157
Socioeconomic Status	-.01	-5.85*	.10*	359	d-.15*	-1.12*	-.07*	157

*Significant at or beyond the .05 level of probability

d-Dichotomously coded

		R	R²
s-Multiple Correlation Coefficient all Midwestern Variables:		.89	.79
t-Multiple Correlation Coefficient all Western Variables:		.89	.79
u-Multiple Correlation Coefficient Legal Factor (Midwestern):		.84	.70
v-Multiple Correlation Coefficient Legal Factor (Western):		.88	.78
w-Multiple Correlation Coefficient Institutional Factor (Midwestern):		.28	.08
x-Multiple Correlation Coefficient Institutional Factor (Western):		.11	.01
y-Multiple Correlation Coefficient Socio-Biographical Factor (Midwestern):		.67	.45
z-Multiple Correlation Coefficient Socio-Biographical Factor (Western):		.32	.10

Certainly, additional research is needed on parole board decision-making. One function they may be serving is reducing the average time convicted offenders might otherwise serve incarcerated if parole and the indeterminate type sentence structure were abandoned. There is differing opinion on this subject (Glaser, 1973), although it has been a major factor some nations have recently used in adopting the parole concept (Elman, 1973). This is certainly an area in which more empirical evidence is needed if practices are to be based upon facts and not simply good intentions. If parole boards in other states are basing their decisions almost exclusively on the legal seriousness of the crime, as the parole boards are in the Western and Midwestern states studied, this is certainly justification for carefully examining the concept of parole.

Notes

1. The Midwestern parole boards did not talk to the inmate or anyone representing him until the decision concerning parole had been made.

2. The records from 1968 were used even though the study was carried out during the 1971-1972 school year. This was done to facilitate a follow-up study and for other comparative reasons. The observations were conducted during the summer and fall of 1971.

3. For those inmates originally given a death sentence subsequently reduced to life and those given life sentences, a score of 500 was assigned. This was arrived at in a somewhat arbitrary manner.

4. Each inmate's prior criminal record was ascertained from the F.B.I. report. From these reports five separate indicators of prior criminal involvement were recorded:
   a. Total number of previous misdemeanor arrests
   b. Total number of previous felony arrests
   c. Total number of previous misdemeanor convictions
   d. Total number of previous felony convictions
   e. Total number of previous prison incarcerations

These five indicators were combined to form a prior criminal involvement scale in the following manner: First, the total number of misdemeanor arrests and the total number of felony arrests in the United States for 1968 were ascertained, as were the number of misdemeanor and felony convictions. These numbers were then divided by the United States population as of July 1, 1968, to get the percentage of the population arrested and/or convicted of misdemeanors and/or felonies during this period. The same procedure was followed for individuals sentenced to prison during 1968. The respective percentages were:

a. 0.04 percent of the population received by prisons in 1968
b. 0.49 percent of the population convicted of a felony in 1968
c. 1.41 percent of the population arrested for a felony in 1968
d. 1.49 percent of the population convicted of a misdemeanor in 1968
e. 2.58 percent of the population arrested for a misdemeanor in 1968

The percentage of the population received by prisons in 1968 was approximately fifty times smaller than the percentage of the population arrested for misdemeanors, thirty times smaller than the percentage convicted of a misdemeanor or arrested for a felony, and ten times smaller than the percentage convicted of a felony. Therefore, the respective weights of 50, 30, 30, 10, and 1 (corresponding to a, b, c, d, and e above) were used to calculate each inmate's prior criminal involvement score. This score was computed for each individual by weighting each time he or she had been arrested, convicted or incarcerated in prison by the above weights and summing the total for each individual.

For an even more detailed explanation and justification of how prior criminal involvement was quantified, see Scott (1972).

5. Parole board members are to have read and taken notes on the cases before the hearing. Thus the eight seconds is, hopefully, not representative of the time devoted to each case. It does perhaps indicate that when there is disagreement the most readily available information will be used to expedite the procedure.

6. Two sets of dummy variables were used to calculate the partial regression coefficient for marital status.

7. Several district courts have recently intervened and imposed procedural safeguards on prison disciplinary hearings: Clutchette v. Procunier, 328 F. Supp. 767 (N.D. Cal. 1971), Bundy v. Cannon, 328 F. Supp. 165 (D. Md. 1971) and Morris v. Travisono, 310 F. Supp. 857 (D.R.I. 1970). For an excellent review of judicial intervention in prison discipline and in particular the impact of the Morris case in Rhode Island, see Harvard Center for Criminal Justice, (1972).

References

Badillo, Herman
    1972   "The Need for an Ombudsman." Social Action 38:24-27.

Bullock, Henry A.
    1961   "Significance of the Racial Factor in the Length of Prison
           Sentences." Journal of Criminal Law, Criminology, and
           Police Science 52:411-417.

Citizens Inquiry on Parole and Criminal Justice
    1974   Report on New York Parole. New York.

Crime and Delinquency
    1973   "Parole Decisions: A Policy Statement." 19:137.

Dawson, Robert O.
    1966   "The Decision to Grant or Deny Parole: A Study of Parole
           Criteria in Law and Practice." Washington University Law
           Review 1966:243-302.

Dressler, David
    1967   Practice and Theory of Probation and Parole, second
           edition. New York: Columbia University Press.

Editorial Comment
    1972   "The Parole System." University of Pennsylvania Law 120:
           282-377.

Editorial Note
    1960   "Statutory Structures for Sentencing Felons to Prison."
           Columbia Law Review 60:1134-1172.

Elman, P. (ed.)
    1973   Policy Consultation on the Rehabilitation of Prisoners
           (Parole and After-Care), Jerusalem: United Nations
           European Social Development Programme in co-operation
           with the Ministry of Social Welfare and the World Institute,
           Jerusalem.

Fitzharris, Timothy L.
    1973   "The Desirability of a Correctional Ombudsman." Institute
           of Government Studies, University of California, Berkeley.

Glaser, Daniel
1964   The Effectiveness of a Prison and Parole System. Indiana-
        polis: Bobbs Merrill and Company.

1973   "Correction of Adult Offenders in the Community." Pp.
        90-93 in Lloyd Ohlin (ed.), Prisoners in America. New
        York: Prentice Hall.

Green, Edward
1966   "Sentencing Practices of Criminal Court Judges." The
        American Journal of Correction 22:32-35.

Harvard Center for Criminal Justice
1972   "Judicial Intervention in Prison Discipline." Journal of
        Criminal Law, Criminology and Police Science 63:200-228.

Miller, Stuart J.
1971   Post-Institutional Adjustment of 433 Consecutive TICO
        Releases. Department of Sociology, Ohio State University:
        Unpublished Ph.D. Dissertation.

Morris, Norval
1966   "Impediments to Penal Reform." University of Chicago
        Law Review 33:627, 638.

Mueller, Gerhard O. W.
1966   "Punishment, Corrections and the Law." Nebraska Law
        Review 45:58-95.

O'Leary, Vincent and Joan Nuffield
1972   The Organization of Parole Systems in the United States,
        second edition. Hachensack: National Council on Crime
        and Delinquency.

Palmer, John W.
1973   "A Preliminary Inquiry into the Exercise of Correctional
        Discretion." Presented at the 1973 Annual Meeting of the
        American Society of Criminology. New York, November 4,
        1973.

Reiss, Albert J.
1968   "Police Brutality—Answers to Key Questions." Transaction
        5.

Schwartz, Herman
   1973   "Let's Abolish Parole." Readers' Digest 52 (August): 185-
           190.

Scott, Joseph Elmo
   1972   An Examination of the Factors Utilized by Parole Boards
           in Determining the Severity of Punishment. Department of
           Sociology, Indiana University: Unpublished Ph.D. Disserta-
           tion: 57-59.

Vasoli, Robert H.
   1965   "Growth and Consequences of Judicial Discretion in Sen-
           tencing." Notre Dame Lawyer 40: 404-416.

The Editors

Marc Riedel, PhD, University of Pennsylvania, 1972; Director, Death
Penalty and Discretion Project, Center for Studies in Crimi-
nology and Criminal Law, University of Pennsylvania; Assistant
Professor, School of Social Work, University of Pennsylvania;
Criminology Book Review Editor, Journal of Criminal Law and
Criminology; Co-editor of Treating the Offender; Issues in
Criminal Justice; Police: Problems and Prospects; American
Society; Sociological Perspectives.

Terence P. Thornberry, PhD, University of Pennsylvania, 1971;
Assistant Director and Research Associate, Center for Studies
in Criminology and Criminal Law, University of Pennsylvania;
Executive Director, International Prisoners Aid Association;
Member, Executive Council, American Society of Criminology;
Associate Criminology Editor, Journal of Criminal Law and
Criminology; Co-editor of Images of Crime: Offenders and
Victims.

The Contributors

Daniel J. Abbott, PhD, University of Wisconsin, 1971; Associate
Professor and Acting Chairman, Department of Sociology,
University of New Orleans.

William C. Bailey, PhD, Washington State University, 1971; Assistant
Professor of Sociology, Cleveland State University.

Mark Bencivengo, MA, University of Connecticut, 1969; Chief Research and Evaluation Unit, Coordinating Office for Drug and
Alcohol Abuse Programs, Philadelphia.

Jeraldine Braff, BA, City College of New York, 1968; Research
Scientist, Mental Health Research Unit, New York State Department of Mental Hygiene.

James M. Calonico, PhD, Washington State University, 1971; Assistant
Professor of Sociology, University of New Orleans.

Arlene Carl, BA, Temple University, 1973; Research Associate-
Statistician, Court of Common Pleas, Family Division, City of
Philadelphia.

Simon Dinitz, PhD, the University of Wisconsin; Professor of Sociology, the Ohio State University.

Ronald A. Farrell, PhD, University of Cincinnati, 1972; Assistant
Professor, State University of New York, Albany.

Franco Ferracuti, MD, University of Rome, 1951; Professor of
Criminological Medicine and Forensic Psychiatry, School of
Medicine, University of Rome.

Gideon Fishman, MA, Carleton University, 1971; Teaching Associate,
Department of Sociology, the Ohio State University.

Peter G. Garabedian, PhD, University of Washington, 1959; Professor
of Sociology, San Francisco State University

Clay W. Hardin, MS, Utah State University, 1973; Research Assistant,
Department of Sociology, Utah State University.

Marvin D. Krohn, MA, Florida State University, 1972; Instructor,
School of Criminology, Florida State University.

Simha F. Landau, PhD, Hebrew University, 1973; Senior Fulbright
Fellow, Center for Studies in Criminology and Criminal Law,
University of Pennsylvania.

Charles E. Reasons, PhD, Washington State University; Assistant
Professor of Sociology, University of Nebraska, Lincoln.

Lawrence Rosen, PhD, Temple University, 1968; Associate Professor
of Sociology, Temple University.

Seymour J. Rosenthal, MSW, University of Buffalo, 1952; Director
and Associate Professor, Center for Social Policy and Community Development, School of Social Administration, Temple
University.

Joseph Elmo Scott, PhD, Indiana University, 1972; Assistant Professor
of Sociology and Associate at the Center for the Study of Crime
and Delinquency, Ohio State University.

Henry J. Steadman, PhD, University of North Carolina, 1971; Senior Research Scientist, Mental Health Research Unit, New York State Department of Mental Hygiene

Richard D. Vandiver, PhD,
Assistant Professor of Sociology, University of Montana.

Donald B. Wallace, PhD, Temple University, 1972; Evaluation Specialist, Center for Social Policy and Community Development, School of Social Administration, Temple University.

J. Homero E. Yearwood, D Crim, University of California, 1972; Associate Professor of Sociology, California State College, Sonoma.

James E. Young, LLB; JD, Georgetown University, 1965; Associate Professor, School of Social Administration, Temple University.

Margaret A. Zahn, PhD, Ohio State University, 1969; Assistant Professor of Sociology, Temple University.

CORRECTIONS: PROBLEMS OF PUNISHMENT
AND REHABILITATION
>
> edited by Edward Sagarin
> and Donal E. J. MacNamara

CRIME PREVENTION AND SOCIAL CONTROL
>
> edited by Ronald L. Akers
> and Edward Sagarin

IMAGES OF CRIME: OFFENDERS AND VICTIMS
>
> edited by Terence P. Thornberry
> and Edward Sagarin

ISSUES IN CRIMINAL JUSTICE: PLANNING
AND EVALUATION
>
> edited by Marc Riedel
> and Duncan Chappell

POLICE—COMMUNITY ACTION: A Program
for Change in Police-Community Behavior
Patterns
>
> Terry Eisenberg,
> Robert H. Fosen,
> and Albert S. Glickman

TREATING THE OFFENDER: PROBLEMS
AND ISSUES
>
> edited by Marc Riedel
> and Pedro Vales

Police Community Relations

A Review of the Current State of Affairs

By Homero Yearwood[1]

Introduction

Any attempt to define police-community relations does in fact indicate the incongruity of the concept. If the police are in the employ of the community, why is it necessary for a department to have a community relations unit?

If the police are serving the community, why should they need apologists. Indeed, one might view the establishment of such units as evidence of failure to meet the specifications of an assignment.[2]

Police-community relations, in effect, should be the total orientation of the department. It should not be the exclusive business of a special unit on any police force. It should be the clear and unambiguous policy of the department, properly disseminated and adapted to all levels of command. All police officers should be held accountable for policy in this area.

Generally, all policemen should be involved in community relations. However, current concepts of police-community relations serve to polarize policemen. Those outside of the police-community relations unit see it as a specialty no different from that of the felony squad, the narcotic squad, or any other special division. Thus, at present, officers frequently refer certain aspects of their work to the community relations unit. This type of specialization creates hostility amongst officers. The patrolman on the beat often feels that he has to do the dirty work while the community relations man gets the credit for easing tension.

Police and their Responsibility to the Community

It is perhaps indisputable that the police cannot operate effectively without fitting into the fabric of the community.[3] This, of course, is an acknowledgement and perhaps an indictment of the current state of affairs.

When police brutality and corruption exist, they usually stem from the personal qualities of particular policemen or from the functioning of the police agency as a social system. It is difficult for brutality and corruption to exist to any significant degree over a long period of time without the support of major segments of the population.

---

[1]*Mr. Yearwood received his B.A. in Social Sciences from New Mexico Highlands University. He has a B.D. degree and a M.R.E. degree from Golden Gate Theological Seminary and he is presently studying in Brazil as a research apprentice in the Professional Schools Program.*

[2]See Appendix for an example of a Police Department's Code of Ethics.

[3]Community here implies the establishment or the majority group in the population.

45

However, the familiar saying that "a community has the police force it deserves" is applicable to the minority community only in the strictest sense. In most minority communities, the only moral consensus under which the police operate is related to the power of control vested in the establishment and/or political machines. The people themselves have little to say about who should police their community.

Fundamental to the problem of police-community relations is the notion that the police in the ghetto are no longer in the employ of the people they police. As Justice Department aide Roger W. Wilkins notes:

> People in the ghettos see the policeman as a whiteman's jailer. They believe, the people in the ghetto, that the police view them all as potential criminals. They believe that there is police brutality of all kinds, police harassment of all kinds. They believe that the police see their role as working for the white community against the blacks. They see as evidence of this attitude the use of dogs, which, at least since Birmingham, has been a symbol of brutality. They see 'stop and frisk' practices applied, they believe broadly and indiscriminately. They believe it is intended for hoodlums. If you are not a hoodlum and you are stopped and frisked, you are utterly indignant [cf. Rogers, 1966, p. 18].

Professor Louis A. Radelet would add that ". . . for most Negroes in the big cities, the white community is rather inaccessible. But the white police officer is always around [cf. Rogers, 1966, p. 9]." He may be perceived as a representative of "Whitey's law," a visible symbol of a social system which the Negro sees as patently unjust and on whom the police officer takes the brunt of his gripes, frustrations, and anger.

Generally, ghetto residents are convinced that police officers do not understand their plight. Today's motorized departments have not accepted the fact that they really need the cooperation of the community they "serve". It appears that they are satisfied with the status quo. As James Baldwin (1962) poetically describes it:

> . . . None of the Police Commissioner's men, even with the best will in the world, have any way of understanding the lives led by the people they swagger about in twos and threes controlling. . . . They represent . . . They represent the force of the white world, and that world's criminal profit and ease, to keep the black man corraled up here, in his place. The badge, the gun in the holster, and the swinging club make vivid what will happen should his rebellion become overt . . . [p. 65].

Clearly, there is no rapprochment in Baldwin's analysis of the present situation. He probably entones the majority ghetto opinion.

In many areas, policemen have become soldiers, performing an eight hour tour of duty in what, for all practical purposes, is an alien community.

Negro Attitudes Towards the Police

The overwhelming view of the police in the ghetto communities is negative, if not outright hostile. Although middle-class Negroes and other minorities are able to conceptualize the theoretical social role of the police in contemporary society, even they relate stories to justify their almost unanimous disapproval of present police policies and procedures.

Despite these negative attitudes, many middle-class persons tend, at times, to feel that the individual policeman is also being victimized by the establishment. Many feel that the policeman is constantly confronted with social effects of problems which are not his responsibility. Many believe that the problems in police-community relations lie with the police system rather than with the individual policeman.

The belief that the police department discriminates is held almost without dissent in all echelons of the minority community. Speaking of this problem, a Caucasian social action leader noted that differential treatment of minority groups is a fact no longer open to question.

Police departments are seen by Negroes as a para-military operation with strong authority exercised from the top. Yet, Negroes believe that there is great permissiveness as regards police conduct in race relations. They wonder how such a rigidly controlled chain of command can lapse so frequently in the area of relations with minority groups.

Many Negroes believe that their community is being used as a "training post" for the police department. They indicate that the strange young faces of rookie "cops" are always in evidence. Many add that the rookie officer can practice in this area because his mistakes will not affect people with influence in City Hall. Others believe that the ghetto is being used as a place to discipline officers banished from other areas. "They come to serve their exile here," many remark. They indicate that the "headbuster" type is often sent to work in the ghetto.

Generally, the most frequent complaint amongst Negroes is not physical brutality. Professor L. A. Radelet writes: "What the Negro community is complaining about when it cries 'police brutality' is the more subtle attack on personal dignity that manifests itself in unexplainable questionings and searches, in hostile and insolent attitudes towards groups of young Negroes on the street and in cars, and in the use of disrespectful and sometimes racist language, behavior collectively called police harassment [cf. Rogers, 1966, p. 11]."

Harassment, according to Joseph Goldstein (1960) is: "the imposition by the police, acting under the color of law, of sanctions prior to conviction as a means of ultimate punishment rather than as a device for the invocation of criminal proceedings [p. 580]." Goldstein noted the extensiveness of police harassment in the district he studied by pointing out the number of persons arrested as compared to the number against whom prosecution was initiated. This, of course, is one point at which it might be said that police personnel frequently antagonize law-abiding Negro citizens and thus increase resentment against the police. By virtue of what might be called indiscriminate harassment, police officials have managed to alienate not only the violators and the poor, but all social classes within the Negro community. Even members of the clergy, who are recipients of preferential treatment, speak of being harassed by police officers. Negro judges and lawyers who would like to speak in favor of the police find it difficult not to innumerate incidents in which they perceived themselves as being discriminated against or harassed by police officers.

Police Attitudes Towards Minority Groups

It is difficult to find published works anywhere in the United States which might uphold the police as objective peace officers. Everywhere, there is mention of unequal treatment towards minority group persons. Further, this situation does not appear to be improving. One could hope that recent studies would indicate some change; however, this is not so.

In Jerome Skolnick's (1965) work dealing with the police in a northern California city, he notes: "A negative attitude towards Negroes was a norm among the police studied, as recognized by the chief himself. If a policeman did not subscribe to it, unless Negro himself, he would be somewhat resented by his fellows [p. 81]."

Albert Reiss of the University of Michigan, in testimony before the National Advisory Commission of Civil Disorders, noted that three out of four white policemen in predominantly Negro precincts of selected northern cities showed prejudiced attitudes toward Negroes. Dr. Reiss cited studies in Boston, Chicago and Washington and said that "close to half of all the police officers in predominantly Negro high crime rate areas showed extreme prejudice against Negroes [San Francisco *Chronicle,* Dec. 6, 1967]."

William Westley studied police operations in a city near Chicago and commented in a similar vein:

> For the police the Negro epitomizes the slum dweller and, in addition, he is culturally and biologically inherently criminal. Individual policemen sometimes deviate sharply from this general definition, but no white policeman with whom the author has had contact failed to mock the Negro, to use some type of stereotyped categorization, and to refer to interaction with the Negro in an exaggerated dialect, when the subject arose [cf. Skolnick, 1966, p. 81].

In his work on police discretion, Joseph Goldstein (1960) has written: "Some policemen feel, for example, that assault is an acceptable means of settling disputes among Negroes, and that when both assailant and victim are Negro, there is no immediately discernable harm to the public which justifies a decision to invoke the criminal process [pp. 575-575]."

In his highly regarded work *The Policeman in the Community,* Michael Banton (1964) writes:

> At no time did I get the impression that white police officers felt the same involvement in the rights and wrongs of life in the Negro district as they did in the white districts.
>
> A captain of detectives in a Southern town told a writer on police matters: "In this town there are three classes of homicide. If a nigger kills a white man, that's murder. If a white man kills a nigger, that's justifiable homicide. If a nigger kills a nigger, that's one less nigger [p. 173].

This author's own research for the President's Commission on Law Enforcement and Administration of Justice confirms these findings (cf. Lohman, *et al,* 1966, Sections III and IV).

Negative police attitudes towards Negroes are not restricted to the general community. These prejudicial attitudes by Caucasion police officers are manifest in their relationships with Negro colleagues.

University of Pennsylvania sociologist William Kephart (1957) found that 59.5 percent of the Caucasian patrolmen felt it objectionable to ride with Negro patrolmen. When asked the question: "Would you have any objection to ride with a Negro patrolman?", those Philadelphia police who found it objectionable responded (p. 79-81):

"The Negro has sweat glands that give off a choking odor."

"Yes. They stink when the windows are closed in the patrol car."

"East is East and West is West. Why should the majority have to ride with the minority."

"Yes, our way of living and outlook on life are entirely different."

"Yes, one time I was assigned with a Negro. I immediately told my sergeant to take me off and put me on sick list."

"Yes, in my estimation they are savages. They have an offensive odor that forty baths a day will not remove. I am also a firm believer in white supremacy."

"Yes, I believe they should work with their own kind."

"Yes, due to the fact that they have a low mentality. Negroes have bad use of languages."

"I have nothing against a Negro patrolman, but I would feel embarassed riding with him.

A further example of the seriousness of the situation is to be found in the fact that 46.3 percent of the Caucasian officers in the above survey responded that there is "no problem at all" in so far as Negro-white relationships in the department are concerned (p. 88).

Police Attitudes Towards Negro Arrest

Another barometer for ascertaining police attitudes towards Negroes is the matter of arrest and arrest procedures. Kephart (1957) found that 75 percent of the Caucasian policemen in his study overestimated the percentage of Negro arrests (p. 83).

Not only do police overestimate the actual number of Negroes arrested, but they are also overzealous in their efforts to arrest Negroes. In a California city, a highly placed police official justified his modus operandi as follows:

> If you know that the bulk of your delinquent problem comes from kids who, say, are from twelve to fourteen years of age, when you're out on patrol you are much more likely to be sensitive to the activities of juveniles in this age bracket than older or younger groups. This would be good law-enforcement practice. The logic in our case is the same except that our delinquency problem is largely found in the Negro community and it is these youths toward whom we are sensitized [cf. Giallombardo, 1966, P. 448].

Clearly, the consequences of this approach are astouding. Dr. Charlotte Epstein (1962) recounts the experience of a Negro youth in a North Eastern city following the beating of a white youth by a Negro gang.

> Several hours after the incident, when the furor in the neighborhood had subsided somewhat, the police official was driving down a street when he saw a disheveled Negro boy of about sixteen or seventeen putting a key into the door of a house. He approached the boy, collared him, and began to hustle him off to the station house. Just then, the door of the house opened, and a Negro woman in the uniform of a public health nurse appeared. "What's the matter?" she asked. "What's wrong Billy?" she said to the boy.
>
> "I don't know, Ma," the boy answered. "You know there's been some trouble in the neighborhood, and we's rounding up all gangs," said the officer.
>
> "My boy isn't a member of any of these gangs. He knows nothing about the trouble. He's just come from basketball practice. Isn't that true, Billy?"
>
> "Yes, Ma."
>
> "How do I know that," the official challenged, and then turned to the boy. "How many times have you been arrested?" "What do you mean by

accusing my son in this way! Do you pick up every white boy in a ten-block radius every time a gang of white hoodlums breaks the law?"
"He might be one of the gang for all I know," the officer protested—somewhat hesitantly, by this time.
"But you haven't one good reason to think he is," answered the mother. And, of course, it was true. Not only were all gangs being rounded up, but, in reality, all Negro boys were being brought in for questioning [pp. 51-52].

It is likely, then, that these frequent encounters with police officials, especially those involving persons innocent of wrong doing, will increase hostility towards the police. The frequency of such encounters serves to reduce their significance in the eyes of those apprehended. They are likely to regard police encounters as "routine". On the other hand, such responses to police encounters are interpreted by the police as disrespectful and the youth are perceived as delinquent (cf. Giallombardo, 1966, p. 449). Such relationships serve to reinforce the officers' prejudices, leading to more arrests among Negroes and a continuance to the vicious circle. This state of affairs is reflected in police statistics. They show a high percentage of Negro arrests which in turn provides "evidence" for police concentration in Negro districts.

Thus, the Negro, who is admittedly stopped more frequently than whites, begins to adopt a more callous attitude towards these "routine" stops. A demoralizing and ever widening circle continues. Police officers persist in their efforts to stop and arrest certain groups with increasing frequency. These groups, in turn, acknowledge these stops and arrests as a *fait accompli*. This situation is not without its damaging side effects both on the police and the people they encounter.

Police Discretion

The issue of police discretion[5] is of transcendental importance to communities of racial minorities. The scope of police discretion is of such magnitude that the police can decide which deviant behavior will be officially registered. They decide whether or not to invoke the criminal process.

Police may choose to warn, apprehend, detain, and/or refer to the courts as they see fit. Concerning this issue, Piliavin and Briar have noted: ". . . the violation per se generally play (sic) an insignificant role in the choice of disposition [cf. Giallombardo, 1966, p. 445]." They discovered that the nature of police action was based on what they refer to as "cues" which emerged from the interaction between the officer and the individual. From these "cues", the officer inferred the youth's character.

---

[5]For an excellent discussion on police discretion not to invoke the criminal process, see Goldstein (1960).

According to Piliavin and Briar, the most important "cues" used by police officers are: "the youth's group affiliations, age, race, grooming and demeanor [cf. Giallombardo, 1966, p. 445]." It should be emphasized that the criteria selected by the police placed the minority group individual at a distinct disadvantage. This type of enforcement which treats a person according to who he is rather than what he does is a major problem in the minority community. Thus, as Gordon Brown (1947) has observed, the true amount of crime in any community is an unknown quantity (p. 66).

All that can be given are such facts as the number of arrests, number of convictions and similar statistics. While these are probably related to the true crime rate, they will also reflect the efficiency and activity of the police force, the varying regulations and customs for dealing with minor offenses and the methods of reporting arrests.

Need for Police Review

As John A. Morsell has written: "Historically, the idea of civilian review did not emerge in a racial context. It arose simply and inevitably from the need for some agency whose evaluations of alleged improper conduct by police officers could be proclaimed and accepted as beyond the influence of group loyalty or self-interest [cf. Stahl et al, 1966, p. 168]." This need for an extra-police agency, as Morsell noted, exists irrespective of the race of the alleged victims, although the preponderance of cases are among the poor. The poor, and especially minority groups, are the people who, by virtue of their enormous contacts with the police, are seen as the enemy.

Police Justice

In a recent study conducted for the President's Commission on Law Enforcement and the Administration of Justice, researchers from the School of Criminology, University of California, Berkeley, made some pertinent observations concerning the Police Board of Inquiry. The following example illustrates the operations of such a Board.

> The case involved the complaints of two citizens—both Caucasians— who alleged that a policeman had extorted a small amount of money from them in order to 'forgive' traffic violations. The other—alleged that this particular policeman had, in separate instances on the same night, demanded money from them.
>
> At this particular hearing, certain obvious deficiences in the hearing process were observed. In the first place, the Board did not convene until forty-five minutes after the scheduled starting time. During the hearing, only the two complaining citizens and the defendant policeman submitted testimony, along with a Lieutenant whose sole purpose was

to introduce the record of investigation. Both citizen complainants were subjected to what appeared to be immaterial and irrelevant questioning. The line of questioning was such that many times it put the complainants on the defensive. One complainant was so visibly disturbed that he suddenly stopped giving his testimony and said that he would answer no more questions without the advice of counsel. Subsequently, however, after assurance from the chairman of the Board that he had no need of counsel, he continued his testimony.

The hearing officer and their advocate did little to control the questioning of any of the witnesses.

Much of the questioning of the complainants by members of the Board appeared to be improper. Perhaps, inappropriately, one of the Board members reemphasized several times the necessity of telling 'the whole truth.' Another pointed out to one of the complainants the gravity of the charge he was making against a member of the Police Department, citing the jeopardy in which he was placing the officer's job.

At the conclusion of the hearing, a member of the research staff asked for a copy of the transcript of record. He was told that it may not be prepared for five or six months, if at all. The Board deliberated for a very short time on the matter. Upon being asked for their findings, the research staff was told they would be submitted to the Commissioner in a sealed envelope, and only he could make the release of the information [Lohman, *et al*, 1966, pp. 198-199].

It is certainly open to serious question whether any citizen who observed the hearing related above would be inclined thereafter to accept the objectivity of any other police judgment.

Attempts at Extra-Police Review

To date, communities in the United States have had little success in their efforts to establish procedures to review police action.[6]

The most illustrious attempt, the Philadelphia Police Advisory Board, cannot be pronounced a failure; however, its success has indeed been limited. The major reason for its lack of success is police resistance and public apathy. Police departments fight any alteration in the status quo, especially as it pertains to any review of their work. At the core of the problem is the need to increase visibility of police actions and hence the reviewability of their decisions. Legal scholars have long concluded, as Skolnick (1966) has observed: ". . . criminal law enforcement can be substantially improved by introducing arrangements to heighten the visibility of police discretion to permit its control by higher authority [p. 71]."

---

[6]For an account of the success of the Danish Ombudsman, see Thomas J. Aaron, *The Control of Police Discretion.*

Conclusion

While there is much talk being generated about police-community relations, there has been little discussion concerning the enormous burden the police are expected to carry. One might well ask whether these expections are anywhere near realistic.

While we hasten to establish new community relations units and review boards, we might also pause to reflect on the fact that police officers are recruited from the lower middle-class, that class of American society which is more threatened than any other by minority groups and their drive for equality. These recruits in turn become leaders in their departments.

As Albert Deutsch (1955) relates: "One of the major causes of inefficiency is that we tend to pick second and third-rate men as executives [pp. 55-56]." He also notes that a psychiatrist who screened applicants for the police departments in Oakland and Berkeley rejected over 35 percent as: "emotionally unstable and immature or otherwise psychologically unfit for police work [pp. 51-52]." Deutsch emphasizes that there are few departments conducting this type of psychiatric investigation.

If better relations between the police and the community are to be developed, it might be necessary to refocus our field of examination. Instead of the current one-sided public relations approach of selling the police department as it is, we might begin to look searchingly at the modus operandi of the police department.

Query: If the Roman Catholic Church can adapt its teachings to the customs and traditions of countries throughout the world, is it too much to ask the police to reduce their inflexibility and bend towards serving people? As Skolnick (1966) suggests: ". . . the common juxtaposition of law and order is an oversimplification. Law is not merely an instrument of order, but frequently its adversary [pp. 7-8]." One need only to look at totalitarian systems to encounter situations of "order" without rule of law.

It is important that the police recognize that order is not the ultimate end in a free society. Dr. Elmer Johnson (1964) of North Carolina University insightfully notes: "Naked coercion is not sufficient as the sole means of social control. Law observance must largely stem from self-policing and habitual behavior of citizens [p. 439]." The efficiency of law enforcement depends on the level of law observance among citizens of the particular community.

Thurman Arnold (1938) puts it well when he writes: ". . . the criminal law should be looked upon by the law enforcers not as something to be enforced because it governs society, but as an arsenal of weapons with which to incarcerate certain dangerous individuals who are bothering society [p. 153]." The function of the police, after all, it not only to su press law-breaking but to prevent it. Sir Robert Peel maintained that the primary responsibility of the force is to prevent crime and public disorder, not simply to arrest the criminal.

A Drastic Change Needed

The field of police-minority group relations is in need of drastic change. The boldness of the change must be commensurate with the degree of the problem. The schism is often wide and sentiment has been running deep for a long time. The atmosphere remains one of accusations and rebuttals. Speeches delivered to audiences composed only of persons who wear badges labelled "Negro leader" cannot be the only device. Neither will efforts which begin at the top and are side-tracked as they come down through the "ranks" be successful.

The measures needed must be drastic enough not to be out-dated and out-moded when recognized by the "man on the street". It is not infrequent that members of the minority community express the view: "The problem is not with the police—it is much wider." These persons usually add that society in general and the power structure sets the tone and "the police are simply following orders". During a personal interview conducted by this author, a highly regarded civil rights worker explained: "I feel sorry for the cop on the beat. He does not recognize that he is a pawn, caught in the middle just as we are."

Many police officers, on the other hand, share the view of the officer who said: "It makes no difference to us; we are here to enforce law and order, and that is all there is to it." The attitude reflected by this officer's thinking must be recognized as part of the conflict.

It is highly illogical for police officials to expect certain stimuli to elicit "normal responses" from the thousands of "purposeless", underprivileged, under-educated and under-employed ghetto residents. It is as though one were to insist on interpreting the responses of a schizophrenic just like anyone else". The Negro expects to be treated unfairly by police officers; police officers expect the Negro to resist arrest. To some degree, each behaves toward the other on the basis of these expectations.

This is the essence of the dual stereotyping process: the "image" of the police officer by the Negro on the one side and the "image" of the Negro by the police officer on the other side. These images tend to be mutually reinforcing, with a certain self-fulling principle operative in both directions.

The facts of "normal life" in the racial ghetto are viewed with astonishment by most visitors. The police officer, whose eight-hour shift is his only contact with those who receive his services, is not exempt.

The most constant factor mentioned by minority group persons is that there is little communication between the people and the police department. The major criticism comes in terms of the apparent failure of the police department to communicate effectively with minority communities. Central to this is the department's lack of contact with indigenous leaders. Police officials are accused of negotiating primarily with middle-class, "titular" leaders. Many of these white collar leaders are rejected by large groups, many of which are in constant conflict with police officials. It is this officially "unrecognized" group that provides the stimulus for much of the current tensions. The police department apparently is of the opinion that it is not respectable to deal with these grass roots people.

The time has come when police departments need to go to the people—not their "representatives". The ghetto residents must provide part of the answer or we shall continue without answers. They, after all, are the ones who hurt; maybe they can point to the pain. Ghetto residents need to have a voice along with those who make decisions in the police department. As L. T. Wilkins has written: "Perhaps a society can control effectively only those who perceive themselves as members of it [cf. Rosenberg, *et al,* 1964, p. 663]."

APPENDIX

LAW ENFORCEMENT
CODE OF ETHICS

As a member of the Philadelphia Police Department, my first duty is to serve the people of Philadelphia.

I will safeguard lives and property; protect the innocent against deception the weak against oppression or intimidation, and the peaceful against violence or disorder.

Above all else, I shall respect the Constituional rights of all men to liberty equality and justice.

I will keep my private life unsullied as an example to all; maintaining courageous calm in the face of danger, scorn, or ridicule; develop self-restraint; and be constantly mindful of the welfare of others.

Honest in thought and deed in both my personal and official life, I will be exemplary in obeying the laws of the land and the regulations of my department

Whatever I see or hear of a confidential nature or that is confined to me in my official capacity will be kept ever secret unless revelation is necessary in the performance of my duty.

I will never act officiously or permit personal feelings, prejudices, animosities or friendships to influence my decisions.

With no compromise for crime and with relentless prosecution of criminals I will enforce the law courteously and appropriately without fear or favor, malice of ill will, never employing unnecessary force or violence and never accepting gratuities.

I recognize the badge of my office as a symbol of public faith, and I accept it as a public trust to be held so long as I am true to the ethics of the police service